MENACE TO THE
FUTURE

Jess Whatcott

Menace
to the Future

A Disability and
Queer History
of Carceral Eugenics

DUKE UNIVERSITY PRESS
Durham and London
2024

Printed in the United States of America on acid-free paper ∞
Project Editor: Ihsan Taylor
Designed by A. Mattson Gallagher
Typeset in Portrait Text by Westchester Publishing Services

Library of Congress Cataloging-in-Publication Data
Names: Whatcott, Jess, [date] author.
Title: Menace to the future : a disability and queer history of
carceral eugenics / Jess Whatcott.
Description: Durham : Duke University Press, 2024. | Includes
bibliographical references and index.
Identifiers: LCCN 2023050759 (print)
LCCN 2023050760 (ebook)
ISBN 9781478030751 (paperback)
ISBN 9781478026518 (hardcover)
ISBN 9781478059745 (ebook)
Subjects: LCSH: People with disabilities—California—
Social conditions—20th century. | Sexual minorities—
California—Social conditions—20th century. | Detention of
persons—California—History—20th century. | Eugenics—
California—History—20th century. | Involuntary sterilization—
California—History—20th century. | Marginality,
Social—California—History—20th century. | BISAC: SOCIAL
SCIENCE / People with Disabilities | SOCIAL SCIENCE / LGBTQ
Studies / General
Classification: LCC HV1568 .W45 2024 (print) | LCC HV1568 (ebook) |
DDC 365/.4—dc23/eng/20240414
LC record available at https://lccn.loc.gov/2023050759
LC ebook record available at https://lccn.loc.gov/2023050760

Cover art: Jacks McNamara, *June* (2017), from *Learning about
Light* (2017–19). Ink on wood panel, 16 × 16 inches. Courtesy of
the artist.

CONTENTS

ABBREVIATIONS

AAC	augmentative and alternative communication
CDCR	California Department of Corrections and Rehabilitation
CHCF	California Health Care Facility
CIW	California Institute for Women
CMF	California Medical Facility
CRC	California Rehabilitation Center
COVID-19	coronavirus disease 2019
CURB	Californians United for a Responsible Budget
CYA	California Youth Authority
DJJ	Department of Juvenile Justice
HIV/AIDS	human immunodeficiency virus/acquired immunodeficiency syndrome
ICE	United States Office of Immigration and Customs Enforcement
IFW	Industrial Farm for Women
IQ	Intelligence Quotient
I/DD	intellectually and developmentally disabled person

LPS Act	Lanterman-Petris-Short Act of 1967 (California)
OMDC	Otay Mesa Detention Center
PPE	personal protective equipment
PSAP	Disability Rights California's Peer Self-Advocacy Program
SP	Southern Pacific Railroad
STI	sexually transmitted infection

ACKNOWLEDGMENTS

I start this ritual of gratitude with the abolitionist organizers who taught me most of what I know. This started with a lucky encounter twenty years ago when a stranger named Sacha Marini gave me a ride to my first protest outside of Pelican Bay State Prison. Sacha later invited me to organize with Bar None, which ended up being the first of many collaborations through which I learned what it means to be an abolitionist. Further conversations with people incarcerated at Pelican Bay, as well as the Bar None collective, including Yvonne Doble, Inés Ixierda, Jahnna Morehouse, and Tonya Netjes, continued to shape my theory. I promise to one day write a more complete story about Bar None. I also thank the San Francisco Bay Area organizations that mentored and collaborated with us. This includes Misty J. Rojo and Cynthia Chandler, formerly of Justice Now, who accepted an invitation to speak at Humboldt State University (now Cal Poly Humboldt) many years ago and allowed me to interview them for a campus newsletter. I thank them for introducing me to the intersection of abolition and reproductive justice. Most of all, I thank my dear friend Sam Page for planting the seed that grew into this book, by summarizing for me the testimony of incarcerated people about reproductive injustice inside of California prisons.

The past three years, as I finished writing this book, I found a community to organize with at the opposite end of the state in San Diego. I am particularly thankful for Alexis Meza, Leslie Quintanilla, América and Ana Laura Martínez, Marcelle Maese-Cohen, and Ymoat Luna. Coming to this work knowing very little about migrant prisons, I am grateful for the education I have been gifted by these organizers. The Detention Resistance collective gave consent for me to write about their work in the book's prologue and epilogue, but any errors or misinterpretations are my own.

Ten years ago, I was lucky to cross paths with Jacks McNamara who taught me about the beauty, joy, and complexity of madness; and with Leah Lakshmi Piepzna-Samarasinha, who introduced me to the work of Sins Invalid, which led me to disability justice. Shortly after, I was invited into the academic field of disability studies by Liat Ben-Moshe, whose influence has richly shaped my research, writing, and citation practice. Liat's scholarship, and the gift of a copy of her first book, put me on this path. I would not be where I am today without the publishing opportunities, networking connections, and friendliness of the Critical Disability Studies Caucus of the American Studies Association. I am grateful to Tanja Aho, Jess Cowing, Lydia X. Z. Brown, Meghann O'Leary, Theodora Danylevich, Aly Patsavas, Margaret Price, and many others. Theodora and Aly get a particular thank you for mentioning me to an editor at the height of the pandemic, when I thought all my career goals were dust. I am also grateful for the disability studies community of the Western Political Science Association, especially Amber Knight and Nancy Hirschmann for convening us. I thank everyone from the virtual community who read and provided feedback on chapters of this book, including Kristin Bumiller for acting as discussant. I also thank Stacy Clifford Simplican for her encouragement.

Late in my process, I met the scholars of eugenics who helped to crystalize my argument. I thank Miroslava Chávez-García and Susan Schweik for convening the California Eugenics Legacies Working Group and for allowing me to be a part of what became an invaluable space to make connections between historic and present-day eugenics. Alexandra Minna Stern and Natalie Lira extended an invitation for me to attend an important symposium at the Huntington Library during a crucial moment of revisions. They have both been extremely generous to me, including connecting me with the Sterilization and Social Justice Lab.

This book could not have been written without the following material support. For encouraging me to pursue funding opportunities, giving me feedback on funding proposals, and providing enthusiastic advice, I am indebted to Erika Robb Larkins and Rebecca Bartel. I thank the College of Arts and Letters Dean's Office at San Diego State University for their support of faculty pursuing first-time book projects, and specifically for the Faculty Book Manuscript Development Workshop, a Critical Thinking Grant, and an award from the Dean's Author Fund. The SDSU Division of Research and Innovation supported this research through two grant awards: a University Grant and Assigned Time for Research, Scholarship and Creative Activities. Start-up research funds and a Jackie Wertz-Deb Carstens Faculty Professional Development Fund from my department at SDSU were invaluable. The Division of Graduate Studies and the Department of Politics at University of California, Santa Cruz, kickstarted this research with a Dissertation Fellowship. And, last but not least, I am eternally grateful to fellow graduate students who provided me with places to stay during research and early writing phases, especially Andrea Miller and Nadia Roche.

I thank the archivists at the California State Archives and the California Historical Society for performing the delicate job of balancing the privacy of institutionalized people with researcher access. I am appreciative of the California Historical Society for allowing me to access a partially processed collection of documents of the San Francisco League of Women Voters, and I thank them for their ongoing efforts to process this collection to make it accessible to more researchers. I am also indebted to many academic and public libraries for providing access to both secondary and primary documents; a special shout-out to the San Francisco Public Library for digitizing California government documents, which made them available during the closures of the early pandemic. I thank the curators of the Patton State Hospital Museum who have collected and preserved invaluable objects, which are now available for researchers and the general public to view. I also thank the staff person who gave me a private tour of the museum even though it was way outside her job description.

Thank you to former graduate students Anna Buckley, Nicholas Villarreal, and Victoria Sulak for providing research assistance across three summers. Spending time thinking about abolition with graduate students at SDSU has been a gift, and I am especially thankful for productive conversations with my students in the Body Politics seminars, as well as with students who explored abolition and disability justice in their thesis research, including Nicholas Villarreal, Jenna Wilson, and Ale Aguirre.

The deepest well of gratitude is offered to everyone who read, gave comments, and asked questions of iterations of writing. I am humbled to acknowledge those who read the very first drafts: Dean Matheowitz, Neda Atanasoski, Sylvanna Falcón, and Elizabeth Beaumont. Neda was the person who most strongly insisted that this research could be turned into a book, and I am eternally grateful for this encouragement. I would never have finished the first draft without Dean Matheowitz taking a chance on me after many others had said "no." On the other end of the process, Liat Ben-Moshe, Joseph Stramondo, and Miroslava Chávez-García were extremely generous with their time, giving incisive comments that made the overall manuscript so much better than it was. I am grateful to my two "anonymous" reviewers for treating my manuscript with thoughtfulness and care. I am delighted to have worked with Elizabeth Ault as an editor, who offered thought-provoking questions and comments that made me consider the big picture rather than get lost in the weeds.

Many colleagues along the way talked through ideas with me, including Jessica Calvanico, Erin Gray, Jasmine Syedullah, Sandra Harvey, Amanda Reyes, Nadia Roche, Sheeva Sabati, and Alena Wolflink at the University of California, Santa Cruz. Colleagues at San Diego State University sustained me with practical advice, humor, and encouragement, including Marie Draz, Priya Kandaswamy, Joe Stramondo, Irene Lara, Anne Donadey, Christine Knott, Roberto Hernández, Catherine Clune-Taylor, Doreen Mattingly, Walter Penrose, and Toni Saia. If I missed anyone, just know I will be kicking myself. Amira Jarmakani deserves an entire acknowledgments section of her own—she is the biggest shooting star in my night sky.

Ending with queer and crip kinship, I express deep love for Sam Page, Hanna Pesha, Iva Dubyak, Leila Whitley, Diana Leong, Elsbeth Villa, and Kate Boersma, who made me food, watched action movies with me, went on adventures with me, and reminded me that I was more than just an academic. Thank you all for never giving up on me and for being my constant hype people. The writing of this book coincided with a deepening relationship with my mother, Michelle Bump. As much as anything, this book grows from the fierce love we have for each other.

Detention Is Eugenics

I first whispered the words "detention is eugenics" in the fall of 2020. In the United States, stories about immigration detention had exploded in news media. Many were outraged by the detention of children and families and the policy of separating parents from children. Yet another example of reproductive injustice took place at Irwin County Detention Center in the US state of Georgia. According to testimony collected by Project South, detained people had undergone unnecessary surgeries at the direction of a private doctor contracted to provide gynecological health care.[1] The sterilizations brought renewed attention to the history of state-sponsored eugenics in the United States.

While horrified by the sterilizations, I was equally disturbed by what happened to the survivors after their surgeries and after public attention to their plight diminished; many were deported out of the United States while others remained in detention for indefinite periods of time, fighting against deportation. The detention and deportation machine is just one of the ways that asylum seekers and criminalized undocumented people face structural violence in the United States every day. Migrant detention centers are sites of pervasive medical neglect, under conditions that cause injury, illness, mental crises, and exposure to contagious diseases.[2] Incarcerated people are more likely to have untreated underlying health conditions and to experience accelerated aging that leads to weaker immune systems.[3] These experiences have long-term effects on reproduction opportunities and parental relationships and also lead to premature death. Some detained people are fighting deportation to places where they have never lived as adults or where they have fled violence, economic insecurity, or climate chaos. At worst, deportation can mean a death sentence for some migrants, and at best it is a massive disruption to partnerships, parent-child relationships, and other forms of life-giving care. Even without surgeries that cause sterilization, detention curtails reproductive autonomy by impacting migrants' ability to parent when, where, and how they choose, as well as disrupting other life-giving-care relationships. Detention in privately run facilities contracted by the US office of Immigration and Customs Enforcement (ICE) is one of the primary ways that the government is involved in the reproductive control of migrants. My realization that reproductive injustice continues even if sterilization surgeries are halted helped me discern the core argument of this book: that detention itself is eugenics. By this I mean that incarceration, in all its forms, continues to function as eugenics, just as policies of institutionalization did in the early twentieth century.

Just months prior to the start of the pandemic, I moved to occupied Kumeyaay territory of the US-Mexico borderlands, also known as the San Diego-Tijuana metro region. Seeking to get involved in prisoner solidarity work as I had done in Northern California, I joined a grassroots organization that wrote letters to people confined in Otay Mesa Detention Center (OMDC) about twenty-five miles southeast of the city of San Diego. I learned that OMDC is run by a private corporation called CoreCivic that contracts with two agencies of the US federal government—ICE and the US Marshals Service—to detain a variety of people, including those seeking asylum; long-term residents of the United States undergoing deportation proceedings; and immigrants with a variety of statuses who are facing federal criminal charges, including but not limited to unauthorized reentry into the United States.

I also learned that facilities like OMDC are relatively new forms of state confinement in the United States. They were first invented in the 1980s to detain migrants from Haiti, Cuba, and Central America, and by 1994 immigrant detention centers in the United States held approximately 6,700 people per day.[4] However, it was two pieces of federal legislation passed in 1996—the Anti-Effective Death Penalty Act and the Illegal Immigration Reform and Immigrant Responsibility Act—that dramatically expanded the categories for which detention of an immigrant was mandatory. These policies incentivized private detention companies like

Corrections Corporation of America to expand from the criminal legal system into contracts to detain criminalized migrants. The company has operated a private detention center in the San Diego border region almost continuously since 1997. By 2019, Corrections Corporation of America had become CoreCivic, and the OMDC facility was part of the national detention of more than fifty thousand people daily by ICE.

The current five-year contract to operate OMDC was signed in 2019 in a midnight deal, an attempt to outrun a California state law outlawing private prisons (since overturned by courts). The contract ensures that a minimum of six hundred beds will be paid to CoreCivic by the federal government at least through 2024 (and potentially ten years beyond that), and for every person detained in excess of six hundred, CoreCivic earns $138.29 per day.[5] Such contracts create an incentive for the two migrant policing agencies (ICE and US Border Patrol) to detain asylum seekers and to aggressively enforce laws against undocumented immigrants. ICE paid CoreCivic $54 million for the fiscal year of 2019 at OMDC alone.[6]

Otay Mesa Detention Center is one of only a handful of facilities in the nation that also holds prisoners of the US Marshals Service, a shadowy federal law enforcement agency that contracts with county, state, and federal agencies to detain prisoners. As local organizers in San Diego, we know very little about this contract. Language appearing in the 2019 ICE contract with CoreCivic indicates that at OMDC, "a minimum of 596 beds will be available to the US Marshals. Of these 96 will be designed for females." What we have heard from individuals being held in US Marshals' custody is that they face a variety of immigration-related charges, including illegal reentry into the United States following a prior deportation.

The stakes of theorizing detention as a form of ongoing state-sponsored eugenics are made clear through an examination of the impact of the COVID-19 pandemic on people in migrant detention. The novel coronavirus had deadly consequences for people in congregate living settings such as nursing homes, and nowhere was this more acute than in carceral settings such as jails, prisons, detention centers, and state hospitals. I had only been writing to people detained at OMDC for a few weeks when the state of California shut down all but essential services to stop the spread of the novel coronavirus. We scrambled to move our letter-writing operations virtually and tried not to panic. From my years of human rights monitoring in Northern California prisons and researching this book, I had witnessed rampant medical neglect, medical abuse, and exposure to premature aging and death inside of institutions. I worried that the disease that came to be known as COVID-19 would kill many loved ones and comrades who were locked up. Indeed, as of July 2023, the COVID Prison Project estimates that 2,933 incarcerated people in the United States have died from complications related to the novel coronavirus.[7] This includes people in state custody, Federal Bureau of Prisons custody, and eleven people in the custody of ICE. This number does not include people confined to other forced congregate living settings; for example, seventy-eight people died while testing positive for COVID-19 in California state hospitals by July 2023.[8]

The first person to die in ICE custody due to COVID-19 on May 6, 2020, was a fifty-seven-year-old man named Carlos Ernesto Escobar Mejia. Escobar Mejia lived in the United States in the Los Angeles area for forty years, having fled the brutal war in El Salvador in 1980 with his sisters.[9] He was unfortunately the only member of his family who never received legal status in the United States. Escobar Mejia was detained in Los Angeles in January 2020 and sent to OMDC to await deportation proceedings back to a country that he had not lived in his entire adult life. On March 22, the organization that I volunteered with received a letter regarding the ill health of Escobar Mejia from another person in the same housing unit. The letter pleaded with us to add Carlos to the list of people for whom local advocates were working to gain humanitarian release on the grounds that they were medically vulnerable to COVID-19. Under pressure, ICE officials conducted two reviews of medically vulnerable detainees in late March and early April and from that review knew that Escobar Mejia had underlying health conditions, including hypertension and diabetes, that put him at risk of severe COVID-19. In addition to these chronic illnesses, Escobar Mejia was also disabled in another way: he had recently undergone a surgery to remove his right foot and used a wheelchair the entire length of his detention. A judge ruled against Escobar Mejia's release on April 15, 2020, citing an arrest that occurred in the 1990s, which, according to the judge's interpretation, made Escobar Mejia a safety risk. At the time, OMDC had the highest number of confirmed cases of COVID-19 within an ICE-contracted facility in the nation—and the official number was probably a vast undercount given the shortage of testing kits at the time and practices of only testing the most seriously ill. It was probably inevitable that Escobar Mejia, stuck inside OMDC, would contract COVID-19. He was hospitalized on April 24, placed on a ventilator three days later, and, like many others, died alone in a hospital during the early stages of the novel coronavirus pandemic.

Escobar Mejia's death was not surprising given the history of medical neglect in detention centers nationwide, but it was still a shock. Even more so because the same week that we learned of Escobar Mejia's death, a lawsuit filed by the American Civil Liberties Union of San Diego and Imperial Counties was successful in forcing ICE to release ninety-one medically vulnerable people from OMDC. Advocates scrambled to provide post-release support in the form of transportation, food, cell phones, and clean clothes.

Meanwhile, we continued to be alarmed about our *compas* who were still inside.[10] On May 11, 2020, I summarized what we were hearing from detained people, including:

- a lack of adequate cleaning supplies (not just hand soap was needed but also disinfectant to spray down surfaces);

- a lack of access to adequate masks and gloves (two masks per month, three gloves shared among a pod);

- that CoreCivic predicated access to masks and gloves on a signature on a form intended to release CoreCivic from liability of detainees getting sick, and the form was written in English only;

- retaliation for refusal to sign release-of-liability forms (April 10) and for making masks from T-shirts (ICE disputed use of pepper spray on detainees for making masks but confirmed removing women who refused to sign the liability form from a pod);

- movement of people within the facility, among pods, without testing or quarantining;

- testing limited to those with only the most severe symptoms (i.e., fever over 104 degrees); and

- inadequate quarantining of people who tested positive for COVID-19 (awaiting test results while still in the pod; returning to their pod after only seven days).

These refusals to protect detained migrants from the virus were later substantiated in multiple reports from local and national organizations.[11]

The unnecessary exposure of people in migrant detention to a highly contagious and deadly respiratory virus is only the latest manifestation of a long-standing practice of what I name in this book as carceral eugenics. During the COVID-19 pandemic, the ways that detention disables migrants and exposes them to premature death became apparent. However, there does not need to be a pandemic for migrant detention centers to function as eugenics. Detention is part of a longer history of state confinement functioning to diminish the life opportunities of populations deemed undesirable. State confinement limits bodily autonomy, cuts people off from parental and other life-affirming relationships, and risks their early death. In this book I historicize the function of detention as a form of state-sponsored eugenics by telling the story of state hospitals, institutions for disability confinement, and reformatories in early twentieth-century California. This history shows that the deadly effects of migrant detention in the twenty-first century are not new problems or the aberration of a xenophobic US presidency. Instead, migrant detention continues a more than one-hundred-year legacy of carceral eugenics.

Introduction

A Disability and
Queer History
of Carceral Eugenics

Detention is eugenics. The seed for this theory was planted during a conversation with a friend who, in 2011, was part of a team collecting testimony from people in women's prisons operated by the California Department of Corrections and Rehabilitation (CDCR).[1] The story that was eventually published focused on those imprisoned people who had received tubal ligations, an irreversible form of surgery that blocks the fallopian tubes to prevent pregnancy, without giving proper consent.[2] However, testimony given by imprisoned people recounted a wider variety of abuses that diminished reproductive autonomy, including pervasive medical neglect that left conditions untreated until surgeries such as hysterectomies were required.[3] At the time we talked about this testimony, my friend Sam remarked to me that the team believed they were witnessing "modern day eugenics" in California prisons and that history was repeating itself. I wanted to know what eugenics was and wondered: What did Sam mean that the state of California had done this before?

The lack of familiarity I had with the term *eugenics* in 2011 is striking given just how popular the movement was one hundred years ago. Although the concept of human breeding can be traced far back in Western thought, the word *eugenics* was coined by a British statistician named Francis Galton at the end of the nineteenth century. Insisting that social and behavioral traits were biologically inherited by humans from their parents and previous generations, Galton called for a socially directed process of human evolution to amplify desirable qualities within humanity. Those who took up the philosophy of eugenics designed programs that manipulated human reproduction with the goal of correcting, curing, improving, purifying, and perfecting the heredity of the human race. Reformers in the United States and across the world called themselves eugenicists and advocated a range of programs that attempted to control the biological makeup of nations.[4] These programs included the promotion of reproduction among elite groups imagined to uplift the race, but also the suppression of reproduction by populations deemed "unfit" or whose heredity was imagined to threaten the health of society. The most well-known of these eugenics programs in the United States are the nonconsensual reproductive sterilizations that several states legislated in the early twentieth century.[5] California had one of the earliest state-sponsored eugenicist sterilization programs, passed in 1909, targeting people institutionalized in state hospitals, homes for the feebleminded, and state prisons.[6]

As I researched California's eugenics history, I was disturbed that the confinement of disability in state institutions was also motivated by eugenics. The segregation of disabled people was described by eugenicists in the early twentieth century as a strategy for controlling human reproduction. No wonder, then, that abolitionists in the present argue that incarceration is a form of reproductive injustice. Building on scholarship on the history of sterilization programs, this study focuses instead on the eugenics policy called segregation.[7] While the most common historical association with the term *segregation* references legal racial apartheid (such as in the US South), the eugenicist usage had a different but not altogether unrelated meaning. Segregation for eugenicist purposes was the long-term confinement in state institutions of classes of people whose heredity was deemed threatening to the body politic. The primary sites proposed for eugenicist segregation were institutions for the confinement of disability, including psychiatric hospitals, homes for the feebleminded, and epileptic colonies. Institutions used for punishment and rehabilitation, such as industrial farms and prisons, were also indicated as sites for segregation. Eugenicists argued that segregation of the so-called feebleminded, mentally diseased, and criminal classes was only partially effective given that there were not enough institutions to contain everyone whose reproduction was a threat.[8] Nevertheless, the managers of state institutions adopted eugenics philosophy to varying degrees, assuming that what they called "custodial care" had a role to play in the project of controlling human reproduction.[9] Eugenics ideology ultimately justified the long-term warehousing of tens of thousands of disabled, mad, neurodivergent, queer, and racialized people in state institutions throughout the twentieth century. Although initially concentrated in institutions for disability confinement, state investment in detention shifted over time into the criminal legal system. County jails, state prisons, and immigrant detention centers have now become primary sites for controlling the reproduction of disabled, impoverished, and racialized communities.

Bringing together a variety of sites of detention, this book investigates the role that eugenics philosophy played in structuring confinement in the carceral state of California. Etymologically, the word *carceral* comes from Medieval Latin to describe a prison, jail, or enclosed space. Scholars use this term to describe how logics of control and confinement have become embedded in the operation of the modern state.[10] While most often applied to the practices of criminalization and the prison industrial complex, disability activists argue that the confinement of disability in institutions comes from the same carceral logic.[11] Liat Ben-Moshe proposes shifting from the term *prison industrial complex* to "carceral-industrial complex" to recognize the shared logics among institutions of confinement.[12] My contribution to carceral studies is to theorize how state confinement was shaped by the philosophy of eugenics in the early twentieth century. To do that, I examine the practice of segregation in early twentieth-century California to theorize what I call *carceral eugenics*. Carceral eugenics is a concept that analyzes how state confinement functions to control the reproduction and life chances of groups of people who have been deemed biologically undesirable. Reproductive control of individuals and groups through detention is legitimated in the name of solving broader social, economic, and political problems that are at least partially blamed on biological inheritance.

Why revisit the early twentieth-century history of eugenics segregation? My theorizing of carceral eugenics is practically oriented toward the movements for disability justice, carceral abolition, and reproductive justice. Disability justice advocates have long sought freedom for all disabled people who are confined against their will, whether in a large state institution or a privately run group home.[13] Motivated by the principles of disability justice as articulated by queer and trans disabled people of color, this book counters the regret that animates the discourse around deinstitutionalization and, instead, bolsters the claim that ongoing disability detention is harmful.[14] Additionally, I and my fellow carceral abolitionist organizers need more information about eugenics to counter historical narratives created by the state. These narratives present eugenics as only existing in the past, as part of some bygone era that has since been overcome or as worthy of attention only when it rises to the anachronistic level of medical abuse in the form of unnecessary tubal ligations. As carceral abolitionists, we can use historical evidence to insist that detention in the present is also eugenics. Further, to recognize the ways that carcerality and eugenics are intertwined strengthens coalitions among the movements for carceral abolition and reproductive justice. If one of the ways that eugenics operates is through detention, then carceral abolition must include an explicit analysis of how eugenicist desires to control reproduction continue to motivate confinement. At the same time, this book contributes to the argument that in order to create reproductive justice, we must abolish carceral logics and structures in all forms.

An Origin Story of Eugenics

How did the philosophy of eugenics come to undergird carceral social policy? Francis Galton coined the term *eugenics* in an 1883 book, wherein he liberally borrowed and mutated Charles Darwin's (his distant cousin) theory of evolution, arguing that human behavioral traits were biologically inherited from parents by offspring.[15] Debating the "competition between nature and nurture," Galton argued that it is biological heredity that determines a person's genius and greatness.[16] Of this process, Galton equated human heredity to dog breeding, implying that "mixed" genetic inheritance in humans created "a mongrel, nondescript type, because ancestral peculiarities are apt to crop out in the offspring."[17] Building on this belief in biologically based behavioral inheritance, Galton demanded direct social intervention into human evolution. He advocated for the breeding of society's elites to increase the percent of the human population with desirable traits, through subtle methods such as incentivizing early marriage of the rich and talented. However, he also wrote about the need for purging humanity of poor "stock" by preventing the reproduction of human weakness, embodied by the so-called defective class. Although not the first to suggest both types of human breeding, Galton's contribution was to create a word—*eugenics*—that gave shorthand to the idea of improving the human race through mathematical and scientific methods. It was a useful word that gave momentum to ongoing fears of degradation of white civilization that plagued imperial and former slave economy states at the end of the nineteenth century. Eugenics organized into a single program multiple efforts to control the reproduction of undesirable members of the human race.

While Galton is credited with coining the term *eugenics*, similar philosophies and organized human breeding projects predate Galton by centuries. According to Dorothy Roberts, the largest ever human breeding project took place during the enslavement of people of African origin in the Americas from the seventeenth century through the nineteenth century.[18] Human breeding was especially heightened after the slave trade was made illegal in some countries while the practice of slavery allowed to continue. These policies perversely incentivized human breeding to perpetuate the population of people who inherited the condition of slavery in the Americas. Eugenics emerged following the outlawing of slavery in the Americas, and this context illustrates the precise danger of the idea of self-directed human evolution: eugenics promoted the reproduction of white elites while pathologizing, criminalizing, and illegalizing the biological inheritance of impoverished, racialized subjects. The philosophy revitalized colonial ideologies of racial purity, recreating Western gendered, racialized, and ableist hierarchies of human value. Drawing on Western philosophies such as Malthusianism, social Darwinism, and racial science, Galton named and revitalized the movement to naturalize social hierarchies by depicting entire classes and races of people as biologically inferior, a threat to the health of the body politic, and therefore legitimate targets of legal restrictions and social control.

Following Galton's coinage of the term, the name *eugenics* became popular among a growing middle class of professionals across the world. Intellectuals took up Galton's term at the turn of the twentieth century to articulate their focus; as the slogan of the Second International Congress of Eugenics proclaimed: "Eugenics is the self-direction of human evolution."[19] While the fantasy of breeding a superior human has since been popularized in science fiction representations of clones and cyborgs, many state-sponsored eugenics programs in the twentieth century focused on excising human weaknesses—and the humans who embodied these weaknesses—from society's biological gene pool. The eugenicist fantasy of human perfection most notoriously authorized the genocide of millions of people under the Nazi Holocaust, wherein Jewish people, homosexuals, and disabled people were targeted for eradication in the name of purifying the so-called Aryan race.[20] The philosophy of eugenics also travelled globally from Europe to the Soviet Union, European colonies, former colonies (such as Australia), Latin America, and Asia.[21]

Eugenic ideas were widespread in the United States at the beginning of the twentieth century and adopted to some degree by people as diverse as President Theodore Roosevelt, the founder of Planned Parenthood Margaret Sanger, and social scientist W. E. B. Du Bois.[22] In California, eugenics theory was embraced by elite men such as David Starr Jordan, the first president of Stanford University and cofounder of the Sierra Club, and Charles Goethe, founder of what is now California State University, Sacramento.[23] Luther Burbank, a Santa Rosa–based horticulturist and agricultural scientist who invented hundreds of strains of fruits, vegetables (including the russet potato), flowers, and grains, espoused many eugenicist beliefs. Eugenics influenced social scientist and educator Lewis Terman, famous for adapting the Stanford-Binet intelligence test and using it to determine the educational placement of thousands of California children. Elite women in California also promoted eugenics, including Dr. Margaret H. Smyth who is credited with "perfecting" salpingectomy surgery for reproductive sterilization in her tenure as a physician and later superintendent of Stockton State Hospital.[24] A sibling to the East Coast's Cold Springs Harbor laboratory, California's eugenicist think tank called the Human Betterment Foundation was founded by Pasadena-based philanthropists Ezra Gosney and Paul Popenoe. Gosney funded Popenoe's study of the state's records on eugenics (to which he was given complete access, patient confidentiality be damned) and published the treatise *Sterilization for Human Betterment* in 1929.[25] This book was once a highly influential argument for eugenics. According to records left by Goethe, the book travelled as far as Germany and inspired intellectuals in Hitler's regime.[26]

Self-proclaimed eugenicists organized programs that they believed would protect the social order from ruin, save the race from degradation, and form a more perfect nation. Eugenicists worked within municipal, state, and the federal governments in the United States to create programs intended to shape human evolution through social and physical interventions. In addition to state-sanctioned sterilization programs, policymakers lobbied for exclusionary immigration laws and aggressive immigrant deportation, enacted marriage restrictions and anti-miscegenation laws, promoted the exclusion of disabled and neurodivergent children from public schools, and argued for the segregation of adults and children in state institutions. In California alone, approximately twenty thousand people were sterilized between 1909 and the 1960s.[27] An untold number of disabled children were excluded from public education throughout the twentieth century. Countless others were divided from their families and exposed to premature death through restrictive immigration laws and the creation of the US Border Patrol.[28] Over forty-five thousand people died while confined to California state hospitals and other disability institutions between the 1880s and the 1960s, the subject of this book.[29] These and other disparate legacies have yet to be fully grappled with by a US public whose cultural, political, and economic systems have been indelibly shaped by the philosophy of eugenics.

Institutions as Reproductive Control

Feminist scholars have demonstrated the ways that Black, Indigenous, Puerto Rican, Chicana, and other people of color in the United States were systematically targeted for reproductive control throughout the twentieth century.[30] Eugenics contributed to these practices of control, including by justifying various state-sponsored sterilization programs. This history is one of the reasons that feminists of color theorized reproductive justice. Reproductive justice shifts the discourse away from choice, which connotes the ability to make decisions about one's body, especially the right to choose an abortion. Reproductive justice emphasizes both bodily autonomy and the conditions necessary to allow people to choose to give birth and to parent—conditions that were historically denied through programs like nonconsensual and forced sterilization.[31]

As a result of the reproductive justice framework, as well as scholarship on eugenics and the advocacy of scholars at the legislative level, more people are now aware of one of California's programs to control reproduction: the Asexualization Act first passed in 1909.[32] Between 1909 and 1964, an estimated twenty thousand people were legally "asexualized," meaning they were reproductively sterilized, in California. However, scholarship also shows that sterilization was not the only reproductive control program undertaken by the state of California in the name of eugenics. Wendy Kline describes how another policy, called "segregation" by eugenicists, was used to control the reproduction of institutionalized people at the Sonoma State Home in Northern California.[33] Kline argues that segregation faded in importance for eugenicists as sterilization took over as the primary strategy promoted by organizations like the Human Betterment Foundation. While eugenicists increasingly promoted sterilization as a cheaper and more comprehensive strategy, the way that California's Asexualization Act was written required victims of sterilization to first be institutionalized. The result, according to Kline, is that eugenicists resorted to temporarily institutionalizing those they sought to sterilize, hinging release from detention on completed surgery.

While this is a startling revelation, I also draw attention to the thousands of people who were considered too disabled or mentally "defective" to parole, whether they were sterilized or not. One way to measure the scale of the impact of segregation comes from a 1928 report by the California Department of Institutions, which reviewed deaths among state hospital patients. Over twelve hundred patients are recorded as having died each year of 1927 and 1928. The department found that one-third of people who died had been institutionalized for over five years, 16 percent had been there for nine years or longer, and a shocking 6.5 percent had lived in the institution for twenty years or longer before their deaths. The vast majority of those who died while institutionalized—estimated to be at least forty-five thousand between the mid-1880s and the 1960s—were buried in unmarked, poorly marked, or mass graves, according to the California Memorial Project.[34] From this heartbreaking statistic, I make the case that medium- and long-term confinement in sex-segregated institutions was an effective reproductive control strategy and a form of reproductive injustice, even without sterilization surgery.

Reproductive justice advocates and abolitionist organizers have made a similar point about present-day incarceration in the criminal legal system. Indeed, I first learned to associate detention with eugenics from organizers who demand carceral abolition to end reproductive injustice. Specifically, my involvement with the prisoner solidarity organization Bar None from 2003 to 2011 connected me with people at the former human rights legal clinic Justice Now, based in Oakland, California. As participants in Justice Now explained it:

> Women's prisons, with their consistent destruction of reproductive capacity, abysmal treatment of pregnant individuals, obstruction of abortion rights, and policing of gender, are themselves tools of reproductive oppression. . . . Our findings specifically focus on: (1) the overuse of often nonconsensual hysterectomies (i.e., surgical removal of the uterus) and oophorectomies (i.e., the surgical removal of one or both ovaries) within California's women's prisons; (2) poor reproductive health care that leads to infertility; (3) the imprisonment of people throughout their reproductive years, in part because of mandatory minimum sentences and three strikes laws; and (4) the specific destruction of reproductive capacity for transgender people.[35]

Even absent surgeries with the only purpose of sterilization, state confinement functionally exerts state control over reproduction, dictating when, where, and how incarcerated people can have and parent children.[36] As Justice Now points out, the disproportionate sentencing of Black, Indigenous, Latine, people of color, queer, trans, disabled, and poor people to jails and state prisons means that incarceration is disproportionately impacting the reproduction of these groups. I argue that the reproductive control enacted by the system of incarceration can be traced back in part to the early twentieth-century policy of segregation. Joining Justice Now, I also argue that reforming the prison system is inadequate to the goal of reproductive justice. As this book reinforces, systems of confinement were first invented in the name of humanitarian reform, and further reform only entrenches carceral systems. Reformism is unable to generate the political will to intervene unless there is egregious medical abuse in the form of nonconsensual sterilization surgery.[37] An anti-eugenics politics demands carceral abolition instead of reform. To create reproductive justice we must build a world without bars, cages, and borders.

In addition to interfering with the ability of people to have and parent children, incarceration and institutionalization cut people off from their parents, biological and chosen families, and other life-giving care networks. This could also be considered reproductive injustice by drawing on Marxist feminist conceptions of social reproduction. Social reproduction identifies how the system of capitalism is reproduced through the labor of birthing the future workforce and of caring for those children, including teaching children the ideologies of capitalism that will make them docile workers.[38] (Resistance to capitalist social reproduction includes the birth strike and forms of motherwork that give people the tools to imagine different futures and organize themselves.) Disability writers, including Akemi Nishida and Leah Lakshmi Piepzna-Samarasinha, have "cripped" the concept of social reproduction, undermining ableist capitalist notions of independence and productivity by articulating forms of crip care work that empower disabled people not only to survive but to thrive.[39] Nishida and Piepzna-Samarasinha expand notions of care work beyond that which is given by parents to children, to include the care that is exchanged with aging, chronically ill, neurodivergent, and mad people, particularly care that takes place outside of the bounds of the capitalist heteropatriarchal nuclear family. While eugenics programs intervene in biological reproduction, carceral forms of eugenics also limit how institutionalized people can engage in the broader spectrum of social reproduction including care work. Eugenicist restrictions on social reproduction are a form of enclosure, constructing borders and boundaries between the collective and institutionalized people, cutting each off from each the vital resources necessary for liberatory social reproduction.

Disability institutionalization was and is a form of reproductive injustice deeply rooted in the philosophy of eugenics. Despite eugenicist concern about the cost of confining the entire defective class, the concepts of heredity and notions of danger attached to disabled bodies naturalized the practice of confinement for decades, with consequences that linger into the present. Long- and medium-term confinement in state psychiatric hospitals, institutions for intellectually and developmentally disabled (I/DD) people, epileptic colonies, and labor colonies was and is an effective way to control sexual contact as well as to deny other methods of conception. Institutionalization was and is part of the spectrum of strategies used to enforce ableist ideologies rooted in eugenics that treat disabled sexuality, reproduction, and parenting as undesirable. Due to these ideologies, the lack of bodily autonomy among disabled persons, especially during institutionalization, is unquestioned. Institutionalization denies detained people relationships with their children, biological and chosen families, and other life-giving and life-affirming community networks of care necessary for social reproduction. For these reasons, medium- and long-term institutionalization, far from being unfair only if there is sterilization surgery, deserves its own historicization as a form of reproductive injustice with roots in eugenics.

Institutions and the Carceral Industrial Complex

Scholars have detailed the carceral history of California from the garrisons built by Spanish colonizers, to the first state prison built on the rocky northern shore of the San Francisco Bay in 1852, to the emergence of some of the biggest jail and prison systems in the entire world.[40] Colonial governance in California has innovated many carceral technologies, from the Spanish mission system in the eighteenth century to the super-maximum prison of the 1990s. However, with exceptions such as Miroslava Chávez-García's *States of Delinquency*, in almost none of this history is there an explicit discussion of the impact of eugenics, nor are the histories of other related state institutions of confinement addressed.[41] The interrelated trajectories of California's institutions of disability confinement with jails and prisons require more historicization.

Kelly Lytle Hernández argues that California has been a settler state developed through the carceral laws, infrastructure, and logics that enact what she calls a "logic of elimination."[42] This logic, I argue, was perpetuated by eugenics and can also be found in segregation in institutions of disability confinement. The extension of the carceral system from the jail and prison system builds on the scholarship of Liat Ben-Moshe who argues that any analysis of the prison industrial complex is incomplete without including institutions of disability confinement.[43] Ben-Moshe, Allison Carey, and Chris Chapman contend that institutions of disability confinement are part of what Michel Foucault called the "carceral archipelago."[44] They explain that carceral logics cross the terrain from the criminal-legal into the medical-pathological, connecting diverse institutions in "what Foucault called a 'protective continuum,' ranging from the medical to the penal.... Differentiated institutions were created, to classify, to control and treat danger, and to safeguard the rest of the population from the dangerous individual."[45] Collectively, jails, prisons, and institutions (usually thought of in more humanitarian terms as sites of care and treatment) operate under shared carceral rationalizations. Disciplinary techniques travel back and forth across institutions of care and punitiveness, subjecting incarcerated people to both punitive practices of neglect and pathological investment as objects of treatment. This present study takes up Ben-Moshe's call to examine how pathologization and criminalization have been used concurrently to develop the carceral state.[46] Further, I take up Angela Y. Davis's point that these concurrent systems are gendered, so that "deviant men have been constructed as criminal, while deviant women have been constructed as insane," resulting in the confinement of women in psychiatric and disability institutions at high rates.[47]

Richard Fox gives the history of California's institutions of disability confinement, focusing on San Francisco's system of civil commitment.[48] Importantly, Fox's book gestures toward institutions as part of the carceral logic of the state. As Bernard Harcourt suggests, studying institutions of disability confinement specifically as carceral technologies creates new timelines for the story of incarceration.[49] The roots of the modern day carceral system in California are often dated to the 1960s, when there was a backlash against civil rights, anti-capitalist, and anti-imperialist movements, as well as the economic gains of the working class.[50] Widening the scope of carceral analysis to include disability institutions, it is necessary to start this history earlier in time—namely, in the Progressive Era. Within this new carceral timeline, the influence of eugenics is unmistakable. Eugenics, I argue, was a pre-"law and order" philosophical justification for confinement, and progressivism was a political movement that fought to construct a carceral apparatus in California prior to the more well-known prison booms of the 1930s to the 1950s and the 1980s to the 1990s.

While California had at least one institution for disability confinement as early as 1851 (Stockton State Hospital), it and the others that followed were deeply transformed by the philosophy of eugenics in the early twentieth century.[51] Other institutions that were built during the so-called eugenics era of the 1890s through the 1940s were established more explicitly for eugenicist purposes. I historicize eugenics institutions by studying together civil commitment in state psychiatric hospitals and so-called homes for the feebleminded alongside juvenile reform schools and the state's reformatory for adult women, more often associated with the criminal legal system. The disability institutions along with the reformatories and prisons were monitored by a single government agency in the early twentieth century: first called the Board of Charities and Corrections and later changed to the Department of Institutions. This shared governance allowed for reform philosophies like eugenics to spread across both the criminal legal system and the civil commitment system. Administrators who embraced eugenics promoted the farm colony model for both the prison and the institution. Under this model, disability institutions and criminal reformatories were hundreds of acres in size and resembled self-contained villages. In the eugenics imaginary, these institutions existed as a parallel world to regular society, fantasized as places where the defective class could indefinitely live out sex-segregated lives, dying humane deaths that prevented them from passing on their socially unwanted heredity.

Just as scholars have examined the racialization of the criminal legal system, groundbreaking scholarship on eugenics history has demonstrated that categories like "feeble-minded" in historical records were specifically gendered and racialized judgments about national belonging.[52] Despite current day narration that state institutions were legitimate sites for the treatment of disability and mental illness, many people were targeted for eugenics that today would be characterized as able-bodied and of normal mentality. Similar to how *criminal* became a code word for racialized and queered people in the late nineteenth century, immoral and sexually deviant behavior was interpreted through racial and gender scripts as disability or, to use the parlance of the time, "defective." This is particularly true of those categorized as female by the state. It is for this reason that scholars have argued that Californian eugenics ideology was not just about direct reproductive control but was also a strategy for enforcing patriarchal gender roles, including limiting sex to monogamous, legal conjugal, nonmiscegenating marriage.[53] Racialized communities in California, especially people of Asian origin and Mexican origin, were coded as gender and sexual deviants due to constructions of womanhood and manhood that revolved around whiteness.[54] At least one eugenics policy, that of sterilization, was used to target these racialized communities in California. As Novak and colleagues have shown, in the southern parts of the state where Spanish-speaking communities were concentrated, people with Spanish surnames disproportionately underwent eugenics sterilization.[55] Marie Kaniecki and colleagues similarly found that people with Asian surnames disproportionately underwent eugenics sterilization.[56] Ethnic groups who were legally categorized as white but also represented as racially "unfit"—namely, people of Portuguese, Italian, and Irish descent—were also targeted.

There is no easy answer to the question of the racial makeup of people institutionalized in California in the early twentieth century due to reasons ranging from inconsistent record-keeping across institutions to evolving racial categorizations. A possible data set with which to explore the race and ethnicity of institutionalized people was recently suggested to me; however, it was beyond my capacities to analyze it for this book.[57] Additionally, any data points of ethnicity and race in institutions need to be read contextually, given that other methods of intervention were used to remove undesirable foreigners (coded as Asian and Mexican) from the country and leave "native" US citizens (coded as white) in expensive long-term custodial care. The point I emphasize is that the discourse surrounding eugenicist segregation reinforced white supremacist views of desirability and national belonging. Importantly, this racist eugenicist discourse sowed the grounds for the disproportionate imprisonment of Black, Latine, Indigenous, Pacific Islander, and some Asian populations in jails and prisons for the remainder of the twentieth century, which continued to reproductively control these communities.[58]

With some notable exceptions, both prison histories and eugenics histories have emphasized gendered and racial disproportionality while neglecting the material ways that carceral eugenics policies also disabled populations.[59] Records of those institutionalized indicate a range of physical impairments that could be recognized as legal disabilities today, including epilepsy, paralysis, limb difference, blindness, and deafness. Also contained in eugenics-era institutions were people experiencing madness, people who today would be called intellectually and developmentally disabled (I/DD), and people experiencing conditions of aging such as dementia. While disability is often coded as white in contemporary discourse, people of color are also disabled people. For one, environmental conditions have always impacted poor and racialized communities disproportionately, including agricultural and industrial exposures and accidents, as well as the trauma of racism, classism, and sexism. Accounts of eugenics that emphasize gender and race without disability run the risk of reproducing the binary distinctions between people of color and disabled people. The race-disability binary implies that disabled people actually did and do belong in eugenics institutions, as long as there was or is no use of institutionalization to unfairly punish (assumed to be nondisabled) people of color. This present study is inspired by the next generation of eugenics history, such as Natalie Lira's account of California's Pacific Colony, that shows how racialization operates through pathologization and practices of disability confinement.[60] This book joins Lira in insisting on a simultaneous race, gender, and disability analysis.

From carceral studies I also bring a feminist commitment to abolition. Carceral abolitionism is a set of practices of liberation rooted in Black feminist resistance to slavery, policing, and the prison industrial complex.[61] In addressing why abolition is necessary, Angela Y. Davis points out that it was through a series of reforms enacted in the name of humanitarianism that the modern carceral system was constructed in the first place.[62] This is nowhere more true than in the system of disability confinement, which was built through intersecting philosophies of eugenics and humanitarian concern for the lives of disabled, mad, and neurodivergent people. Carceral abolitionists use the phrase "reformist reforms" to refer to policy changes that legitimate and reestablish social reliance on the carceral system, and nonreformist or abolitionist reforms to refer to dismantling the carceral system and rebuilding a new world.[63] From an abolitionist perspective, the danger of reformist reforms is that they re-entrench carceral logics, and, therefore, reforms themselves can become a means of biopolitical discipline.[64] Feminist abolitionism instead seeks to dismantle the structures and logics of oppression that sustain cages, borders, and policing by employing what Liat Ben-Moshe calls "dis-epistemologies of abolition."[65] Abolition is not simply (as if it were simple) a matter of dismantling carceral systems—it is also the practice of imagining new horizons for possible futures and of creating new worlds by forming networks of mutual aid and transformative justice. In contrast to reformist reforms that purport to solve problems with quick fixes, abolition is an unfinished project, always a collective becoming.[66] As a perpetual practice of both unlearning and re-creating, carceral abolition is an essential framework for offering life-giving and life-affirming futures that can counter ongoing practices of eugenics.

Critical Disability Studies

Encountering Julie Avril Minich's essay on critical disability studies while in the early stages of writing this book gave me much-needed direction to interpret the archive of carceral eugenics.[67] Minich identifies a version of disability studies not organized around the object of taken-for-granted disability but as a methodology of analyzing texts for how disability is produced. With this insight, I revisited my archive. No longer did I seek evidence for how people were falsely labeled as disabled to justify their institutionalization, but instead I identified how institutionalization was a material process of disablement.

This concept is rooted in an older and now-contested theory, that of the social model of disability. Until disabled people began articulating alternatives in the 1960s, the dominant model of disability identified disability as a problem, an inherent pathological condition of the body or mind.[68] Under the "individual" or "medical" model of disability, to say that someone is disabled is to point to a physical or neurological condition—such as paralysis, autism, or limb difference—that renders their body and/or mind incapable of performing the tasks needed for social reproduction, such as completing schooling, holding down a job, or feeding themselves. The medical model is deeply rooted in the eugenicist assumption that biology is destiny. The dominance of the individual/medical model legitimates disability exclusion and inaccessibility by depicting the problem as emanating from a body or mind that is not up to the standards of modern life.

Social models of disability, articulated by activists as early as the 1960s, argue instead that variable bodyminds (a term chosen to reject Cartesian dualism) are not inherently defective but, rather, are constructed as limited through social, political, and economic understandings of normal and abnormal.[69] Alison Kafer points out that the version that gets called "the social model" of disability draws a distinction between "impairment" as a limiting property of the bodymind and "disability" that refers to the social barriers that prevent access for people with impairments.[70] Kafer insists that impairments are also constructed as such by social, economic, and political contexts. Kafer coined the term "political/relational model" to emphasize that body and mind differences are filtered through discourses that structure understanding of which so-called impairments constitute suffering or limitations of functioning. Dominant understandings of impairment and disability may or may not have a correlation with a person's visceral experience of pain or suffering. For example, many people who use wheelchairs do not necessarily experience pain or suffering until they encounter a built environment that is inaccessible or the bias of people who make assumptions about wheelchair users. Some impairments and disabilities, especially chronic illness, do cause pain that people wish to be rid of. This discrepancy between social assumptions and individual experience has led to a debate within the field of disability studies about how to attend to the materiality of pain and suffering and the interests of some for pursuing medical interventions while still critiquing the denial of access to those who have been socially dis-abled. For my purpose of explaining critical disability studies as methodology, I will summarize that these social or political and relational models emphasize that people become legally disabled not through a necessary limitation associated with a biological impairment but through a process of being categorized as abnormal and excluded from access to public space. These models shift disability from an immutable property of the bodymind to a socially constructed "sign of and justification for inferiority."[71] These models draw attention to how "problem bodies"—to adapt a phrase from Clare Sears—become the targets of cure, rehabilitation, or elimination by naturalizing the source of their difference as immanent to their bodies.[72]

Accepting disability as socially constructed rather than immutable, the methodology of critical disability studies is a practice of "scrutinizing . . . the social norms that define particular attributes as impairments, as well as the social conditions that concentrate stigmatized attributes in particular populations."[73] That is, rather than disability studies as a genre that tells the stories of the lives of people who are generally accepted as disabled (a move that reproduces the medical model and also tends to reinforce the whiteness of the field), critical disability studies instead reads texts to analyze how disability, and related categories such as crazy or fat, are produced and re-produced. Mobilizing cultural studies and discourse analysis methods, what counts as a text is broadly construed, including visual, sonic, performative, and archival. These texts are analyzed and interpreted for how they produce social understandings of normality, as well as how the resulting discourses obscure or justify differential material treatment of people based on whether they are considered abnormal.

Applying this methodology to my archive, I join others in pointing out that categories such as "feeblemindedness" and "mentally defective" were deployed in the early twentieth century to justify eugenics interventions. However, rather than take these terms as arbitrarily deployed merely to justify institutionalization, I use critical disability studies to interpret these as meaningful categories of disability within historical context. Instead of arguing that a person was falsely labeled feebleminded to justify their confinement, I instead analyze the ways that categorization as feebleminded materially "disabled" people and cut off their access to public space. Disability was—in the eugenics era, just as in the present—created in and through gender and racial formations. A *critical* disability studies methodology requires also examining the assumptions of gender and whiteness that attend the concept of disability. In this case, those who were disabled by eugenics policies include those people institutionalized due to gender deviance and white supremacist notions of national belonging. For example, a person assigned to the category of female who was diagnosed as a moral imbecile in the 1910s was materially disabled by the state of California, just as were Mexican American youth diagnosed as feebleminded and confined to the state's epileptic colony.[74] This emphasis on disability opens up the possibilities for crip kinship with institutionalized people, a chosen family that crosses the timespan of the twentieth and twenty-first centuries.

Critical disability studies as a methodology is driven by what Merri Lisa Johnson and Robert McRuer name "cripistemologies"—what they define as the ways of knowing and forms of "prohibited knowledge about disability" that emerge from a collective, politicized reflection on the experience of disability.[75] Deriving from the derogatory term *crippled*, the term *crip* has been reclaimed by some scholars and activists as a political affiliation among those who practice anti-assimilationism and reject unwanted efforts to cure, treat, or fix the disabled body.[76] Crip epistemologies, genealogically descended from women of color feminisms (according to Johnson and McRuer), disrupt the expectation that knowledge about disability will come from nondisabled experts and prioritize instead the knowledges of those whose bodyminds cannot or will not be cured into normativity. Critical disability studies centers the reading practices developed by those of us who are disabled, sick or chronically ill, mad, unwell, and neurodivergent. Although the conception of a eugenics history from below is most strongly theorized in chapter 4, the prohibited knowledges of disabled people drive the analysis throughout the book.[77] For example, it is from talking about my own experiences with bodily impairment and neurodivergence that I learned to conceive of the medical exam as a possible form of violence and to understand the ways that treatment can veer into punishment for deviant behavior. This understanding allowed me to critically interrogate descriptions of medical examinations in the archive that others may have interpreted as routine or unremarkable. However, as a white, queer, nonbinary, neurodivergent person with invisible physical impairments, including an autoimmune disorder, I do not believe that my experiences give me inherent access to disability knowledge, and I also recognize that I have missed many things that a person with a different socially located disability might have emphasized. I have cultivated a critical mode of disability analysis through being in relation with queer and trans disabled scholars, activists, and friends of color, but although my mode of analysis is collectively generated, I take personal responsibility for any ableism or carceral logics that crop up in this book.

As a white person trained in ethnic studies, I am especially attentive to challenging the white-centric cripistemologies and understandings of disability that have been dominant within disability studies. I am humbled to be writing this book at a time when the field that Jina B. Kim calls "crip-of-color critique" is being foregrounded in disability studies.[78] Crip-of-color critique reconstructs a genealogy of knowledge about disability grounded in women-of-color feminisms and queer-of-color critique, one that reads disability in and through its coproduction with race, class, gender, and sexuality. Crip-of-color critique is aligned with the nonacademic movement for disability justice, which centers "disabled people of color, moreover queer and gender non-conforming disabled people of color."[79] Just as critical forms of disability studies have intervened in academic fields, disability justice pushes back on disability movements that seek rights through appeals to the state. According to the Sins Invalid collective, "Our understanding of able-bodied supremacy has been formed in relation to intersecting systems of domination and exploitation. The histories of white supremacy and ableism are, after all, inextricably entwined, both forged in the crucible of colonial conquest and capitalist domination."[80] As such, the disability justice movement challenges the technologies of the state that materially disable racialized and classed populations, including through surveillance, policing, borders, imperialism, militarism, and incarceration. Both crip-of-color critique and disability justice inform my methodology, calling me to examine how states and their empires "debilitate"—a concept used by Jasbir Puar to decenter white and settler-infused notions of preexisting disability—racialized, gendered, and poor communities.[81] Disability justice is a guiding frame for this examination of eugenics as a form of state violence that invaded the body in order to limit reproductive potential, and institutionalization as a form of state violence that created illness, injury, and premature death.

By enacting disability justice as an ethic, the stories of violence in this book attend to the epistemologies of institutionalized people who repeatedly asserted the value of their lives. Their yearnings for freedom resisted the carceral state. While some institutionalized people voluntarily chose to be institutionalized, this experience has been overblown into a fantastical Hollywood trope.[82] Those who were targeted for carceral eugenics were also unruly, rejected cultural norms and the law, escaped, pursued legal remedies, and engaged in everyday acts of refusal that constitute civil disobedience. Throughout the descriptions of state violence in these books are also many moments where those with problem bodies resisted state efforts to contain them and articulated yearnings for life that can be interpreted as anti-eugenicist. These crip epistemologies of institutionalized people in the early twentieth century are the roots of anti-eugenics practices that today can propel our movements toward the horizon of feminist, queer, and crip abolition.

Destroying Crip Futurity

In Alison Kafer's description of the cultural imaginary of disability, she demonstrates that a healthy future is secured by obliterating disability and disabled life.[83] This ableist imaginary of a future without disability is

pervasive in the archive of eugenics confinement, such as when the superintendent of the California State School for Girls in 1920 had a "vision of
a society in which heredity will be so controlled that children will not be
born with handicaps that can not [sic] be overcome and in which home,
school, amusements, church, courts—all factors of environment, in short—
will so function that segregation of young girls in schools like the California School for Girls will be unnecessary."[84] The superintendent describes a
utopic future that arrives by eliminating disabled people and disability itself
through the strict control of reproduction. As this example demonstrates,
eugenics was at the root of many Californians' early twentieth-century
imagination of the future.

In addition to a physical intervention through confinement, eugenics
was a form of temporal enclosure. By attempting to control the timeline
of human evolution, eugenicists also diminished the possible futures that
could unfold. Those people deemed "bad stock" were, as the title of this
book references, considered "a serious menace to the future" of society, the
race, and civilization itself.[85] As threats to the future, the defective class was
subjected to what Ruha Benjamin calls a "temporal penitentiary."[86] Theorizing the "carceral imagination," Benjamin writes, "Black people routinely
are either degraded in popular representations of progress or completely
written out of futuristic visions . . . , a kind of temporal penitentiary in
which oppressed people are locked in to a dystopic present."[87] Benjamin
uses this concept to describe the discursive strategies of excluding Black
people from imaginaries of the future. Similarly, eugenics institutionalization both physically contained the defective class and denied people categorized as defective the possibility of being part of the future. In addition
to functioning as sexual control, confinement exposes populations to disablement, premature aging, and eventually premature death. The social
acceptance of carceral exposure to premature death is rooted in eugenicist
ideologies about the value of human lives.

Temporally, institutionalization also induced a kind of social death. By
this I mean that institutionalized people had little opportunity for imagining their own futures because they had limited access to cultural creation
and expression of their own. People institutionalized in the early twentieth century were offered infrequent religious, recreational, educational,
or other programming; they were more frequently denied the resources
necessary for the independent creation of art, music, writing, and other
expressive artifacts. Although undoubtedly within institutions there were
affirming spaces, most likely created by institutionalized people themselves,

the evidence of temporary autonomous zones and other unsettled places for intimacy (such as within the tunnels underneath the Oregon State Hospital described by Diane L. Goeres-Gardner) is ephemeral or recorded only in ableist ways in the archive.[88] Forms of social reproduction and creativity did occur inside of institutions; however, the practice of segregation limited the reach of such creation to the outside world by attempting to disappear the defective class and any evidence of their ideas. Institutionalized people may have created alternative embodiments and occupations of time, including the cultivation of chosen family that offered alternate lineages exceeding blood inheritance. These practices had the potential to disrupt eugenicist timelines for human evolution. However, through practices of confinement, eugenics limited the possibilities for creating potentially transformative culture, ultimately diminishing the horizons of crip futurity.

Eugenics institutionalization not only foreclosed on the futures of those who were labeled as defective but also delimited the possible futures for us all. The mere existence of eugenics institutions impacted noninstitution-alized individuals by incentivizing the adoption of the time-telling, time-keeping, and future planning required to be liberal workers and citizens. If individuals did not or could not embody liberal time properly, they ran the risk of being categorized as defective and committed to an institution. Disabled people who could not learn to embody liberal time and progressive timelines included gender-nonconforming, sexually deviant, neurodivergent, and mad people assigned to the category of women and girls and racialized as other. In this way, eugenics detention perpetuated a carceral logic that subtly terrorized the population against experimenting with other ways of being and being-in-relation in the world. Normative regimes of time and temporality were consolidated by the threat of physical enclosure. Through carceral eugenics practices, the state in California claimed jurisdiction over which possible futures could be allowed to unfold. As a result, the carceral logic of eugenics has never been safely contained in the past but has always been reaching through time, attempting to control both our present and our futures.

A Queer Desire to Touch the Other across Time

Archival work can be an isolating enterprise. Yet, as I squinted into the microfiche screen or carefully handled illegible and delicate papers, I rec-ognized kin in the state's records of the defective class. I recognized kin in the girls with goiters (enlarged thyroid glands in the neck) and low vision requiring thick glasses. I cringed to know that for eugenicists, this was proof of our hereditary weakness and degeneracy. I recognized kin in the assigned women that were declared "peculiar," "excitable," and "nervous"—early twentieth-century code words for *neurodivergence*. I recognized my appendectomy scar and my missing tonsils in the records of tens of thousands of institutionalized people experimentally operated upon. I recognized kin in the family histories of those who surrounded themselves with queer family and questionable friends. I recognized kin in the troublemakers, the unruly bodies, the strange affects, and the awkward, chronically ill people.[89]

Employing the queer concept of chosen family, I imagine these archival figures as lost ancestors. I use *queer* as a concept in the ways it has been taken up in Black feminist thought for at least twenty-five years. Described succinctly by Sarah Haley, queer is a racialized, subjugated subject position "produced outside of binary oppositional gender categories as something else altogether."[90] This understanding of queer as a material process of weaponizing sexuality to subjugate populations is applicable in relation to disability that is treated as an asexualized subject position. This usage of queer also works to explore how deviant sexualities were disabled in the early twentieth-century eugenics era. As far back as Cathy Cohen's seminal essay, the interventions of Black feminism and queer-of-color critique demand political implications, shifting movements to embrace as family those whose struggles may not look exactly like ours or who do not match the identity formations we mobilize to seek recognition.[91] Instead of biologically essentialist notions of solidarity with those who we presume were "just like us" in the past, I propose forms of queer kinship that are created by acting as accomplices to those rendered materially deviant in the past, a methodological practice that opens up new possibilities for collective queer futures.[92]

This kinship-building exercise is what Carolyn Dinshaw describes as "contingent," in the etymological sense of the word: a queer genealogical method that tries "to 'touch' bodies across time. Resurrection is the aim of this history, unreached but nonetheless signaled."[93] The resurrection is unreached because the histories of those who lived and died in institutions for disability confinement "[strain] against the limits of the archive," to borrow from Saidiya Hartman, requiring accounts that grapple with the impossibility of representation.[94] The straining toward resurrection is necessary in the case of state institutions, however, in order to counter the logic of eugenics that attempted to obliterate dysgenic populations both physically and temporally. Through queer reading and reaching across time, I do not attempt to recuperate the truth of the eugenicist past or include all histori-cal details about California's institutional history, but I insist on remem-bering the dysgenic other locked in the past by the ongoing circulation of eugenicist ableism. I offer this genealogy as a form of anti-eugenics—that is, I counter the imaginary of a future without disabled people by deconstruct-ing eugenicist logic, opening up queer and crip possibilities of an otherwise.

Michel Foucault theorized that the method he called "genealogy" is necessary to challenge historiographies that posit a seamless teleology from the past to the present in order to uphold sacred ideas and sentiments.[95] According to Foucault, a genealogical method demonstrates the historical contingency of these sacred ideas and reveals them instead as "unstable assemblages." Genealogical history is highly speculative, because, as Din-shaw theorizes, "queer historical projects aim to promote a queer future."[96] In contrast to liberal temporalities, queer genealogy is not congratulatory about an imagined queer present that we have collectively arrived at due to a steady overcoming of the oppressive past. Nor is queer genealogy invested in establishing an inevitable final destination, which we will collectively ar-rive at if only we keep marching forward. Queer genealogy draws on tem-poralities that are nonlinear, not inevitable, and not teleological. Instead, queer genealogy is a practice of what José Esteban Muñoz names as criti-cal hope: a methodology that "can be best described as a backward glance that enacts a future vision."[97] Although grappling with queer and critical disability theory snatches from us the assurance of inevitable future free-dom through steady reforms, the alternative temporality offered is far more powerful. By tracking the carceral eugenics technologies through which queer and crip futures were foreclosed, I reveal this present dimension of existence as historically contingent and therefore changeable. Genealogy is a practice of yearning for what Muñoz calls a queer "then and there," a future we can feel but have not yet arrived at.[98] Marking these "days of future past" gestures toward other possible ways of living and being in the world, modes of social reproduction, and ways of organizing human value, countering the future imagined by eugenicists.[99] Queerly reaching across time to touch the other splits the future wide open from carceral eugenics logics to create the space for anti-eugenicist abolition to emerge.

The core archive of this study is a compilation of state records that provide a sense of the day-to-day operations of early twentieth-century eugenics institutions in California, including written records of individual institutionalized people, staged group photographs, and observations from visiting the physical campus of Patton State Hospital and its museum of mental health. A significant component of this archive is state records of long-term plans for institutions, including administrative reports submitted to the state legislature. Examining these reports reveals the role that eugenics theory played in constructing who should be confined to state institutions in the long term, how differences between treatment and punishment were collapsed, and how spending on state institutions was justified through eugenics rationale. Meeting records and correspondence of the League of Women Voters of San Francisco, a club that visited institutions and lobbied the state to build additional facilities, provide insight into the contributions of reformers outside of the government in developing carceral eugenics specifically for wayward girls and women. To provide additional context of the social imaginary in the early twentieth century, I describe two novels written by authors with California connections: *The Octopus: A Story of California*, by Frank Norris; and *Herland*, by Charlotte Perkins Gilman.[100] Through descriptions of these novels, I draw out the dystopic and utopic visions of Progressive reformers. Finally, in addition to reading the state archive against the grain, seeking the perspectives of those targeted for carceral eugenics, I located limited correspondence of institutionalized people and newspaper columns and letters to newspaper editors published in the book *Alice: Memoirs of a Barbary Coast Prostitute*.[101]

Chapter 1 uses "defective class," a term repeated in the archive, as a heuristic device to explore how agents of the state of California created a population of people that could justifiably be segregated in state institutions. By analyzing the documentation of people committed to state institutions between the years 1900 and 1940, I show how agents of the state used the process of commitment, including medical examinations, family histories, and psychological testing, to attach difference to bodies. Through routine practices that physically invaded the body, the discourse of defectiveness was made material—no longer living just in the pages of administrative reports but embodied in the defective class. A body made materially different could legitimately lose autonomy in the name of public health. I examine the process of losing autonomy through the interrelated and coconstitutive frameworks of disablement, racialization, and queering.

Chapter 2 tracks the everyday experience of life at a eugenics institution in the early twentieth century, specifically focusing on the types of care, treatment, and rehabilitation that institutionalized people were purported to receive. Building on Ben-Moshe's identification of eugenics institutions as part of the carceral industrial complex, this chapter identifies the many ways that care, treatment, and rehabilitation also acted as punishment.[102]

My purpose for this line of inquiry is to draw out the ways that pathologization and criminalization overlap and operate simultaneously to create the carceral state. This expands on what Angela Y. Davis calls the "punishment continuum"—specifically, I build on Davis's point that psychiatric institutions operated as an additional site for the punishment of those assigned to the category of girls and women.[103]

Chapter 3 follows the money, situating eugenics institutions in the political economic transformation of California at the turn of the twentieth century, from laissez-faire to administrative state. According to political economist Thomas C. Leonard, Progressives sought to establish a scientific, administrative state as the solution to the threats of economic greed of the corporate trusts and the growing population of defectives.[104] Where Leonard leaves off, I pick up to examine how surplus value continued to be extracted from the defective class, even after confinement in institutions. As Natalie Lira has discussed, eugenics institutions were places for disciplining gendered and racialized labor.[105] To this I add that institutions also extracted nonlabor surplus value from disabled populations. If part of the transition away from laissez-faire was through building state capacity to discipline labor and extracting surplus value that could be funneled for capitalist interests, my point is to emphasize that institutions played an important role in expanding this state capacity.

Drawing on Gilman's utopian novel *Herland*, chapter 4 starts by describing the imaginaries of middle-class and elite activist women of a maternal, caring state that enacted eugenics consensually.[106] The second half of the chapter resists consensual eugenics by telling the stories of unruly and undisciplined patients in state institutions. While locating the consciousness of institutionalized people is difficult for a variety of reasons, I insist on trying. To forget the perspective of the institutionalized person is to collude with eugenics, to disappear those labeled as dysgenic, and to obliterate the other possible futures that disabled and queer people could have created. By reading against the grain in the archive of institutions, I work toward a eugenics history from below.

To make the case that detention is eugenics, chapter 5 jumps ahead in time and provides a compressed history of California's institutions, from the 1950s into the present. While the population of people living in institutions for disability confinement has declined dramatically, and many institutions have been closed and converted for other uses, institutions are still here. Today, these institutions resist closure through the integration of publicly supported practices of criminal incarceration and containment of the so-called mentally ill. I also describe how the California Department of Corrections and Rehabilitation (CDCR) has, since the 1950s, leveraged public fear of the so-called mentally ill and substance abusers to build innovative prisons that continue to conflate care, treatment, rehabilitation, and punishment. However, I show that this fantasy of state care is undermined by endemic medical neglect and other forms of death-dealing that reproduce the logic of eugenics in a variety of carceral settings.

Chapter 5 makes clear the stakes for engaging in this archive: grappling with the policy of segregation is part of the process of recognizing that eugenics continues to be one of the philosophies motivating carceral systems. Programs that segregate populations functionally control human reproduction. They also cause disablement, premature aging, and premature death. Carceral projects separate people from their children, families, and life-giving and life-affirming support networks. Although it may no longer be done explicitly in the name of eugenics, detention continues to promote old fantasies of self-directed human evolution. Even when laws are put in place designed to prevent eugenics, civil servants and the increasing number of private contractors who carry out government services under neoliberalism have found loopholes or acted in violation of the law in order to continue enacting what they understand to be necessary forms of social control.[107] Even when actions do not rise to the level of medical abuse, I observe eugenics in the rationales used for incarceration and detention, the adaptation of eugenics institutions for new carceral purposes, and the acceptance of massive carceral budgets at a time when voters reject all other forms of state spending.

While I am cautious of reproducing violence through the repetition of stories of abuse and neglect inside institutions for disability confinement, I am frightened by the ongoing abuse and neglect of disabled, impoverished, racialized, queer, and gender nonconforming people in a variety of institutions. Even as some forms of confinement have become limited, one of the adaptive forms of detention that has emerged with a vengeance is immigrant detention. The epilogue returns to where the prologue left off, discussing how organizers in accompaniment with detained migrants are resisting confinement. While this book is not a detailed study of migrant detention, reconfronting historic state violence is one small piece of undermining the romance of detention as a solution to political, economic, and social problems, including mass global displacement. This book is my act of anti-eugenics. I define anti-eugenics as a counter-philosophy, one that is expressed by those deemed broken and threatening, as a will for creating life beyond the carceral state. Wherever the practice of carceral eugenics is exposed, an epistemology of anti-eugenics can be found. As much as this book is an examination of truly horrific state violence in the form of carceral eugenics, witnessing it is also an articulation of an abolitionist anti-eugenics that revalues disabled, mad, neurodivergent, queer, gender nonconforming, and immigrant life. To borrow from Muñoz, it is to feel toward an anti-eugenicist, abolitionist horizon that I tell the stories in this book.[108]

1

Making the
Defective Class

In a photograph submitted to the California State Legislature in 1919, people institutionalized at Sonoma State Home stand in clusters among shoulder-high bushes in front of scenic hills. Although most are too distant to make out their faces, their full-sleeved white dresses and wide-brimmed hats stand out against bushes that make up half of the frame. According to the caption, they are picking berries. However, the one person whose face is somewhat discernible stands at the center of the picture, neither chatting nor picking. Instead, this person, hatless and still, stares at something out of the frame (see figure 1.1). This image captures the haunting likeness of feminized people targeted for eugenics by the state of California in the early twentieth century.

1.1   Berry picking, Sonoma State Home. Photographer unknown. Published
       by California State Printing Office, 1921.

Juxtapose this photo to a report sent to the legislature two years prior,
wherein the government body in charge of regulating state institutions fa-
mously outlined its adoption of the theory of eugenics:

> We must make it our business to awaken the people to a realization
> of the fact that it is as foolish to permit human defectives to repro-
> duce themselves as to permit defective domestic animals to beget
> offspring. The whole stream of human life is being constantly pol-
> luted by the admixture of the tainted blood of the extremely defec-
> tive. If this source of contamination could be cut off, the beneficial
> effects would begin to show in a single generation, and in a very few
> generations the average level of human society would be very ma-
> terially lifted.[1]

As this passage illustrates, state government employees advanced the eugenicist view that so-called human defectives passed on biological weaknesses to their children that caused social problems. These agents of the
state were granted the power to control sex and reproduction among those
categorized as defective in the name of protecting the health of human society. The person in the foreground of the photo is treated in the archive
of eugenics as equivalent to a diseased animal, a source of pollution and

contamination. Her presence in the photo is made spectral and her gaze haunting because agents of the state of California imagined a better world without her in it.

I use the concepts of the defective and defective class in this chapter as heuristic devices to discuss how the state of California created a population of people that could justifiably be segregated in state eugenics institutions. *Defective* described the "neuropathic taint" of "a vast class of nervous and mental conditions embracing insanity, epilepsy, and feeblemindedness on the one hand; alcoholic tendencies, vice, eccentricities, absence of the moral sense, undue excitability and various anomalies of conduct and disposition on the other."[2] This "hereditary class" included the feeble-minded, the insane, imbeciles, morons, idiots, epileptics, the mentally diseased, delinquents, dependents, cripples, the handicapped, the mentally deficient, perverts, moral degenerates, the unnormal, the subnormal, and the immoral.

The adjective *defective* described a class of people, but the word also worked as a noun for individuals, as when state administrators expressed alarm about the growing presence of defectives—with an *s*—in state prisons, reformatories, and county institutions, including almshouses, county hospitals, and maternity homes. Of concern was the sense that a significant proportion of defectives had not yet been segregated by the state, posing a continued menace to social order. Defectiveness was conceived of as a fluid possibility for all bodies that carried inherited weakness. The Board of Charities and Corrections warned that the "normal," those who were "able to care for themselves, or [be] cared for by their families, relatives or friends" could easily slip into "unnormal status"—those "dependents, defectives, delinquents, and the aged" destined to "ultimately fall into the hands of the state."[3]

The category of "defective" was thus broad and edgeless. State agents may not have agreed on a specific definition, but they knew defective when they encountered it. It was a concept that productively conflated physical disability, madness, neurodivergence, and unruly behavior that challenged the social order. *Defective* operated as a discourse of difference that drew on existing social hierarchies and repackaged them in occasionally surprising ways, resulting in a hierarchy of bodily difference that may be nonsensical outside of that space and time. This non-sense does not mean that the category of "defective" was randomly deployed but, rather, that the category materialized a specific subject of state power.[4] Elaborating on the ways this process appears to be unfair and nonsensical in the present is precisely the point of historicizing this concept. This exercise invites us to question the non-sense of other formations of disability, race, and gender in the present.

This chapter tracks how the state of California constructed official knowledge about the defective class between the 1890s and 1930s. During this period, California systematized points of contact between bodies and agents of the state—points where those bodies could be read and scientifically interpreted as defective. The state constructed a defective class of people through the newly formalized systems of legal commitment and increasingly invasive medical, psychological, and familial assessments of institutionalized people. I identify these processes by analyzing state archival documents, particularly case books and registry logs for inmates at Sonoma State Home, Stockton State Hospital, and the California School for Girls in Ventura, as well as annual reports sent to the state legislature by medical superintendents, psychologists, general superintendents, teachers, and institutional oversight boards. I also analyze the text of legislation governing commitments to eugenics institutions.

Defective as it appears in these texts can be read as a euphemism for disability, race, or gender nonconformity. My interpretation is that defective is all of these but not reducible to one of these categories. The concept of *defective* drew on and elaborated ideologies of ableism, racism, and heteropatriarchy simultaneously. Eugenics revitalized colonial ideologies that have long prioritized men over women, bodies with clear binary sex over intersexed bodies, light-skinned over dark-skinned bodies, and body-minded normativity over disability, madness, and neurodivergence.[5] The eugenicist imaginary reestablished the notion of human normality as a white, binary-gendered male, one who has no visible disabilities or chronic illness, and whose mental processing is considered sane and normal.

However, in addition to drawing on these older colonial discourses, eugenics constructed new understandings of properties of the body. Through eugenics, naturally occurring human variations were observed and categorized as biologically abnormal. Social interventions into these variations, up to and including eradication, were legitimated using the discourse of scientific medicine.[6] To counter the eugenicist assumption that these differences are natural signs of inferiority that reside in the body just waiting to be discovered by medicine or the law, I describe how institutionalization produced differences in human bodies. The frameworks of disablement, racialization, sexing, and gendering each illuminate different aspects of the heuristic object of defectiveness, but none alone ever fully capture it.

Consequently, disability, critical race, intersectional feminist, and queer readings are each necessary to understand how carceral eugenicist practices made the defective class.

Institutions for State Inspection

There was no way to scientifically prove the existence of the defective class until they came into legal contact with the state. At the end of the nineteenth century, the United States began to systematize more pathways for people to be formally inspected by the agents of the state. On the heels of the federal government inventing immigrant inspection at ports of entry, the state of California created points for inspection of those already living in the interior. These internal inspection points were codified by the state's short-lived 1897 insanity law, which attempted to create a civil commitment process for the state hospitals, and the longer-lived 1903 juvenile court law, formalizing referrals to the state reform schools. For Sonoma State Home, the assessment process was not governed by the courts but through an application process and waiting list. The assessments at Sonoma culminated in a patient diagnosis that provided the rationale for commitment. Once a person became an "inmate" of these various institutions, they went through further inspection and classification by state agents, including physicians, nurses, social workers, and psychologists. A medical exam, eugenics-based social case history, and psychological testing allocated the placement of persons within the various wards, wings, and cottages of eugenics institutions. Together these practices of bodily and psychological inspection represent the process through which the state of California scientifically made a defective class of people.

One of the pathways to state inspection was civil commitment for reasons of insanity. Although short-lived, the insanity law, passed by the California legislature on March 31, 1897, illustrates some of the features of civil commitment for reason of mental disorder. Under the language of the 1897 law, family members, friends, police officers, city and county officials, and hospital officials could file an application for the commitment of a person accused of insanity with a county court. The court would then issue a warrant for the detention of the accused insane person in a county setting, including jails, unless provisions could be made for the insane person in their own home, the home of a family member, or in a private facility, pending the court hearing. Two court-approved physicians were to be solicited to examine the accused. If each physician agreed to the diagnosis, they completed a certificate of lunacy that was attached to the application for commitment. A judge was to review the application and certificate, declare the accused person insane, and order indefinite civil commitment to a state hospital. Transportation to the state hospital was to be carried out by the county sheriff's deputies. The 1897 insanity law provided that a friend or family member of the accused could call for a full hearing with the presentation of evidence, including but not requiring the appearance of the accused insane person in court. Similarly, after a declaration of insanity, the person declared insane, or "any friend in his behalf," had the legal right to appeal the decision to a superior court, yet they only had five days from the original court decision in which to make the appeal. The person who filed the appeal also had to submit a money bond for the court proceedings, unless they could prove that the committed person and anyone acting on their behalf was indigent.

The insanity law's lack of due process was the core issue in the 1901 decision *Matter of Lambert*, wherein the California Supreme Court ruled that the aspects of the insanity law that allowed for detention without notice and ability to be present at the hearing were unconstitutional.[7] In response, the right of persons to receive notice that an application for commitment had been filed against them prior to judicial review was affirmed. After the *Lambert* decision, the state's commitment process reverted to the earlier California Political Code language that allowed for indefinite civil commitment on the finding of two medical examiners that a person was "dangerously insane" and convincing a judge that the person was "so far disordered in his mind as to endanger health, person or property."[8] The ability of family, police officers, and medical officials to petition the court; the requirement that a judge make a final determination on the petition; and the transportation to a state hospital via county sheriff, all continued. This broad interpretation of involuntary commitment on the basis of danger to health, person or property lasted until 1969, when the Lanterman-Petris-Short (LPS) Act dramatically narrowed the criteria for forced commitment.

The other significant codification of detention at the turn of the century was California's 1903 juvenile court law. This law formalized the process of referring minors (boys up to the age of eighteen; girls up to the age of twenty-one) to the state's reform schools through a declaration of dependency (abandonment or neglect on the part of parents) and/or delinquency (inability of parents to control the unlawful behavior of the child). The juvenile court law allowed any person in the state to file a petition with a county court, initiating a citation to the youth's parent or guardian that required their appearance in court. A judicial finding of delinquency and/or dependency gave the judge authority to commit the minor to state custody. State custody options included placing the youth with a "reputable citizen with good moral character," a charitable organization, the care of a probation officer, or at one of the state's reform schools.

Juvenile delinquency was determined by the commission of a legally designated crime, including what are now called status offenses—acts that are only criminal because of the status of the accused person, in this case a legal minor. Dependency was a more nebulous category indicating parental abuse, parental abandonment, or some other inability of parents to keep a minor out of delinquency. The treatment of delinquency and dependency through a single legal process meant that youth could come under state surveillance for a wide variety of behaviors on the part of the minor, as well as for various failures to protect on the part of legal adults in their lives.[9] Some youths who entered the reform schools were labeled as mentally normal or even exceptional. However, this wide net caught many minors that state agents would later construe as defective, and their confinement at a state school sometimes facilitated their later placement in state homes and state hospitals.

However they arrived at a state hospital, state home, or reform school, committed people then underwent another, arguably more intensive, round of state assessment. In the eugenics era in California, agents of state surveillance were stationed at eugenics institutions to read bodies and interpret them as defective. Each individual entering an institution was subjected to intrusive state inspection that included at minimum a medical exam and at times also included a family history assessment and psychological testing.

The records of the medical exam are by far some of the most disturbing materials I encountered in the archive. I am wary of reproducing the violence of the state's inspection process, particularly when the only archival memory about those institutionalized is of their violation. At the same time, confronting this trauma is necessary to undermine the romance of institutions of disability confinement and to connect historical eugenics with the continued operation of carceral eugenics at multiple sites. I recount this violence of the past with the critical hope that it contributes to abolishing carceral eugenics in the present.

Entrants into eugenics institutions were closely examined for inherited weakness and congenital pathology. The intake form used by Sonoma State Home from 1913 to 1920 calls for blood and urine samples and a visual and physical inspection of the body, including hair, teeth, throat, breasts, external genitalia, and the vagina. Testing for venereal diseases—the Wassermann test for syphilis antibodies and Gram staining tests for gonorrhea—was routine. Reading the individual records in the Sonoma State Home casebook reveals the markers collected through these exams that staff considered deviant; bodies and minds were sometimes literally recorded as "normal" or "abnormal." Unmarked boxes are presumably normal while specific observations indicate anomalies or irregularities. Some observations mark conditions that are recognizable as chronic or even terminal illness, which in the eugenics era became evidence of bad heredity. For example, "enlarged goiter," evidence of a thyroid disorder that can be environmentally produced, could be constructed in eugenicist terms as "congenital." Other notes of irregularity indicate bodily difference that constitute a social judgment under the guise of an objective medical condition, such as the note: "Very obese, short stocky figure." Numerous records are opaque as to their medical import, including repeated concerns at the Sonoma State Home with "pendulous breasts" and "abundant hair." Practitioners interpreted these observations through gendered and racialized narratives that helped to construct notions of defectiveness.

The Sonoma State Home form also included a section devoted to what the California Bureau of Juvenile Research called a social case history—specifically, a family history and psychological testing for mental age.[10] In training manuals, social workers from the bureau called for collecting evidence of defectiveness within the body, invisible to the eye. This was accomplished through an examination that, at its most extensive, included assessments of intelligence, temperament, moral character, conduct, quality of associates, education level, job history, home and neighborhood conditions, and a family history. Trained social workers were deployed by the bureau to visit institutions to conduct lengthy entrance interviews with newly committed people; interviews that, under ideal circumstances, were followed up by interviews with family members, former employers, and institutional administrators. This ambitious project appears to have had success at Whittier State School under the superintendent Fred C. Nelles, but the translation to Sonoma State Home, at least until 1920, consists of a page of questions in the casebook that staff who were likely not trained in the emergent field of social work frequently left mostly or partially blank.[11]

The lack of engagement at Sonoma State Home with the social case history is indicative of the procedure as an emergent technology of state surveillance, one that was directly influenced by eugenic science and specifically the guidance of the Eugenics Record Office.[12] The family history was an effort to identify weakness in the vitality of the family, evident through the insanity, alcoholism, epilepsy, or criminality of family members. The first superintendent of Mendocino State Hospital, Dr. Edward Warren King, described the purpose of the family history this way: "What is transmitted to the child is a weak physical organization endowed with only a moderate amount of vital force, and a lessened resistance to the encroachment of disease.... What was the cause of this abnormal heredity? In order to get at the real facts we must ascertain the history of the patients' ancestors in each case."[13] Dr. King clarified that inherited weakness interacted with environmental factors: "Original weakness of nervous make-up is commonly the predisposing factor that makes habit, stress or overwork, environment, modes of life, joy and sorrow, with the high pressure of modern business life, active in the productions of insanity."[14] Here he illustrates that eugenics accommodated theories of defectiveness that considered environmental factors but ultimately rooted problems in direct biological inheritance.

In the case of both biology and environment, the premise of the family history was that defectiveness could be directly traced back to the mother and father. Diagnosed conditions such as feeblemindedness, insanity, and alcoholism were construed as stemming from the family. Behavioral histories of parents and family members also constituted evidence of defectiveness of a person. The traits that social workers or intake staff were encouraged to notice in new commitments included: alcoholic, criminalistic, epileptic, feebleminded, insane, pauper, sexually immoral, syphilitic, tubercular, wanderer, and potentially delinquent. Normal persons were those "who are free from mental defect, insanity, and epilepsy and who are known to be capable, intellectually, of managing themselves and their affairs with common prudence."[15]

Part of the social case history was a determination of mental age, a test that solicited the efforts of psychologists to examine newly committed inmates to California eugenics institutions. However, there appears to have been inadequate psychological staff to test all people inside California's eugenics institutions. Only some of the people committed to Sonoma State Home prior to 1920 have annotations indicating they underwent enough psychological testing to scientifically determine a mental classification on the Binet-Simon scale. The California Bureau of Juvenile Research focused their efforts on Whittier State School and the School for Girls in Ventura, adding the Pacific Colony after it opened in the late 1920s.[16]

In the 1910s at the California School for Girls, psychological testing was conducted as soon as possible to avoid cheating through other inmates;

this was no easy feat, because the testing could take up to ten hours total, spread across four separate sessions.[17] Using the Binet-Simon IQ test, and later the Stanford-Binet modification (or "Stanford Revision") published by Stanford psychologist and eugenicist Lewis Terman in 1916, the result of psychological testing was a determination of a person's mental age. Psychological testing purported to determine mental defect scientifically by measuring the mental age in relation to physical age. The tests delineated gradations of defectiveness: idiots had a mental age up to two years and were incapable of protecting themselves from physical danger; imbeciles had a mental age between three and seven and were incapable of earning a living; and morons had a mental age of eight through twelve.[18] So-called borderline cases marked those whose test results fell between moron and normal. In the state's reform schools, psychological testing also uncovered individuals with "unusual mentality" or who were otherwise "precocious."[19]

The consequences of psychological testing could be significant, especially at the state reform schools where both normal and defective people entered state custody through the same port of entry. Reflecting on her experience with testing at the School for Girls, Dr. Grace Fernald (who would go on to fame for inventing a kinesthetic reading method for remedial learners) outlined the practical application of psychological testing. According to Fernald, testing allowed institutions to "segregate the mental defectives from the normal" and the "degenerate (those most perverted and morally contaminated) from all others," including through separate sleeping, schooling, and recreational quarters when possible.[20] Segregation within segregation institutions facilitated the creation of different tracks for work assignment and formal schooling, with only limited opportunities offered to those determined to be feebleminded and therefore of limited potential for rehabilitation. The determination of mental defect by the state justified permanent custodial care in the view of Fernald, who argued, "Every feeble-minded girl who has gone out for the school as the law allows, at the age of twenty-one, has come to disaster. . . . [Society] must understand thoroughly that every feeble-minded girl who is turned out to make a living under the complex social and economic conditions of the present day has just one life open to her."[21] Fernald here meant to advocate for the state to take care of young women who were at risk of the life of prostitution or some other ill repute. Yet the effect of Fernald's maternalistic version of eugenics was to promote the indefinite detention of portions of the girl population determined to be defective.

The search for markers on and in the body, through the medical exam, the social case history, and psychological testing, culminated in a diagnosis written in the state's documentation of institutionalized people, including the casebook or registry log. In both the Sonoma State Home casebook and the Stockton State Hospital commitment register, diagnosis is the final category at the bottom of the form. The "cause" of detention in the Inmate History Register for the California School for Girls plays a similar function. It is here that all the evidence amassed by state actors justifies the designation of an individual body as part of the defective class. Occurring at the conclusion of the assessment process for new inmates, the diagnosis signals the moment when a body became officially conscripted as a defective subject. This medicolegal utterance materialized a body as defective.

The more in-depth assessment of people at the point of entry into the institution sometimes contradicted the findings of county judges. To illustrate, consider that shortly after the passage of the insanity law and prior to its overturning, state hospital staff had to establish diagnoses for those who had already been determined socially and legally insane. A chart dated from the year 1900 shows the range of diagnoses at the five state hospitals. Approximately 90 percent of patients were sorted in broad categories, including mania, melancholia, and dementia.[22] However, slightly more than 10 percent of patients in state hospitals were considered "unclassified"—meaning that one in ten people had been legally committed but had no official medical reason for their institutionalization in a state hospital.

Evaluations of people entering Sonoma State Home, California School for Girls, and Stockton State Hospital are evidence of the state's process for constructing defectiveness. Through judicial commitment processes, medical exams, social case histories, and psychological testing culminating in a diagnosis, institutional staff created persons as defective and thus deserving of state confinement with the rest of their class. The category of defective was attached to the body through the invasive medical practice of prodding the body, measuring the vitality of family lineage, and rendering state judgments on the psyche. Drawing attention to these material practices of making difference unravels the presumption of eugenicists that defectiveness was inherent to the bodymind. Defectiveness, like all difference, did not emerge organically from human bodies. Instead, difference was attached to the body through a scientific apparatus that materially invaded and marked the body as proof.

Defectiveness and Disablement

One way to interpret the category of defective is that it labeled the group of people that today would be identified as disabled. Records of individuals entering institutions indicate impairments that would be recognized as legal disabilities today, including epilepsy, limb paralysis, limb difference, blindness, deafness, Trisomy 21 (Down syndrome), or psychosis. However, in some cases understandings of these conditions were plain erroneous. An example is that persons with physical differences and impairments were assumed to be intellectually disabled, a discourse that persists into the present. Further, understandings of impairments in the early twentieth century were entangled in moral judgments and economic imperatives around heredity. Many people were institutionalized for reasons that would not be categorized as legal disabilities today or for conditions that have been depathologized—namely, immorality and sexual deviance. Examining defectiveness through a critical disability methodology is not about drawing a direct lineage from people confined in eugenics institutions to people legally categorized as disabled today. Instead, the eugenicist conception of defectiveness highlights the mutability of disability across space and time.

Eugenicists described bodily impairments and mental disorders as congenital conditions, the inevitable result of a biologically inherited weakness. Yet it was only through a legal process of detailed inspection that bodyminds could become categorized as defective. *Defective*—and other similar terms, such as *feebleminded*—conscripted heterogeneous qualities and behaviors into a single category with legal force. Those who were recognized by the state as defective could legally be stripped of their bodily autonomy by being committed to a state facility and subjected to other eugenics policies, including sterilization. Rather than essentialize institutionalized people as being targeted for preexisting disabilities, I am arguing that it was through institutionalization that the defective person became disabled, denied access to public space in the extreme form of removal from society.

Nirmala Erevelles argues that this process of disablement is not just a discursive shift from one subjectivity to another but a material transformation. In her analysis of disablement and racialization in the writing of Hortense Spillers, Erevelles writes, "Black subjectivity as an impaired subjectivity is neither accidental nor should it be conceived of as merely metaphorical. . . . Black and disabled are not just linguistic tropes used to delineate difference, but are, instead, materialist constructs produced for the appropriation of profit in a historical context where black disabled bodies were subjected to the most brutal violence."[23] Attending to the materiality of disablement requires confronting the physical violence of capitalism that produces visceral "marks" on "the flesh"—to borrow from Spillers—that cause physical impairment.[24] The example of material disablement that Erevelles gives is of the physical abuse of enslaved Black people, such as whipping, that tore the flesh and caused extreme pain and suffering. This process of disablement was also material in the sense that it occurred as a routine process of capital accumulation. Erevelles flips conventional wisdom of disability on its head by illuminating at least one site where bodies became both racialized and disabled through the extraction of surplus value. Erevelles opens the door for identifying other historical moments in which capital is extracted from human bodies through the use of violence in processes that also produce disablement.

Viewing the state's assessment of those entering eugenics institutions through Erevelles's theoretical approach indicates the early twentieth century as a historical moment that materially produced disablement. I am thinking of the medical exam through which physicians physically invaded the orifices of the body. The medical exam was the precursor to future surgeries and other medical treatments that scarred the flesh, and, by removing tonsils, appendixes, ovaries, and uteruses, created literal "bodies without organs" (to reference to Erevelles's discussion of Gilles Deleuze and Félix Guattari). I put forward that contact with the state would have also left invisible markings on the body in the form of trauma that constitute material acts of disablement.

Erevelles insists on attending not just to the body but to the political economy enabled by marking the flesh. The defective class was culled from the social population that Grace Hong calls the "existentially surplus," which indicates people who were not necessarily exploitable by capital as laborers—not Karl Marx's industrial reserve army of labor—but people who scraped by outside of regular licit labor markets in turn-of-the-century California.[25] Prefiguring the neoliberalization of global labor markets, I submit that the conceptualization of the defective class supported a new system of political economic relations. The shifts and movements of capital transformed by eugenics programs in California are discussed further in chapter 3.

Erevelles is talking specifically about the disablement of Black people globally, and by using her scholarship I do not mean to imply that the population of disability institutions was majority Black. The racial makeup of the defective class in early twentieth-century eugenics institutions does not mirror the populations of those institutionalized and incarcerated today, who are vastly disproportionately Black, and more likely to be Indigenous, Latine, or Pacific Islander. However, even for white populations institutionalized in the early twentieth century, disability was also constructed through race, gender, and sexuality. A normative body that is white, male, gender conforming, sexually normative, middle class, and a citizen can be materially disabled through discourses that interlock with racism and heteropatriarchy. Erevelles (among others) points to the ways that the process of disablement constructs racial formations.[26] Liat Ben-Moshe calls this relationship "race-ability," or "the ways race and disability, and racism, sanism, and ableism as intersecting oppressions, are mutually constitutive and cannot be separated, in their genealogy (eugenics, for example), current iterations of resistance (in the form of disability justice, for example), or oppression (incarceration and police killing, for example)."[27]

I insist on starting with disability in my analysis of commitment to state institutions. Other scholarship has taken as a starting place that eugenics policies targeted racial-ethnic groups for reproductive control and women for immoral sexual behavior and gender deviance.[28] This scholarship argues that eugenics policies were (and are) unjust because they were racist and sexist, meaning that they targeted people specifically for their race, ethnicity, and gender. However, without a disability analysis, the danger is of inadvertently implying that "actual" disabled people, those who were not targeted solely for their race, ethnicity, or gender, may have been justifiably institutionalized and sterilized by the state. Starting with disability is necessary to insist that those categorized as defective were simultaneously victims of racism and disablement. Some of the racial-ethnic populations as well as gender and sexual deviants targeted by eugenics programs did meet the criteria for legal disability today; they were disabled people in terms we would recognize today. They did not deserve to be institutionalized or have their reproduction controlled any more than those who did not have a disability that would be recognizable today. However, even if institutionalized people did not have a disability that we would legally categorize as such today, all of those assessed as defective were materially disabled in their historical context, at the same time as any negative racialization or gendering that they also experienced. The categorization of "defective" made them disabled in the eyes of the state, and that designation made it acceptable to deny them bodily autonomy and to remove them from public space. Why does it matter to remember institutionalized people as disabled by the mere fact of their institutionalization? Soliciting outrage about segregation in the past is one way to challenge the legitimacy of confining disabled, mad, and neurodivergent people in the present.

Defectiveness and Racialization

While racialization has been identified as a core component in the emergence of the prison industrial complex in the United States, fewer scholars have assessed the centrality of race to disability institutionalization.[29] Although I do not have comprehensive evidence of racially disproportionate levels of institutionalization, the concept of defectiveness reproduced the logic of white supremacy. Placed in the middle of a historic period of animosity against nonwhite populations in California, including Asian and Mexican people, carceral eugenics was an important strategy of racial hierarchy formation.

A compressed history of racial projects in California will be necessary to understand racialized language that appears in the archive of carceral eugenics. As in the rest of the Americas, and especially in resource-rich areas like the Pacific coast, hundreds of thousands of diverse Indigenous peoples have belonged to the place now called California since time immemorial. However, the trajectory of their colonization by Europeans differs from other parts of what is now the United States. The place that is now called California was first claimed by the Spanish crown in the early 1500s. While Spanish galleons that included sailors from the Philippines touched Pacific shores as early as the sixteenth century, the first waves of Spanish-citizen settlers did not arrive until Jesuit priests established a series of missions, starting with Mission Basilica San Diego de Alcalá in 1769. Missionization and forced conversion to Spanish Catholicism, which many California Indians have likened to slavery, fragmented and culturally decimated the highly populated coastal areas of the state as far north as present-day Santa Rosa, just across the San Francisco Bay.[30] Indigenous people in the inland areas and northern third of the state were not actively colonized until after the discovery of gold at Sutter's Mill in 1848, when the territory was annexed by the United States after the invasion of Mexico forced the signing of the Treaty of Guadalupe Hidalgo. Some Indigenous Californians still recall great-grandparents who lived through the post–Gold Rush wave of Anglo colonization and the genocidal policies of the early state of California. California Indians also have grandparents and parents who lived through the forced boarding school era of the late nineteenth and early twentieth centuries.[31]

These federal Indian boarding schools were a separate system for confining Indigenous youth, and their existence may explain why there are limited records of Indigenous people institutionalized by California in state facilities for disability confinement. Regardless of the rate of institutionalization, the records of eugenics institutions reproduced settler-colonial discourses that legitimated the containment of Indigenous people. For example, one note from the Sonoma State Home casebook reads: "Genitals: Normal, not clean" on the record of an "Indian" child. In an etymology of racist slurs, Deborah Miranda explains that Anglo settlers discursively linked Northern Californian Indians with dirt and dirtiness, which was used to justify genocide.[32] In the example from the Sonoma casebook, depicting the genitals of a Native child as "not clean" established that the child was defective and consequently deserved to be institutionalized. The discursive link between "Indian" and "defective" was reestablished in such notes, through which the agents of the state reaffirmed settler superiority.

While settler colonialism may have been the original racial formation of the state of California, another quickly followed: nativist orientalism. The Gold Rush brought non-Anglo immigrants to California from around the Pacific Rim. Chinese, Japanese, Pacific Islander, Southern American, Indian, Fijian, and Southeast Asian migrants arrived in the mid-nineteenth century and contributed greatly to the culture and landscape of California.[33] However, white supremacist policies were passed against Asian peoples almost immediately after their arrival, starting with the Foreign Miners' Tax Acts. After immigration law was preserved as the privilege of the federal government, prominent Californians promoted and then enforced national nativist laws, including the 1875 Page Act, the 1882 Chinese Exclusion Act, and the 1892 Geary Act.[34] Each of these national laws affected people with Chinese, Japanese, and other Asian ancestry, including those born in the United States. Eugenics programs that emerged around the turn of the century reinforced this existing nativist orientalism.[35] While some Asian-origin people were institutionalized, and at least one article suggests they were disproportionately sterilized, this evidence must be held simultaneously with the state heavily enforcing restrictive immigration laws to expel Asian populations.[36] Dozens of people of Chinese descent were deported directly from California institutions as early as 1891. Identifying potential deportees and facilitating their deportation limited the number of non-whites in both the nation and within institutions, distorting evidence of racially disproportionate detention.

During the time period in which Chinese populations declined due to the exclusion laws and deportation efforts at the end of the nineteenth century, people of Mexican origin were increasingly migrating to California, eventually replacing Asians as a cheap labor force. California had previously been part of Mexico, grafted to the United States at the end of the so-called Mexican-American War. Years of resistance to the land consolidation policies of Mexican president Porfirio Díaz pushed increasing numbers of poor farmers to migrate north of the border, joining the Mexicans who had stayed when the border crossed them.[37] The nativist infrastructure that had been built to devalue Asian laborers then targeted Mexicans. Attacks did not discriminate among recent arrivals and people of Mexican origin who were born in the United States, or whose families had lived in the United States since the annexation of northern Mexico. The construction of a physical US-Mexico border and enforcement of laws regarding crossing stepped up in the 1910s to the 1920s, specifically to regulate the flow of migration from Mexico.[38]

This border containment program was just one of the eugenics strategies against people of Mexican origin, who were presumed to be highly fertile and a threat to the Anglo nation. There is specific evidence collected by the Sterilization and Social Justice Lab that California's so-called Asexualization Act, first passed in 1909, disproportionately targeted Mexican Americans, particularly at the Pacific Colony in Southern California.[39] Given the lack of routine statistical collection by each of the state institutions, Novak and colleagues reintroduce the early twentieth-century census method of counting Spanish surnames to provide evidence of this disproportionate targeting.

Prior to the 1930s—when there is evidence that Mexican-origin youth were targeted for confinement in places like the Pacific Colony and Whittier State School—there were concerns about whether the state could afford the cost of institutionalizing Mexicans.[40] State agents made arguments that institutions should be reserved for the legally white "natives" of California and denied to racialized foreigners attempting to access resources. In response to the increasing reliance on Mexican-origin farmworkers and other laborers during World War I, one of the state commissioners in lunacy lamented, "California is sure to receive her share of this influx and her public institutions are bound to be called upon to care for those who fall by the way. The Mexican does not make a good eleemosynary charge. He will not work and is sullen and surly."[41]

This commissioner's argument was an articulation of what would become a common refrain: people of Mexican origin were not worthy of state charity. Charity meant institutionalization, with the perverse implication that only some defectives were worth the cost of segregation. Therefore, whatever evidence there is about the rate of Mexican-origin youth being institutionalized must be read critically. Other eugenics solutions were possible to deal with undesirable people of Mexican origin. Specifically, California's deportation agent put considerable effort into deporting Mexican-origin youth directly from institutions, arguing that it saved the state money in the long term to deport Mexicans from California rather than to institutionalize them.

In the 1920s and 1930s, anti-Black sentiment in California exploded during the Great Migration, which brought large groups of African Americans to California cities like Oakland and Los Angeles.[42] Kelly Lytle Hernández provides evidence that after this migration, Los Angeles County jails disproportionately incarcerated Black people. I was unable to track whether institutionalization was also racially disproportionate for Black people given inadequate recording of race on California state forms. Statistics sent to the state from the California State School for Girls in the 1910s and 1920s indicate that at any given point the population of "African" or "Colored" girls was 5 to 10 percent.[43] Because of how institutions were understood as sites of care and rehabilitation rather than as sites of punishment, it is possible that arguments would have been made against the institutionalization of Black youth and adults. However, this changed over the course of the twentieth century, especially as the system for disability confinement became integrated with the criminal legal system. Black people are now vastly disproportionately committed to California's psychiatric hospitals compared to their overall population in the state.[44]

Regardless of evidence of racial disproportionality in rates of institutionalization, anti-Blackness appears everywhere discursively, and sometimes in startling ways. For example, a record in the Sonoma State Home casebook lists "Hottentot suggest" for a "white, German descent" child. Hottentot was a derogatory, colonialist term invented by Dutch settlers in the Western Cape region of what is now South Africa to refer to non-Bantu Indigenous peoples in the seventeenth century. It entered the English lexicon and became a widely used derogatory term for Black people, especially when Sarah Baartman, a Khoikhoi woman from South Africa, was put on display in a travelling freak show across Great Britain and France billed as the "Hottentot Venus."[45] While in France and after her death, Baartman became the object of study of Georges Cuvier, one of the founders of comparative anatomy. As Janell Hobson discusses, it is through Cuvier's work that "Hottentot" came to be associated with the particular body type of large buttocks and elongated external genitalia.[46] Curiously, this note in the Sonoma State Home casebook attaches racial difference to a specifically white child. Although not used in this instance to institutionalize a Black person, this usage still reinforces the discursive link between Blackness and the defective class.

The white "Hottentot" child is also a reminder that in the pre–World War II era, legally white people who belonged to ethnic groups, including Portuguese, Italian, and Irish, were racialized as foreign and threatening to the Anglo nation. I use the term *legally white* to refer to centuries of colonial law, federal legislation such as the 1790 Naturalization Act, and supporting case law that maintained differential legal status (such as withholding citizenship) for people who were formally determined to be nonwhite.[47] As numerous examples in US history illustrate, legal categorization as white for the purpose of claiming certain rights can co-occur with de facto racialization through nationality or ethnicity. In the early twentieth century, legally white people were racialized through eugenics discourses of degeneracy and defectiveness that portrayed them as threats to the purity and health of civilization. However, in the post–World War II era, this form of racialization was proven to be temporary, as ethnic groups, including Irish, Italians, and Jewish people, were deracialized and assimilated.[48] While men and women constantly threatened to degenerate in eugenics discourse, and consequently join the ranks of racialized populations, the shift in status could never go in the other direction. That is, manhood and womanhood were achievements that could only be made by those who embodied legal whiteness.

Efforts to exclude racialized groups from state care, including through direct deportation from institutions combined with nationwide efforts to prevent racial-ethnic migrants from entering the country, may have whitened the institutionalized population in the early decades of the twentieth century, especially in Northern California. Yet eugenics programs consistently upheld white supremacy. While eugenics reproduced racial formations, including the settler-colonial logic of elimination, orientalism, and anti-Blackness, eugenics as a discourse was also racializing on its own. Jodi Melamed describes racialization as a process that constitutes "differential relations of human value and valuelessness according to reigning orders while appearing to be (and being) a normative system that merely sorts human beings according to categories of difference."[49] In this definition, racialization describes the active and adaptive creation of distinctions between some lives that are understood as valuable or worthy and other lives that have no value and are unworthy. Through concepts such as "defective," eugenics constructed a hierarchy of human value, helping to constitute the human by denying humanity to others. Eugenics articulated what a valuable bodymind is and devalued bodyminds that deviated from this norm of embodiment.

Eugenics discourses specifically worked through discourses of time and temporality, reproducing the white supremacist logic of recapitulation. Western Enlightenment philosophies conceive of time as linear, unidirectional, progressive (always moving away from the past and toward the future), teleological (always moving toward some destiny), and universally synchronous (we are all in the same time and on the same timeline). Johannes Fabian's description of colonial knowledge regimes shows a theory of time that created a temporal distance between "us" and "them."[50] Because colonization brought bodies into the same physical space, Fabian theorizes, the colonized other was relegated to a different time. Through the assumption of universal time and the teleological privileging of the future, the colonized other was relegated to the past through discursive categorizations such as primitive, backward, and atavistic. This temporal distancing could then be made geographic, locating civilization in the West, experiencing time in the "here and now," while the savages of what Stuart Hall calls "the rest" were conceived of as existing in prehistorical worlds on the periphery "then and there."[51]

Nineteenth-century racial science applied this colonial time in the theorization of recapitulation. As Siobhan Somerville recounts, "According to the stages of evolutionary 'progress' . . . the children of 'superior' groups embodied phases equivalent to the mature adult phases of 'inferior' groups . . . adult African Americans and white women were at the same stage as white male children and therefore represented an ancestral stage in the evolution of adult white males."[52] The brain of a racialized adult was conceived as equivalent to the brain of white infants so that racialized adults were perpetually considered to be backward in time—in the "then." Somerville points out that this logic of recapitulation was subsequently borrowed by sexual science in the early twentieth century. The diagnosis of an abnormally sexualized individual was also placed on a developmental scale and conceived of as backward and an anachronism. The abnormally sexual individual (in Somerville's case study, the homosexual) was viewed as having stalled in their development, having not progressed into normal heterosexuality.

The logic of recapitulation reemerged in the eugenics era of the early twentieth century. As the California Bureau of Juvenile Research described their methodology of psychological testing: "It is now possible, by reason of recent comparative research, to predict, within reasonable limits, the probable intellectual development of individuals whose present status we learn through psychological tests. Mental development, like every other natural process, follows an orderly procedure. The laws of mental growth are now sufficiently well understood that we can safely rely upon the psychological laboratory for predictions of intellectual achievement."[53] Similarly to how racial scientists organized human skulls to show the evolution of human intelligence, psychological testing arranged people according to mental age, built on the presumption of universal, linear development of the mind.[54] The normal individual was understood to have progressed to the here and now while the defective mind was plotted further back in the timeline.

Some psychologists, social workers, physicians, medical staff, and teachers employed by California eugenics institutions undoubtedly understood themselves to be helping needy individuals by creating systems of classification that exempted defective youth and adults from having to struggle to survive in the normal world. Yet these humanitarian gestures trafficked in eugenicist discourse that fundamentally understood defectives to be biological threats to the body politic. Exemplifying this is a report from the superintendent of Mendocino State Hospital, where he claimed:

> Here we find the real cause of much of the crime and insanity that is the bane of civilization.... Every healthy, normal man who from any cause, either from serious disease, alcohol, or sexual excesses, or through a life of debauchery, lowers the tone of his vital forces and afterwards propagates the species, is preparing the soil which will surely bring forth a class of degenerates, many of whom will be insane or criminals, and many of whose children will be feeble-minded, or perhaps idiotic.... In order to correct this condition of affairs we must strike at the causes which produce so much vicious heredity, and allow the race to return to a normal, healthy condition.[55]

It is impossible to escape the racialized valence of the term *civilization*; its invocation reproduces the logic of recapitulation. It is a concept that produced a binary opposition between those at a normal stage of development who have advanced beyond, but constantly threaten to revert to, a less desirable state of existence and those whom the superintendent called a "class of degenerates." The threat to civilization came from within the men and women who behaved immorally and then passed on defectiveness. The race that was threatened by this behavior was both the generic human species and the white race, which is the unmarked standard for humanity.[56]

While the discourse of carceral eugenics in California drew on and reproduced preexisting racial formations in California, the discourse also offered useful material for racializing a broader population of people. This class of so-called defectives was racially generic and frequently unmarked in the records of the state, even as they were racialized through formations of value/valuelessness. Race-neutral language, such as referring to civilization and pretending to imply all of humanity, obscured the material ways that the discourse and practice of carceral eugenics specifically upheld white supremacy. Even when legally white people made up most of the population in institutions for disability confinement, the discourse around their racial status helped to buttress the white supremacist system of carcerality. This had dire consequences for communities of color, who became over-institutionalized and over-incarcerated in the second half of the twentieth century.

Defectiveness and Queering

When I started presenting on this research, I was asked to discuss the "actual queer people" who were part of the defective class.[57] Queers do appear in the eugenics family history record, usually as an adjective for male family members:

> Father queer.
> Her brother paralyzed and queer.
> Mother's brother was a little queer.
> Maternal grandfather queer.
> 5 brothers on father's side queer.[58]

In her etymology of the term *queer*, Siobhan Somerville explains that it has been used in American English to refer to an eccentric or unconventional person.[59] Yet the use of queer for only assigned-male persons is notable, providing evidence to support George Chauncey's claim that queer had a specific connotation of an effeminate male in the early twentieth century.[60]

This usage prefigured the eventual transformation of queer in the mid-twentieth century to signify a person engaged in same-sex sex, or at least professing same-sex sexual attraction. It is these kinds of "actual queers" that my audiences wanted to hear about.

My interest in queering the history of carceral eugenics, however, is more aligned with how Black feminists use the concept as a material process of subjugation through attacks on sexuality. I argue that eugenics institutionalization materially queered institutionalized people in two ways: (1) through the process of sex assignment at the point of admission, and (2) through attacks on girls' and women's sexual behavior.

First, state confinement was a way of constructing the sex binary and conscripting people into gendered subject positions. The policy of segregation was effective as a reproductive control strategy only insofar as institutions were internally segregated by sex, to prevent sexual activity that could spread undesirable inheritable traits. Prior to the turn of the twentieth century, carceral institutions in California were not necessarily organized along binary sex. In 1872, California passed a state law mandating that county jails segregate males and females. As late as 1905, however, reformers observed that jails in the remote parts of the state did not have the facilities to enforce this law, and people of all sexes and ages were placed together in large cells. Women reformers lamented that these conditions allowed for the abuse of imprisoned women by "passionate, brutal men," pointing to reports that the women's quarters at San Quentin State Prison had been used as a brothel.[61] Women reformers promoted strict sex segregation as a solution to sex scandals: they sought to protect their fallen sisters by insisting that separate state and county institutions be established for women and girls. Further, they advocated that the women's institutions be operated by women who were invested in preventing immoral sexual contact between men and women. The women's jail in San Francisco provided a model for the completely sex-segregated institution, followed at the state level by the School for Girls in Ventura in 1914, the Industrial Farm for Women in 1922, and the California Institute for Women in 1933. The superintendent of the new State School for Girls celebrated these accomplishments by declaring: "The present condition of the school now established at Ventura enabled the state of California to properly and scientifically segregate ... the girls who have become its wards."[62]

Where separate sex-segregated institutions could not be built, such as at state hospitals and homes for the feebleminded, separate living quarters were established by designating female cottages or locked wings. Separate facilities for assigned women with a history of promiscuous sexual behavior were especially desirable, because girls and women were presumed to be responsible for the reproduction of the defective class. A State Commission in Lunacy report explained: "This condition [high grade defectiveness] is bad enough among the boys, but in the girls the misery and anxiety are increased a hundredfold in the families."[63] When the State Board of Charities and Corrections called on the legislature in 1914 to make additional appropriations "for Care of Defectives," it was for the express purpose of building additional facilities to segregate girls and women, because "many of these are girls and women of child-bearing age who constitute a serious menace to the future."[64]

The desire for sex-segregated institutions that could prevent sexual activity required the state to determine the sex of a person at the point of entry. As the medical intake records disturbingly show, sex determination included visually and physically inspecting secondary sex characteristics such as breasts, as well as visually and physically examining external genitals and interior organs. Observations about "enlarged clitoris," or "enlarged labia minora," indicated concerns about sexual deviance; one note makes the connection explicit: "Clitoris prominent (masturbation?)."[65] In addition to viewing and touching external genitals, medical practitioners inserted their fingers and instruments into the vaginas of patients, so that they could note: "hymen ruptured," "vulva very red," or "Uterus child's size. Vagina admits one finger." During this portion of the exam, medical practitioners used these observations as evidence of whether a patient was a "virgin." Claims about the intactness of the hymen and the normality of the internal reproductive organs built evidence for the diagnosis of immorality. Formerly incarcerated people and their advocates have argued in recent decades that this component of the contraband inspection at prisons constitutes a form of state-sponsored sexual assault, particularly for individuals with a vagina.[66] The tragedy of this practice during the early eugenics era is that behavior that could be construed as an assault—in blunt terms, the insertion of a finger or object into a person's vagina—was then deployed to make judgments about a person's own sexual deviance.

Judith Butler describes sex as being materialized through an iterative and repetitive process of gender formation, one that "stabilizes over time to produce the effect of a boundary, fixity, and surface we call matter."[67] Queer approaches to carceral studies argue that incarceration operates as an important site for materializing the binary sex system, for bodies both inside and outside of the institution.[68] What I propose is that California also materialized binary sex through institutionalization in the early twentieth century. The process of institutionalization reproduced the social fact that there are two, opposite biological sexes among humans. In the present, the carceral state's binary sex assignment causes difficulties for at least two types of people: first, intersex persons whose sex characteristics do not match ideologies of male or female typology; and second, persons whose gender identity does not align with official sex assignment. In these cases, people are forced, often violently, into binary state institutions based on state assignments of sex that do not account for intersexed or trans bodies. It is reasonable to conclude that some people institutionalized in the early eugenics era found themselves in a similar situation of epistemic and physical violence due to an official state sex assignment that was not, to use Butler's term, "self-identical" to understandings of one's body.[69] Intersex and trans people would have been among the defective class, uniquely affected by the policy of segregation that forced them into a binary sex category.

Second, gendered expectations that emanate from sex assignment were enforced on institutionalized girls and women through control of sexual behavior. Gendered sexual behavior was first regulated at the point of admission to a state institution, through further material invasions of the body that included the collection of blood and other bodily fluids. Specifically, the medical exam at institutions in the prewar period routinely included a Wassermann's test for syphilis and a Gram staining test for gonorrhea. Although testing enabled medical staff to implement (at that time still experimental) treatment protocols for new patients, the process also facilitated an additional level of segregation for those testing positive for syphilis or gonorrhea. Despite a high rate of false positives, institutionalized people who tested positive for a sexually transmitted infection (STI) were sometimes internally segregated during a period of quarantine. At the state's reform schools, all incoming youth were isolated until a medical examination and clinical tests could prove they were free of communicable STIs. At the School for Girls, "not until pronounced free from disease [were] they allowed to go into a home cottage" or to take on chores in the kitchen and dining areas.[70] These internal segregation policies would have prevented institutionalized people from accessing limited training and recreational programs and, I argue, materially queered inmates as sexual deviants. In the mid-1920s, both the California School for Girls and Whittier State School had at some point implemented policies against even admitting people who had tested positive for syphilis—constituting some as too sexually deviant for reform school. After appeals by probation officers from around the state, this policy was changed by 1928.

Investigations of the genitals, internal organs, and bodily fluids built evidence toward diagnoses of immorality for assigned-female subjects. Immorality as a diagnosis weaponized sexual behavior into a legitimate reason for state confinement:

> Girl has no moral sense. Supposed to be married has had two children. . . . Was arrested in Sac[ramento] for illicit relations with man.
> Moral imbecile. Mental age 11^4. Sexually irresponsible.
> Is addicted to masturbation. No moral sense.
> No moral sense; lazy; filthy in care of person.
> Moron. Vicious immoral type.[71]

An administrator at the California School for Girls declared that "ninety-eight per cent of the girls committed to this school are sexually immoral."[72] She went on to elaborate:

> Seventy-five per cent of the girls received at the school have had sex relations with boys or men, or both, before they were 14 years of age.
> Fifty per cent had such relations before they were 12 years of age.
> Fifty-four per cent are known to be victims of deplorable sex practices, and another 10 per cent might safely be added to this number. In these two years 180 of 233 girls (79 per cent) have been treated for gonorrhea. . . .
> Fourteen per cent are or have been married.
> Twelve and a half per cent of those married have borne children (most of them were forced marriages and the girls continued their delinquency).
> Seven per cent of the 233 have given birth to illegitimate children. None of them have married.
> Eight and a half per cent have produced abortions before coming here. . . .
> Six per cent have been victims of the lusts of their own fathers or brothers, or both.
> One 20-year-old feeble-minded girl has borne two children by her own father. Her mother is dead.

> Another feeble-minded girl, with the knowledge of her parents, had one child by a white man and a second one by a Chinaman. Semisexualism is not uncommon.

This gendered sexual deviance was presented as proof of legitimate confinement by the state. Yet Regina Kunzel points out that it was a circular logic, wherein "feeble-mindedness both caused illegitimacy and could be deduced from the fact of out-of-wedlock pregnancy."[73] To be assigned as female by the state, and to perform one's gender immorally, was proof of defectiveness, but, vice versa, all sex and reproduction by female defectives was defined as deviant. Not all the offenses caused socially unwanted pregnancy—notably, masturbation and same-sex sex, marked in this text as "semisexualism."[74] Immorality was not just about socially unwanted reproduction, but it was also a queer signifier because it signaled the unwillingness of assigned-female people to limit themselves to the narrow gender role of proper human reproduction. Pursuing their own pleasure without concern for propriety rendered women and girls as sexually deviant.

The superintendent claims that 14 percent of inmates had been heterosexually married, and that a portion of these people already had children. Under the logic of eugenics, even inside of heterosexual marriage an assigned girl or woman could produce defective children, and so she was still considered sexually deviant according to eugenicists. Like the ostensibly heterosexual welfare queens who emerged as targets of state regulation in the 1980s described by Cathy Cohen, all sex for defective girls and women was potentially illegal and open for state intervention, whether it was inside of legal conjugal marriage or not.[75] Disability was constructed as inherently sexually deviant, and, at least in the eugenics era, gendered sexual deviance was a disability.

Perversely, the discourse of immorality denied women and girls the capacity to make a claim to sexual trauma. Girls and women were routinely considered defective after being the victim of sexualized violence. Case histories tracked the forms of both "brutality and immorality"[76] that left a mark on the defective body:

> Patient addicted to masturbation—sexual intercourse with old men and boys. Supposed to have had intercourse with father (syphilitic).
> Man said to have [indecipherable] sexually [indecipherable] with her from 9 y.o.

Father of child is father of child's mother. Cause of deficiency: Consanguinity and depravity.

Child sexual abuse, referred to in these notes as "brutality," left physical marks on assigned-female bodies, including gonorrhea and syphilis. Under eugenics discourse, child sexual abuse, including abuse that occurred in prior generations, also left physical marks, resulting in "consanguinity," or an increased risk of inheriting recessive genes that caused a variety of disorders. There is serious slippage between having an STI and consanguinity, the form of inheritance presumed by eugenics. The father's (or another adult male parental figure's) depraved behavior was evidence of vital weakness that was necessarily passed on to the assigned-female child and manifested as symptoms of defectiveness.

Child sexual abuse also materially queered girls and women into sex offenders. Eugenicists Paul Popenoe and Ezra Gosney illustrate this in two comprehensive surveys of patient files related to California's sterilization program, released in 1925 and 1937.[77] Popenoe and Gosney describe those girls "of the lowest level of intelligence" who were at risk of socially unwanted pregnancy.[78] They report on two "girls" sent to Sonoma State Home: "It is worth mentioning, in passing, that the mother of the lower of these (IQ 16) noted on the application blank that the patient is 'fond of men.'" The second girl's parents thought she was so physically "deformed" that no man would want her, yet she was "raped by a delivery man, and gave birth to a child, whereupon she was sent to Sonoma to be sterilized."[79] Popenoe conflated both examples, one of potential consensual sex and the other of likely rape, to argue that "mentally deficient" girls were "oversexed."[80] Because girls were unable to consent to sex, any sexual contact—whether consensual or not—was grounds to reinforce the categorization of defective. Within this discourse, the solution to child sexual abuse was not to punish the perpetrators but to categorize girls and women as defective and treat them accordingly.

Once diagnosed as immoral or otherwise defective, people became candidates for another materially queering process, that of reproductive sterilization. Sterilization rendered the body deviant, removing an assigned-female person's capacity to reproduce and consequently destroying one of the few social roles available to women—that of mother. In another example of the circular logic of defectiveness, sterilization disciplined the patient for her failure to embody normality, yet sterilization disabled the gendered body's capacity to reproduce, making her freakish and monstrous. Here becomes evident that material practices of constructing defectiveness were a self-fulfilling prophecy. The discourse of defectiveness claimed to be able to locate the truth of the defective body, to discipline the body into normality, and at the same time continuously rendered the body defective, different, and other. This dynamic of eugenics is paradoxical, as it seems to indicate a simultaneous disciplining of the body and reification of the body's status as other that cannot hope to achieve normality.

The gendering effects spread outward from eugenics institutions to society at large. In her essential study of women's reformatories in the United States, Nicole Hahn Rafter argues that "prisons function to control gender as well as crime."[81] She continues: "Founded by middle- (often upper-middle) class social feminists, reformatories extended government control over working-class women not previously vulnerable to state punishment. In addition, the reformatories institutionalized bourgeois standards for female propriety, making it possible to 'correct' women for moral offenses for which adult men were not sent to state penal institutions. And reformatories feminized prison discipline, introducing into state prisons for women a program of rehabilitation predicated on middle-class definitions of ladylike behavior."[82] This program of gender conformity is evident in the superintendent's description of the girls locked in the California School for Girls described above. By delimiting the facts of the type of girl locked up in the girls' reform school, the superintendent helped to constitute a queered, immoral girl who deserved to be segregated from normal society. The articulation of who belongs in a reform school helped to, in turn, consolidate a dominant understanding of the type of girl—the normal girl—who did not belong in an institution. This normal girl had internalized a sense of sexual propriety, so that she did not engage in sex outside of marriage, she did not allow herself to be sexually victimized by her male family members, she did not masturbate or have same-sex sex, she did not have interracial sexual relationships, she did not contract venereal disease, she did not have sex too young, and she was not feebleminded or mentally defective. The normal girl was both of good genetic stock and asexual, until the point at which she became sexual within the confines of able-bodied, white, heteropatriarchal marriage. In short, the normal, nondisabled girl performed her gender in ways that buttressed ableist heteropatriarchy.

Building on Rafter's point, I conclude by suggesting that the construction of bodies as defective through the intake process at California state institutions had disabling, racializing, and queering effects that extended beyond state facilities' walls. Knowledge that people called "defectives" could justifiably be contained in eugenics institutions would have affected not only those institutionalized and their families. The practice of carceral eugenics must have also incentivized disability masking, racial passing and assimilation, and heterosexual gender conformity by those at risk of institutionalization. In this way, carceral eugenics shaped society far beyond the bodies captured at the institution.

2

The Carcerality
of Eugenics

One of two museums of its kind in the western United States, the Patton State Hospital Museum examines "the history of psychiatry and treatment of mental illness in California state-run facilities."[1] The museum is built on the campus of a still-operational state institution in Riverside County, east of Los Angeles. Opened in 1893 as Southern California State Asylum for the Insane and Inebriates, Patton State Hospital continues today as a secure forensic psychiatric hospital. The museum is housed inside a historic cottage near the entrance to the campus, and entry is possible through an appointment with hospital staff. I start this chapter with a tour of the museum, because its location next to a forensic hospital is indicative of the ongoing entanglements of carcerality and the treatment of disability.

One of the museum's exhibits is a jarring mashup of the technologies used over 175 years of Western treatment of mental disorders. In the center is a hydrotherapy tub covered with a canvas restraint sheet, with a single opening for the head of a patient. A photograph dated circa 1960 shows the tub in use by two patients being supervised by three nurses (see figure 2.1). The caption to the photo explains that "hydrotherapy was a common and inexpensive means of treating patients, particularly those who were deemed depressed or acutely disturbed.... Canvas covers were often placed over the hydrotherapy tub to insulate the water temperature and/or to restrain patients." The "and/or" in the sentence, joining the therapeutic with the carceral, is one of many such juxtapositions in the room. Right next to the tub is a chaise lounge with an unsmiling (and unlabeled) picture of Sigmund Freud, the founder of psychoanalysis. Freud's gaze is away from the two display cases across the room, which feature a straightjacket (manufactured by the Humane Restraint Company), a variety of arm and leg restraints, a transorbital lobotomy pick, a trephination instrument (used to drill holes in the skull), a magneto-electric machine, and an electroshock therapy machine. A smaller display case features funnels and bottles filled with liquid and labeled with homeopathic formulas.

Visible through an open doorway is a replica of a mid-twentieth-century patient room. Among the sparse accommodations is another leather restraint that has been placed at the foot of the bed. This serves as a reminder that it was not just in the tubs that patients were restrained; the bed and bedroom were also carceral technologies operating within the institution. Photographs in another room of the museum indicate that the privacy of a single room was likely unavailable to most patients at Patton in the first half of the twentieth century. These photographs depict a crowded hallway lined on either side with cots full of sleeping people.

While the Patton State Hospital Museum bills the hospital as the site for the treatment of mental illness, I argue that in the early twentieth century an equal or greater priority for the state was the eugenics function of institutionalization. The state of California implemented a variety of programs with the purpose of protecting society from unfit and dangerous populations, a partial scope of which is laid out in a 1914 report to the state legislature. There the Board of Charities and Corrections called on the state to invest in "(a) more definitive and stringent laws for the commitment of feeble-minded persons, (b) establishment of farm colonies for feeble-minded, (c) segregation of the sexes, (d) sterilization when necessary, (e) laws preventing the marriage of feeble-minded, (f) immi-

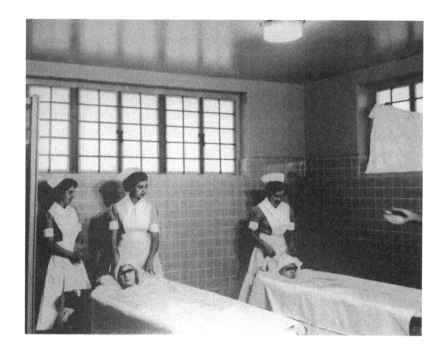

2.1　Hydrotherapy tubs in use, ca. 1960. Original photographer unknown. On display at Patton State Hospital Museum. Photograph by the author.

gration laws to exclude the defective classes, (g) special schools for the backward child."[2]

The Department of Institutions later reiterated techniques a, b, and c in 1922, determining that "those defectives whose tendencies are such as to make them undesirable members of the community should be permanently segregated in the institution."[3] Permanent segregation combined with sex segregation worked as a prophylactic to prevent socially unwanted pregnancies that, according to eugenics, threatened to diminish the vitality of human stock. Some of the state of California's most prominent eugenicists, including Paul Popenoe, objected to the cost of institutionalization for the purposes of eugenics when other programs like sterilization were significantly cheaper.[4] Even as eugenicists emphasized sterilization, the state of California continued to segregate thousands of people in state hospitals, other institutions for disability confinement, and juvenile prisons. Even beyond the time when any administrator would explicitly use eugenicist discourse to justify institutionalization, long-term confinement functioned as a form of reproductive control and social death. Interwoven through the memorialization of mental health treatment, the Patton State Hospital Museum implicitly commemorates this history of segregation for the purpose of eugenics.

This chapter rewrites the museum's exhibits, describing life inside California's state hospitals, state homes for the feebleminded, and juvenile reformatories in the early twentieth century. I analyze data within the annual reports sent to the state legislature regarding the institutions, physical plant descriptions, populations, gender and race demographics, and death rates. I read the state archive against the grain for evidence that despite the museum's portrayal of these sites as oriented toward treatment and rehabilitation, these purposes were undercut by carceral architecture, medical abuse, and indefinite detention. To flesh out the scene of life inside of the eugenics colonies, I draw on the limited correspondence of institutionalized people available in the state archive and newspaper reporters' accounts of eugenics institutions.

In the museum's narrative, the state hospital was ostensibly built to provide treatment to those who would today be categorized as mentally ill, intellectually or developmentally disabled (I/DD), and dependent. This narrative is a continuation of early twentieth-century discourse, when agents of the state portrayed eugenics colonies as a respite from the harsh demands of modern life, as sites of relaxation and recovery, and even as zones of freedom. However, in the early twentieth century, the eugenics purpose of segregation through long-term custodial care was also explicit, moderated only by the claim that the institution was a humanitarian alternative to the outright execution of the defective class. The fussiness of reformers over surface details, like whether someone was transported to a hospital in restraints or merely in the back of a sheriff's vehicle, whether the barred windows had curtains, or whether someone was relaxed by being tied into a bathtub, obscures the carceral architecture, logic, and experience of the eugenics institution. The early twentieth-century program of permanently segregating the defective class in eugenics institutions was a carceral project.

Indeed, accounts of life on the eugenics colony depict an architecture that was not dissimilar to state prisons. These descriptions reveal that the technologies of restraint and punitiveness infiltrated the eugenics institution, blurring the distinctions among punishment, care, and rehabilitation. Moreover, carceral practices and reforms were developed in eugenics institutions before travelling back to state prisons and jails. In prisons and jails, treatments were deployed as punishments, and the recovery rule informed the invention of indefinite detention. An examination of daily life in the state institutions establishes that what Liat Ben-Moshe calls "the carceral-industrial complex" in California was built through the intersecting pathways of pathologization and criminalization.[5]

California's Eugenics Institutions

At the turn of the twentieth century, the state of California officially linked together prisons, juvenile reform schools, hospitals for the insane, and homes for the feebleminded by placing them under the shared oversight of the Board of Charities and Corrections. The stated mission of these institutions was to offer treatment, care, and reformation to the insane, epileptics, the feebleminded, delinquents, dependents, and other defectives. At the time of its formation in 1903, the board oversaw operations at five hospitals, one institution for the feebleminded, two state prisons, and two juvenile reform schools:

- Stockton State Hospital (founded 1851)

- San Quentin State Prison (1852)

- Napa State Hospital (1875)

- Folsom State Prison (1881)

- Sonoma State Home (1883, as the California Home for the Care and Training of Feeble-Minded Children)

- Agnews State Hospital (1888)

- Whittier State School (1891)

- Preston School of Industry (1892)

- Patton State Hospital (1893, as Southern California State Hospital)

- Mendocino State Hospital (1893)

Between the board's founding and World War II, five new institutions were built. These included a third juvenile reform school, the first sex segregated institution specifically for girls in Ventura in 1913. Shortly after, the growing Anglo population in the southern part of California spurred the establishment of Norwalk State Hospital just south of Los Angeles in 1915, as well as a second state home for the feebleminded called the Pacific Colony, which accepted inmates in 1927. The Industrial Farm for Women opened in 1922 in Sonoma County, north of San Francisco. The farm was barely in operation for a year before a fire destroyed the main building, and the newly reorganized State Board of Institutions (which replaced the Board of Charities and Corrections) declined to rebuild. Reformers instead turned their attention to lobbying to build the California Institute for Women (CIW), the state's third prison, and the first one exclusively for women. The CIW was slated to accept prisoners in 1933 but was hindered for four years by public outrage over an architectural style that was declared not prisonlike enough, as well as a struggle over whether it would be women that would staff and operate the prison.

In 1900, the total population of the five state hospitals and the state home was 5,276 people, with 37 percent of patients classified as female. Twenty years later, in 1920, the population of six state hospitals had almost doubled to 10,119, with an additional increase in the percentage classified as female—up to 42 percent. The Board of Charities and Corrections calculated the commitment rate in comparison to the overall population of California in 1916, observing that the commitment rate to the state hospitals alone (excluding all other institutions) was one to every 285 people residing in the state. At the time, the overall population in California was just under three million people.

The commitment rate to the state hospitals far exceeded that of the state's prisons. In 1900, the state's two prisons held a total of just 2,131 people, with a 36 percent increase by 1920 to 2,911. (Enlistment during World War I strongly affected the incarceration rate but less so the institutionalization rate, with both types of facilities experiencing impacts on the level of staffing.) The difference is even more stark when focused on those assigned as women by the state; as Black feminist scholar Angela Y. Davis points out, in the twentieth century women were institutionalized at far greater rates than they were incarcerated.[6] Compared to the thousands of females listed as residing in state hospitals, records indicate that less than a dozen people were held in the women's quarters at San Quentin at the turn of the century and none at Folsom. Twenty years later, in 1920, the population in the women's prison quarters had tripled, to around seventy-five people. Even with this explosive growth in women's incarceration, the scale was far outpaced by the thousands confined in disability institutions. This was true even after the state's first prison for women accepted prisoners in the late 1930s.

What were disability institutions physically like? Some of the oldest state institutions, including Agnews, were built in the early nineteenth-century Kirkbride asylum model: a congregate plan where all patients lived under one roof. Mimicking the construction of a teacher's college, Kirkbride institutions were multistoried brick and masonry buildings with two wings that formed a shallow V shape spreading from a central entrance.[7] These buildings could be easily sex segregated by floor or wing. The so-called cottage plan for the state hospital became increasingly popular in the post–Civil War period, where smaller wooden buildings served as dormitories for patients. As the sciences of mental medicine and disability evolved, the smaller dormitories were useful for segregating the increasing variety of categories of patients. Carla Yanni notes that the cottage plan did not immediately or entirely replace the large hospital.[8] Even in the late nineteenth century, large brick and masonry buildings continued to be built, with cottages added to supplement, while other institutions were made primarily of the smaller cottages. Yanni suggests that the cottage system coincided with the growth of the number of so-called incurable patients in the latter third of the nineteenth century, who were thought to need to live indefinitely in institutions. While Yanni does not discuss eugenics, the timing of the shift in architectures of state institutions coincides with the popularization of the ideology. As more and more people were imagined to be defective, the cheaper cost and speedier time frame for constructing cottages became more desirable.

After the 1906 San Francisco earthquake destroyed Agnews State Hospital (located on the southern tip of the San Francisco Bay), the drawbacks to the large brick and masonry buildings were even more apparent. Dr. Leonard Stocking, medical director at Agnews, appealed to the state legislature to use the opportunity to reconceptualize the hospital:

> I think this hospital, as it is, should be for the acute and treatable cases, with an outlying colony for those who need care rather than treatment. . . . Better to colonize them on a large tract of land within a few miles of the parent institution. . . . I believe a colony on a sufficient quantity of good land in this valley could be made nearly, if not quite, self-supporting by horticulture and agriculture, if properly organized and conducted. I think that at as early a date as possible we should acquire a tract of land for this purpose, and begin our colonization.[9]

Although the urban site of Agnews hindered its ability to function as a site for eugenicist segregation, Stocking's vision of a colony a few miles out of town was implemented at many other facilities. Throughout the California state archive, the most desirable site for segregation was imagined as a large acreage colony that could be self-sufficient, with its own dairies, vegetable gardens, fruit orchards, laundries, bakeries, and kitchens, in part staffed by institutionalized people themselves. By the turn of the century, Sonoma State Home, for example, had grown much larger than its name suggests, occupying a total of 1,640 acres, approximately two and a half square miles. The site was lauded for its "ample water supply, drainage, and two railroad lines that passed through the property," ensuring that the facility could supply its own water, deal with its own waste, and receive shipments of goods by train.[10] Siting issues similar to Agnews's impacted the segregation function of other institutions, even as they tried to replicate the colony model on smaller scales. California School for Girls hosted a small population of less than eighty when it opened in 1913, occupying only 125 acres crammed with a hospital, four cottages (each housing about thirty people), a manor house for the superintendent, a commissary building, farm buildings, and a garage. In 1916, the superintendent requested appropriations to purchase an additional fifty-seven acres containing a functioning apricot orchard in order to increase the buffer between the school and seasonal fruit pickers, who apparently distracted the girls at the school from their reformation.[11]

Southern California State Hospital (now Patton State Hospital, where the museum of mental health is located) was built originally on the Kirkbride model on an over three-hundred-acre tract located about sixty-five miles east of downtown Los Angeles. In 1903, a newspaper reporter for the *Los Angeles Herald* attended a hearing about accusations of the physical and emotional abuse of patients by hospital staff on the campus. His description conveys the scene in ghostly imagery:

> The half windows that look out upon the pretty hospital grounds from the basement board room were haunted by the harmless patients, who are permitted freedom of the grounds, and almost constantly some distorted face was pressed close to the heavy woven wire screen that protected the window or the shrubbery was agitated by a patient who, with stealthy steps, was stealing to the windows. The institution was never quiet. Throughout the twenty-four hours some unfortunate was either reciting his woes, howling and screaming in fear or singing. The hospital was never at rest.[12]

The colony model allowed patients, at least the "harmless" ones, the freedom to wander the grounds at will. The large acreage of the facilities combined with the physical and mental impairments of patients acted as a natural barrier to escape, although escapes did routinely occur. Restraint was also regularized, with some patients consigned to locked-down wings, buildings, or beds.

The originators of the asylum in the nineteenth century proposed that the fresh air of the countryside was vital to the treatment of insanity. As states took over the operation of the asylums, the economic justification of the colony-style institution was more of a driving factor: such a facility could be made self-supporting. Sites in California were selected for water wells that could be driven and for the quality of farmland. With water and land, the institution could produce its own food through the raising of livestock, dairies, fruit orchards, and vegetable gardens. With water and land, institutional staff could live on-site, and patients could be put to work on the farms, in addition to working in the laundries and kitchens, acting as cleaning staff, and providing care for other patients. The possibility of self-sufficiency appealed to eugenicists, who claimed that removing defectives from the body politic, and allowing them to live out their lives in sex segregated colonies where there would be no opportunity to reproduce the next generation of defectives, was the humane alternative to execution.[13]

If the institutions were as self-sufficient as possible, this further reduced the possible contact that defectives would have with the outside world: "The farm colony means the creation of a new world for him [the feeble-minded] where he will be largely or entirely self-supporting under proper supervision."[14] Here the institution was imagined as a parallel world to normal society, removed from the demands of capitalism and modern citizenship, at which the feebleminded could not adequately compete. Social death was a humanitarian gift to feebleminded boys and men, but, for women and girls, institutionalization was necessary to protect society. The state institution slipped even further away from treatment and toward custodial care, functioning as reproductive control. Whether it was to be a home for untreatable insane women, sexual delinquents and dependents, girls in need of reform, or feebleminded women, the farm colonies facilitated eugenics demands—namely, to save the human race by preventing unchecked reproduction of the defective class.

The eugenics institution was still within the geographic boundaries of the settler nation—a colony within a colony. I imagine the eugenics institutions of California as something like the penal colonies of Britain, where poor and criminalized people were used to settle stolen territories. Instead of loading undesirables onto the ship of fools that would take them outside of the spatial bounds of the mother nation and the temporal bounds of history, California committed defective people to internal occupations of land claimed by the United States. The fantasy of the self-contained eugenic farm as a "new world" for the defective was colonialist in that it was foundationally premised on settler claims to Indigenous land and resources. Once the defectives died off and were prevented from reproducing, the land they had occupied would again be terra nullius, available for other settler uses. The construction of eugenics institutions in California expanded the carceral infrastructural footprint of the settler state; later, the land was available for other uses. Insofar as eugenics legitimated the establishment of carceral state infrastructure on lands that Indigenous people had lived on since time immemorial, it was also a settler-colonial project of modernization.

Carceral Pipelines and Carceral Architectures

Accepting that state institutions served a eugenics function does not mean that life for institutionalized people and staff was wholly terrible. Indeed, the archive registers ambivalence about life in state institutions. On the one side are depictions of colonies as peaceful places offering the restorative properties of farm life. The image of the berry pickers at the beginning of chapter 1 conveys some of the potentially appealing attributes of living in the country: digging in the dirt and eating fresh berries off the vine while the beautiful hills stretched into the distance. Institutionalized people must have found other like-minded people with whom they could share friendship, commiserate over struggles, and imagine new worlds. Sex segregation on the farms introduced a homosociality that some may have found queerly pleasant. Although it must be read critically, the state Board of Charities and Corrections claimed that some formerly institutionalized people took comfort in farm life and attempted to return after being discharged: "Very frequently one of the discharged patients, who is unable to get along on the outside, voluntarily comes back and says he wants to stay. Paroled men are allowed to go out to look for work, and, if after three or four days they have been unsuccessful, they are allowed to return to the hospital."[15] Institutional life in this description was a kind of refuge for deviantly bodied people understood as having difficulty surviving in modern society.[16] Similar to the ghostly description from the newspaper reporter, this passage implies that people confined to the state hospital were free to come and go as they pleased.

However, whatever freedom people found at the eugenics institution was constrained at the start by the fact that most people were forcibly committed, and in many cases travelled to institutions through carceral pipelines. In the nineteenth century and into the early twentieth century, county jails in California were not limited to the detention of those convicted of crimes, but also contained accused insane persons, witnesses subpoenaed for court, and those accused of public-order infractions, including vagrancy and commercial sex work. Additionally, prior to the scientific innovations of the Progressive Era and enforcement of state rules, all persons, regardless of age or gender, were detained together in jail cells. The civil commitment process developed in the early decades of the twentieth century created local psychopathic wards in the five urban areas of California, where accused insane persons could be confined against their will.[17] Once the short-lived state insanity law was nullified, these psychopathic wards became the primary pipelines for moving people into the hospital system.

County sheriff involvement in civil commitment continued with the task of transporting people to the state hospitals, frequently in restraints. Even the administrators of state hospitals understood that for the committed person, the process mimicked a criminal conviction. The superintendent of Agnews State Hospital called on the state legislature in 1904 to change "the present method of committing the insane, the method of their care, and the manner of their transportation to the Hospital" because

> rulings of the courts and legislative amendments have so changed the manner of committing that it now partakes too much of a criminal proceeding, and it is often difficult to convince a patient, who does not recognize his own confusion of mind, that he has not been tried and committed for some criminal offense. . . . The law now provides for the handling of the insane by the Sheriff's office. . . . Too much the method of handling the criminal, and not the sick, prevails. By far too much restraint is used.[18]

Although the superintendent expressed regret that patients arrived at the state hospitals convinced they had been convicted of a crime, he did not go so far as to question the forcible commitment practice itself.

A similar problem was created by the 1903 juvenile court law, which allowed for the detention of youth through a legal process that conflated juvenile dependency and delinquency. Juvenile delinquency was determined by the commission of a crime, while dependency was signaled by parental abuse, neglect, or abandonment. Under the law, and well into the twentieth century, a youth who had been found the victim of parental abuse or abandonment could be remanded to the juvenile reform schools through the same process as a delinquent youth who had been accused of a crime.

Once institutionalized, people encountered the carceral architecture of eugenics institutions. In some cases, this included being housed in facilities that were locked down. The superintendent of the Southern California State Hospital argued in 1904 for more secure housing options:

> This [new] ward should be constructed with special reference to security. The locks, doors, windows, and window guards should be made especially strong and secure. . . . I would not have you think that we desire a miniature penitentiary in connection with a hospital, but nothing short of the safeguards offered by a penal institution would meet the requirements in some cases that we are obliged to receive and care for. Therefore, separate provision should be made so that the wards of a hospital for the mentally sick should not assume the appearance of an institution for the care of criminals.[19]

The superintendent's solutions to the feel of a "miniature penitentiary" were aesthetic measures such as installing curtains, tricking the eye into maintaining visual boundaries between a hospital and a prison. Underneath the curtains, the carceral infrastructural remained.

Treatment as Punishment

The carceral infrastructure of the eugenics institution proliferated further entanglements, as medical treatment collapsed into punitive discipline. A warning: the cases of medical abuse discussed in this section are particularly disturbing. Operating under the rubrics of care and rehabilitation, these examples of experimentation, disciplinary uses of medical treatment, and carceral forms of surgery show that eugenics institutions developed new, medicalized technologies of containment. These technologies then circulated to jails and prisons, becoming available for use on criminalized populations into the twenty-first century.

Like later twentieth-century medical experimentation on prisoners, which has been documented, institutionalized people were also subjected to bioethically questionable studies.[20] In one example, a medical practitioner at Napa State Hospital authorized several experiments on patients. One of those took place at the tail end of the 1918 to 1919 global novel influenza pandemic. Four hundred people at the hospital were subjected to an experimental influenza vaccine administered by an assistant of Dr. McCoy of the Hygienic Laboratory in Washington, DC. Three weeks after the administration of the vaccine, a wave of influenza swept through the hospital, affecting at least four hundred people. Following the outbreak, administrators concluded that the vaccine had no preventative effect. While the possible benefits to both the population of the hospital and society could have been great had the vaccine had even a modicum of preventative effect, the now-accepted principles of respect, beneficence, and justice were violated.[21] No mention is made of any attempt to solicit volunteers and gather consent, to weigh individual risks and benefits, or to collect data on possible side effects to the experimental vaccine. Nor was there discussion, at least in the state report, of the ethics of using a confined population as a captive site for experimentation. Given what has been recently learned about highly contagious viruses and congregate living settings during the novel coronavirus pandemic, it was also unethical to not consider the most reliable prophylactic against influenza, which would have been to release everyone from the institution.

Another experiment at Napa is even more troubling, given that it required regular invasive extraction of bodily fluids for a study of epilepsy that was never concluded. In that case, the medical superintendent reported that a

> bio-chemical study was begun by C. G. Mc Arthur, Ph.D., the late acting pathologist, at the temporary laboratory rooms under the kitchen of the Acute Quiet Hospital. About thirty of our patients, male and female, who were suffering from epilepsy, were singled out for the study of their blood, urine and spinal fluid. The specimens of these body fluids were secured at certain fixed times, bearing on the relationship to the epileptic seizures (before, during and after attacks). Dr. McArthur did an enormous amount of chemical analysis in this connection, but had not brought matters to a satisfactory conclusion when he left the institution August 1, 1920.[22]

In this instance, the principle of beneficence, the requirement to maximize benefits and minimize harm, was especially violated, because there was no clear benefit to either the individual or society for a series of extremely painful procedures such as the extraction of spinal fluid.

Medical treatments also violated the principle of beneficence when they were used for the purpose of disciplining unruly patients. In one example, a grand jury investigation into reports of abuse at the Southern California State Hospital in 1903 discussed the use of apomorphia, a medication derived from morphine that was used as a "counter-stimulant" and an expectorant, but which could also induce vomiting. According to a newspaper reporter who attended the hearing, "The use of apomorphia in disciplining patients in lieu of mechanical restraint was admitted by the physicians in certain cases."[23] The grand jury concluded that this use was done "in accordance . . . with the authorities cited" as experts on the use of the drug.[24] That is, medical experts testified that apomorphia was used properly to calm agitated patients so that they would not need to be physically restrained. Treatment of agitation here slips into discipline, not to mention that one of the prescribed uses of apomorphia as an emetic would have been an additional punishing side effect—sending the message to patients that if they became agitated the staff would calm them down by making them vomit.

The common practice of hydrotherapy gives yet another example of the complicated relationship between medical treatment and discipline. Hydrotherapy was used in the early half of the twentieth century in state hospitals, state homes, and reformatories for nervous conditions and incorrigibility alike. Despite the image that accompanied the tub at the Patton State Hospital Museum—that of patients soaking in a warm bath—hydrotherapy also included patients being plunged into ice-cold water or being restrained in the tub for hours or even days, a practice called a "continuous bath."[25] While some patients testified that the warm bath version of hydrotherapy was an effective treatment, it also had serious risks. In 1912, a man was killed at Napa State Hospital following an aggressive use of hydrotherapy where he was forced by staff into a tub that was filled with scalding hot water.[26] The commission convened to investigate determined that the death was accidental and justified the death by insisting that the patient was already near death due to the medical condition of paresis (lack of voluntary movement). The commission also determined that the attendants who scalded the man were not at fault because Napa, like all other state institutions, suffered from severe overcrowding and staff shortages.

When the scalding occurred, only two attendants were present to care for forty-four patients on the ward.

The disciplinary possibilities of hydrotherapy proliferated as the treatment spread to other kinds of institutions. The Board of Charities and Corrections reported in 1920 that the "California School for Girls has installed hydrotherapy equipment which is of distinct value in treatment for the prevention of hysteria and in quieting girls with psychopathic tendencies."[27] This instance demonstrates that hydrotherapy was conceptualized as a tool for containing not just the insane but also the criminal. Hydrotherapy was in at least one instance adopted as explicit punishment in a state prison, when the "continuous shower" was used on a prisoner who was tied naked to a cross and sprayed with a high-pressure water hose.[28] This carceral medical practice continued into the later twentieth century. In a case that was disturbingly like the 1912 death in Napa, in 1994 a man named Vaughn Dortch, with a documented history of mental unwellness, was plunged into a tub of scalding hot water at Pelican Bay State Prison in Northern California.[29] Guards then scrubbed his body with a wire brush while shouting that they would turn the African American man white, causing third-degree burns over 80 percent of Dortch's body. Unlike his predecessor, Dortch lived to sue the state for this tortuous use of hydrotherapy.

The practice of reproductive sterilization is perhaps the most compelling example of how medical treatment was punitively disciplinary. As the state Commission in Lunacy put it bluntly, "We find sterilization makes the patient more amenable to discipline and less restless."[30] Sterilization was imagined as taking the vinegar out of patients, sapping their will to resist. As in other treatments, bioethics went out the window for sterilization, as the law explicitly stated that consent was not required from either the patient or their closest relative. Sometimes husbands or family members were asked to consent as a kind of courtesy; however, their requests to not sterilize were not necessarily respected. As other scholars have documented, one of the biggest problems with sterilization surgery was that it was used as a gate between the institutionalized person and release from the institution.[31] The original 1909 Asexualization Act had purported to offer sterilization as a form of treatment for defectiveness and recommended the surgery in instances when it would be "beneficial and conducive to the physical, mental, and moral condition of the inmate." By 1917, however, the discursive emphasis in the law was instead on the protection of society from the inmate. The version of the law in place until 1978 provided three paths to sterilization, the first being:

Before any person who has been lawfully committed to any state hospital for the insane, or who has been an inmate of the Sonoma State Home, and who is afflicted with mental disease which may have been inherited and is likely to be transmitted to descendants, the various grades of feeble-mindedness, those suffering from perversion or marked departures from normal mentality or from disease of a syphilitic nature, shall be released or discharged therefrom, the state commission in lunacy may in its discretion . . . cause such person to be asexualized, and such asexualization whether with or without consent of the patient shall be lawful.

Hinging release on sterilization surgery further disrupted the possibility that an institutionalized person or their family could willfully provide informed consent. The only other option would have been to remain confined, which is no choice at all. Sterilization treatment expanded the reproductive control of the state from confinement of the body to inside the body.

Of course, sterilization was not a guarantee that an institutionalized person would be released, and there are many examples of people who underwent surgery yet remained institutionalized. Others, who remained in long-term custodial care, were presumably deemed too defective for release and never underwent sterilization surgery. These people still suffered eugenics, because their containment functioned to diminish the reproductive possibilities of their lives.

Indefinite Detention

The defective class was stalled in time during the debate over which people required permanent segregation vis-à-vis which persons could be reformed enough to release. Because of what I call the *recovery rule*, once committed to a state home or state hospital (whether voluntarily or forcibly), a person's confinement was indefinite. The superintendent of each state hospital retained authority to release "1. A patient who, in his judgment, is recovered; 2. Any patient who is not recovered, but whose discharge, in the judgment of the superintendent, will not be detrimental to the public welfare, or injurious to the patient."[32]

While these guidelines were ostensibly designed to support the medical judgment of the practitioners who knew each institutionalized person, superintendents were empowered to use eugenics philosophy to determine recovery based on whether the person was a threat to public welfare. Some, such as the general superintendent of the Commission in Lunacy F. W. Hatch, were skeptical that defective persons could ever recover: "Mental defectiveness is not a disease that can be medically treated. It is due to hereditary defect that results in a defect of development. We find a brain development very much like that of an infant. Feeble-mindedness in the parents brings about the same condition in the progeny. The untrained mental defectives are incapable of self-support and must be pensioners on their more intelligent fellows. A cure cannot be expected."[33] Denied rehabilitation under the rubric of eugenics, defectives were excluded from the possibility of reconstruction and the opportunity to catch up with their normal peers. These patients were imagined as properly living and dying in long-term segregation.

Even avid supporters of sterilization—such as the superintendent of Sonoma State Home for almost twenty-six years Dr. Fred Butler—declared that while "some cases only need to come [to the institution] for a short time," and that many cases could be handled by sterilizing patients before they exited the institution, "those defectives whose tendencies are such as to make them undesirable members of the community should be permanently segregated in the institution."[34] This statement is remarkable because Butler initiated a process at Sonoma State Home whereby patients were institutionalized temporarily, just long enough to make them candidates for sterilization under the state law.[35] Post-operation, Butler could then determine whether these patients were recovered and capable of being released. However, this quote shows that even someone like Butler, who was highly invested in sterilization, agreed that permanent segregation was necessary for some people. In his words, long-term institutionalization was appropriate for those who showed "vicious tendencies," were disobedient or lazy, and were part of extended defective families that were incapable of properly caring for them.[36] Even prosterilization eugenicists promoted indefinite detention as a part of the total solution of destroying the line of defective heredity.

Indefinite exclusion from society meant that peaceful, natural death could occur while simultaneously restricting the reproduction of the future defective class. The state of California estimates that forty-five thousand people died while institutionalized in state hospitals between the mid-1880s and the 1960s (this total does not include other state institutions).[37] The vast majority of that total were buried in unmarked or mass graves. Through the efforts of the California Memorial Project, three disability rights organizations have worked with the state to identify the location of gravesites and to research death records to restore the names of those who died. The sheer number of those who died is not surprising, given that congregate living settings cause what Ruth Wilson Gilmore calls "premature death."[38] Forced congregate living settings accelerate the aging process through overcrowded, high-stress environments, lack of nutritious food, restrictions on movement and exercise, limited positive human interaction, and lack of access to sunshine and fresh air, not to mention systematic medical abuse and medical neglect. Further, overcrowding and understaffing in institutions create ripe conditions for the spread of infectious diseases, exacerbating existing illnesses and impairments, as well as introducing new illnesses and disabilities.[39]

Many people entered institutions not only with mental unwellness but with preexisting chronic conditions, such as dementia, syphilis, and tuberculosis. Napa State Hospital reported in 1920 that the rate of syphilis infection among incoming admissions was as high as 23 percent, with almost 12 percent of new admissions showing advanced stages of the disease, including "syphilitic invasion of the nervous system."[40] After the 1910 discovery that Salvarsan, a derivative of arsenic, was effective against syphilis, patients were able to at least receive treatment for their conditions, although the treatment itself was painful (it could burn the veins), and side effects could also be debilitating.[41] It was this combination of preexisting conditions and premature aging that led to high rates of premature death. In Stockton State Hospital, 154 patients died in the year 1900. Given that the daily total of patients in the facility was around 1,593, and many of those patients would have lived in the facility for the entire year, the death rate was close to 10 percent.

Exposure to contagious diseases on-site also contributed to the death rate. One-third of the deaths at Napa State Hospital in 1920 were due just to tuberculosis, a highly contagious respiratory infection. The influenza pandemic of 1918–19 hit Southern California State Hospital, Mendocino State Hospital, and Sonoma State Home particularly hard, causing 518 cases of the flu and resulting in 192 deaths in just a few short months.[42] Permanent segregation paid off for eugenicists in some cases sooner rather than later, as the defective class died due in part to the conditions of congregate living.

The temporality of incarceration is often referred to as "serving time" or "doing time." Ruth Wilson Gilmore describes jails and prisons as extracting time from prisoners, while Regina Kunzel depicts the prison as a place that is "out of time."[43] The recovery rule and likelihood of premature death created a temporality out of sync with the occupation of normal time and participation in progressive timelines. It narrowed the future horizons of the defective class. How did institutionalized people occupy this time out of time? In addition to basic care, treatment, and any labor that was extracted from people working in the laundries, picking vegetables in the garden, or providing care for each other (especially when labor shortages drove staffing levels to even more dismal levels), institutionalized people were often bursting with free time. This "free" time of the eugenics institution, for those forcibly committed and indefinitely detained, meets the definition of what Neferti Tadiar calls "excessive remaindered life-time."[44] This surplus time, in excess of what was extracted for capitalist production, was constrained by living in the colony. Institutionalized people were suspended in interminable, useless time outside of the normative temporalities and horizons of citizenship. Meanwhile, through segregation normatively timed citizens were protected from the menace posed by the backward, the anachronistic, and the untimely—those whose mental age did not match their physical age.

The recovery rule prefigured the indefinite time that California state prisoners would serve throughout much of the twentieth century. The practice of indefinite detention is another example of how carceral logics were developed within eugenics institutions before travelling back to state prisons. The indefinite sentence that organized institutions was incorporated into California state's penal code in 1917, where it shaped the lives of people with prison sentences for over sixty years. Describing the desirability of the indeterminate sentence, the State Board of Charities and Corrections declared:

> There is no legal recognition of the fact that some persons who never have committed serious crimes should be permanently segregated, while others whose overt acts are rated as felonies may early be restored to good citizenship. With the principle of the indeterminate sentence as a starting point, the legislature should consider a revision of the entire Penal Code. Instead of punishment there should be corrective treatment which should be based on the character of the offender instead of on the nature of the particular act for which he was arrested. . . . It would provide for all offenders' treatment until cured or permanent restraint.[45]

The board advocated for "permanent restraint" of inmates whose "character" (read: defectiveness) restricted the possibility of reformation. This conception borrows heavily from the principle of recovery already established in the state hospital system. Extending the authority of medical superintendents, the board advocated for giving administrators the authority to determine when a prisoner was cured of their criminal tendencies while allowing for some to remain permanently segregated in institutions.

The state's adoption of the indeterminate sentence meant that for decades state prisoners served wildly varying amounts of time for the same crime. A famous example is George Jackson, one of the Soledad Brothers. His original 1961 sentence was one-year-to-life imprisonment for participation in an armed robbery at the age of nineteen, in which he and a comrade stole seventy dollars from a gas station at gunpoint. For Jackson, the indeterminate sentence was ultimately a death sentence, although not because he died of old age, as increasing numbers of prisoners in California have become prone to in the three-strikes era. After a long battle to defend himself from accusations that he had killed a guard during a prison riot, Jackson was shot and killed by another prison guard.[46] Under the indeterminate sentence, the possibility of death was a likely horizon, especially for Black and Latine people. California's indeterminate sentencing law was eventually repealed in 1978, the same year that California's other great eugenics practice—the asexualization law—formally ended. And yet, when I was a human rights monitor for Pelican Bay State Prison in Northern California in the early 2000s, I corresponded with several people who had been sentenced prior to 1978 and continued to serve time indefinitely; they explained that the repeal of indeterminate sentencing had not automatically resentenced them.

Although I include reformatories in this study of state institutions because of the way that the discourse of eugenics invaded their operation in the twentieth century, reformatories were an exception to the indefinite detention rule. Even with extensions given for girls, the School for Girls could detain only until the age of twenty-one for most, and in some rare cases, the age of twenty-three. Given this limitation, the superintendent of the school called on the legislature to develop a plan to transfer as many as one-third of the inmates to other eugenics institutions because:

> One out of every three girls admitted to the school is definitely feebleminded. These girls should never be permitted to return to society, nor should they be associated with dependent defectives. In our opinion, provision should be made at this institution for the

care of all defective delinquent girls. . . . We believe there should be established in the southern part of the state a colony for the permanent custodial care of such defectives as would be a menace to society and whom no amount of training or education would ever fit to take a normal place in the community.[47]

Such an institution for permanent segregation in the "southern part of the state" was established as the Pacific Colony in 1927. Prior to this, women and girls labeled as defectives circulated between the institutions as the state sought more permanent custodial care: those convicted of crimes and later deemed insane were transferred to state hospitals, and those who failed to be adjudicated as insane were prioritized in the application process for the state home. Despite the age limitations, the reformatory and the reform school were part of a chain of confinement that could lead to the indefinite detention of women and girls for eugenics purposes.

To borrow a phrase from Neda Atanasoski, institutionalization constituted a kind of "humanitarian violence."[48] The paradox of indefinite detention is a specific form of temporal distancing, through which the other is permanently deferred from the promise of freedom yet subjected to arbitrary demands to strive for inclusion. Through exposure to premature death and the interminable time of indefinite detention under the recovery rule, eugenics institutions foreclosed on the possibility that those labeled as defective could occupy the present or imagine a future.

Carceral Logics

The ideology of eugenics also contributed to the development of theories of incarceration, such as the logic of incapacitation—a discourse just as valuable a resource as labor, land, and capital in inventing the mid-twentieth-century prison industrial complex.[49] By insisting that some individuals' autonomy was a risk to a healthy body politic, eugenics justified their removal from society.

State confinement as strategy of removing those who are disruptive to the social order was theorized by abolitionists like Bettina Aptheker in the 1970s: "What then is the political function of the criminal and the prisoner as they are created and described by the bourgeois penologists and criminologists? Consider penology as one aspect of the theory and practice of containment on the domestic front; that is, consider penology as the confinement and treatment of people who are actually or potentially disruptive of the social system."[50] When the scientific state labels a person as a criminal, it constitutes a subject who is deserving of social death.[51] Under social death, criminals are denied legal recognition of civil and political rights, public empathy for their dispossession of these rights, and any form of resistance against this dispossession. Criminalization adapts the colonial racial projects that came before, making the disparate treatment of racialized subjects—now labeled with the race-neutral term *criminal*—legal under the Thirteenth Amendment to the US Constitution and palatable under the regime of liberal multiculturalism. The racialization of the criminal is obscured by race-neutral laws that demand equal punishment in the form of incarceration for a crime committed.

What is not often considered in critical criminology is that pathologization of the defective class coconstructed the carceral in the twentieth century. Eugenics institutions were another form of social control, albeit through the alternative rubrics of treatment, rehabilitation, and care. Both the discourse of crime and the discourse of defectiveness worked to turn some into "problem bodies" (to borrow from Clare Sears) from whom the body politic needed to be protected.[52] Corollary to the criminal class, the defective class was constructed as deserving of, even requiring, separation from law-abiding and nondefective people in the name of protecting the health, order, and futurity of society. The ideology of eugenics can be read in the criminological concepts of (1) desert, which dictates that confinement is justified if someone has done something to deserve their treatment; (2) disposability, which treats some as if their lives are worth less than others; and (3) social protection, which declares some acts that violate the individual are acceptable if done in the name of protecting the social as a whole. Eugenics discourses are essential to carceral governance in that they grant to scientific state managers the capacity to detect a fundamental difference between normal people and abnormal people, and the power to legally partition people into essentialized categories of normal/defective, citizen/inmate, reformable/unreformable. Through pathologization, the defective class was targeted for assimilation and rehabilitation programs, expulsion programs, or outright death. Among the defective class, those who could not be deported or assimilated were quarantined and contained internally. The institutionalized person existed in two spheres, the criminal and the civil, their bodily difference labeled criminal, defective, or both. In each overlapping discourse, problem bodies were relegated to social death by becoming inmates, whether that was to a prison, a state hospital, a state home, or an epileptic colony.

Through the discourse of eugenics, an internal other to the body politic was created, joining the colonial gaze onto the criminal class, the racialized Indian that needed to be conquered, and the immigrant alien that needed to be expelled. Eugenics induced another practice of identifying internal threats to the health of the body politic and intervening to contain these threats. Eugenics institutionalization in the early twentieth century created a new racializing discursive economy that devalued some and created value for others. My intention in identifying the carceral logic of eugenics discourse is not to displace the enormity of criminalization. Rather, I draw attention to the ways that defectiveness, as a discourse of difference/normality and a structure of feeling (to borrow from Raymond Williams) that made defective others into a threat, was then available as an ideological resource.[53] This was important in the 1960s when California political elites sought to, according to Ruth Wilson Gilmore, deal with problems of surplus labor, surplus land, and surplus capital generated by transformations in the global political economy through the expansion of the state prison system.[54] The discursive memory of carceral eugenics was a valuable resource that shaped how these surpluses were channeled into building a prison industrial complex.

Carceral Eugenics on the Punishment Continuum

Recognizing the entanglement of carcerality and eugenics is also important specifically for the history of state confinement of people assigned to the categories of women and girls. Separating state institutions for disability confinement from jails and prisons leads to the erroneous conclusion that non-Black women and girls were not targets of carceral governance in the early twentieth century. Segregation was a strategy for confining women and girls who were unlikely to be confined in California state prisons due to capacity issues and discourses about the inability of women to be reformed. In this section, I build on Angela Y. Davis's now classic observation that the gendered construction of deviance has meant that women are more likely to be sent to psychiatric institutions than to prisons.[55] Eugenics, rather than criminality, was used to justify the indefinite detention of women and girls in California.

The California Board of Charities and Corrections argued that permanent segregation of girls and women on farm colonies would "reliev[e] society of one of the greatest menaces that now confront it."[56] Institutionalization was simultaneously imagined as a humanitarian gesture of protection from the crushing pressures of modernity and served the eugenics function of reproductive control of the defective class. This dual purpose was gendered, with men and boys benefiting from protection from capitalist competition, while women and girls, construed as the vessels of defective reproduction, were locked up for the purpose of reproductive control. This gendered split in rationale can be seen when the board discussed so-called rescue homes for unmarried pregnant girls, young prostitutes, and girls with venereal disease:

> The serious problem of the rescue home, as touched by this board, is . . . a girl problem. The girl is usually the victim of a bad home environment. She has already demonstrated her inability to protect herself. The type of unfortunate girl who seeks refuge in the rescue home is frequently of low mentality and unable to care properly for her child. She needs most careful guidance after her return to the community and only too often should have permanent custodial care.[57]

Here the board transformed what Regina Kunzel calls the "fallen woman" discourse of the nineteenth century into the need to indefinitely detain the defective girl.[58] No longer did the fallen woman deserve to be cast out on the street for commercial sex work but instead required permanent placement in one of the state's eugenics colonies to protect the future from her menace.

As a result of gendered arguments for segregation, thousands of women and girls were confined in state institutions each year, many during prime reproductive years, and others until their deaths. In the year 1904, a count of 2,192 patients in the state hospitals and 238 people in the state home were categorized as female, making up 38 and 44 percent of those institutions, respectively. A chart showing the populations in state reformatories, hospitals, Sonoma Home, and state prisons between the years 1915 and 1918 tells a similar story, that anywhere between 38 and 46 percent of people in state hospitals and state homes were classified as female. By 1928, when the total population at the state hospitals had almost tripled from the turn of the century, assigned females made up 43 percent of state hospital patients and 48 percent of people at Sonoma State Home.

These statistics challenge assumptions that only a small number of people assigned to the category of women and girls were under state custody in the early twentieth century. Girls and women make up a tiny numerical minority of people in jails and prisons compared to men, leading to histories of the carceral state in which women and girls are all but absent. I was unable to find an official year-by-year account of assigned women incarcerated in California's prisons, but the numbers I did find show some overall trends. At year's end in 1904, twenty-eight people assigned to the category of female were incarcerated in the women's ward at San Quentin State Prison, and no females were incarcerated at the state's other prison at Folsom. This figure represents slightly over just 1 percent of the state's total prison population of 2,384 recorded that year. Similarly, in the midyear count of the same year, ninety-six females were recorded in the statewide county jail population, out of a total 1,253. In 1937, when the state's third prison opened, this one specifically for women in Tehachapi, there were 172 women incarcerated there, representing a small fraction of the state's total 8,108 prisoners. In the prewar decades, however, the population of people categorized as female in state hospitals and state homes was roughly equivalent to the total population of the entire state prison system. Expanding analysis to include more than just state prisons shifts understanding of the carceral state as only affecting male-assigned people. Including eugenics institutions in the picture of the carceral industrial complex brings into view the much larger population of women and girls under state confinement in the early twentieth century.

This offers another challenge to the narrative that girls and women were confined primarily to the private sphere from the Jacksonian era of the 1830s and 1840s through the mid-twentieth-century second-wave feminist movement. The concept of the cult of domesticity, also known as the cult of true womanhood, describes a shift toward distinct gendered public and private spheres in the Jacksonian era. Women and girls were limited to laboring in the domestic sphere, working to socially reproduce the home and family, and to create a haven for male breadwinners to recover from their productive labor and political engagements in the public sphere of market and politics.[59] In this period, only men would have encountered the carceral, for only men would have been disciplined in the public sphere through criminal sentencing to jail and prison. The 1830s through the mid-twentieth century is construed as a time when women and girls were instead primarily disciplined in the private sphere by family members and religious leaders.

Late nineteenth- and early twentieth-century reformers in the Northeast and Midwest United States advocated for the semipublic disciplining of white women. In their view, women had been excluded from the promise of carceral reforms due to the persistence of the nineteenth-century discourse of the fallen woman. The fallen woman hypothesis rested on the assumption that women did not possess rational individuality and therefore could not be reformed, which was the ostensible purpose of the penitentiary.[60] This discourse conceptualized women as morally unsalvageable after falling into lives of disrepute, justifying their exclusion from the sphere of feminine protection. According to Estelle Freedman, reformers "claimed that, if given a chance to bring their feminine influence to bear, the fallen could be redeemed and made into true women."[61] The establishment of girls and women's reformatories was a successful departure from the narrative because women were given the opportunity to reintegrate into society through the completion of rehabilitation, rather than being permanently shunned. Even so, Nicole Hahn Rafter argues that the women's reformatory movement offered only "partial justice" because women's reformatories insisted on reproducing the domestic scene in a carceral space, and consequently these programs did not receive the same amount and quality of state resources for rehabilitative programming that men's institutions did.[62]

Angela Y. Davis complicates this story by arguing that only white women could become fallen because only they were conceived of as "true women."[63] Instead of being governed by the legal doctrine of coverture, Black women in the United States were historically constituted as property, denied the right to privacy of home and family, including the right to protection from public punishment. Davis argues for conceptualizing a "punishment continuum," where modes of racialized "gendered punishment" have been delivered in both private realms, through domestic violence, and in public realms, specifically through the convict leasing of Black women in the US South during Reconstruction.[64] In Sarah Haley's account of punishment in the US South, there is ample evidence that it was only white women who were (mostly) protected from public punishment (incarceration and convict leasing) in order to uphold racial economic logic, which required the labor exploitation of Black people of all genders.[65] White women were the object that white men claimed needed to be protected from Black criminality, even as white women continued to be subjected to private violence in the domestic sphere from white men. According to Davis, these private and public modes of racialized gendered punishment all reinforced each other, with the result that Black women were disciplined at a greater magnitude and across a wider diversity of sites than men for deviance.

Elsewhere, Davis makes the observation that women, including ethnically and class-marginalized white women, were also subjected to public punishment when they were committed to institutions for disability confinement (such as state hospitals) beginning in the nineteenth century.[66] I argue that Davis's concept of the punishment continuum implicitly includes state institutions as one of the carceral sites used for disciplining racialized gender nonconformity and sexual deviance.[67] Rafter describes women's reformatories as sites of social control, where imprisoned people were targeted for a variety of gendered offenses that were not considered crimes when committed by people assigned to the categories of boys and men, especially sexual delinquencies such as sex outside of marriage.[68] Joining these reformatories were disability institutions, including state hospitals and state homes, which also were used by the state to punish girls and women for immoral and unruly behavior. These institutions became significant in early twentieth-century California for the public regulation and containment of those assigned as girls and women. The disciplining of gender operated through discourses of defectiveness in addition to criminality, and in sites of care and treatment in addition to prisons and jails. In this way, the punishment continuum dispersed through the language of care and treatment, becoming a technology for extending carceral state jurisdiction over bodies assigned as girls and women.

This expansion of the concept of the gendered punishment continuum does not challenge its racialized logic. Instead, the call for permanent segregation in disability institutions left intact the racialized discourse of criminality and carefully avoided the racialized and gendered politics of incarceration. Carceral eugenics deftly transformed the white fallen woman, who had lost the sphere of domestic protection/punishment, into a feebleminded woman from whom society needed to be protected. In this way, disability confinement buttressed the growing prison system in the early twentieth century, helping to both entrench and expand the reach of the carceral industrial complex.

3

The Political Economy
of Carceral Eugenics

A photograph dated circa 1919 shows two columns of people on either side of a large laundry room at Sonoma State Home in Northern California. Each person stands behind an ironing board draped with cloth. The person closest to the camera on the right-hand side is of indeterminate race and gender. Their hair could be short or pulled back in a ponytail, and their white shirt sleeves peek out from under a white apron. Unlike the rest of the people in the photograph who are standing with their arms to their sides, this blurry person in the front is in action, pressing a hot iron firmly to the cloth on the board (see figure 3.1).

Among thousands of pages of reports to the California state legislature from the oversight Board of Charities and Corrections, this

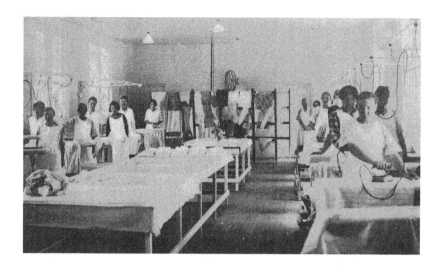

3.1   Laundry room, Sonoma State Home. Photographer unknown. Published
by California State Printing Office, 1921.

photograph is a rare depiction of the labor required to maintain an institution for disability confinement. Most of the few images in the legislative reports capture the grounds of state institutions or the recreational
and therapeutic activities of institutionalized people. However, there is
nothing idyllic about the laundry room. A passage in a newspaper column
published in 1913 gives a multisensorial account of the conditions of such
laundry work: "Ten hours a day, and on my feet shaking out clothes the
whole time—that was part of it. Heat and steam all around—that was another part. . . . I would go to bed at night so tired I could hardly walk, and
I would get up in the morning pretty near as tired—with all the time that
empty gnawing feeling in my stomach."[1] As a depiction of the difficult
work that it took to maintain institutions, the photograph is in some ways
a revelation. However, the image also raises questions. Who are the workers in this photograph and what is their relation to the institution? At least
some of the people portrayed in this image were patients at Sonoma State
Home. Patients were conscripted into as many jobs as possible at eugenics institutions, their unpaid labor justified under the concepts of occupational therapy or vocational training. This chapter describes the use of
inmate labor as one of the cost-saving and income-producing strategies of
Progressive reformers facilitating the transition from laissez-faire to the
administrative state. Some patients who received this so-called therapy in

the laundry may have later paroled out to a family in the community as live-in domestic laborers.

For many reasons, race in this photograph also merits attention. Two people behind the first figure with the iron catch the attention of the viewer because they appear to be Black women.[2] The lighting in the room is dim, but other persons at work in the laundry could also be Black. Natalie Lira's tracking of racial descriptors at the Pacific Colony (the sister institution to Sonoma located in the southern part of the state) found that of 4,165 racial descriptors used between the years 1927 and 1947, 191 individuals were marked as Black, or 4.5 percent.[3] Although I do not have the same kind of data for Sonoma, there are a few instances where individuals were marked as "colored" in the casebook. Either the Black people committed to Sonoma home were conscripted into the difficult labor of the laundry room or Black workers were hired into one of the most dangerous jobs on the campus.

Both because of what it shows and because of what it does not, the photograph of the laundry at Sonoma State Home is a starting place for teasing out the political economy of carceral eugenics in California. This chapter follows the money, situating eugenics institutions in the political economic transformation of California at the turn of the twentieth century. Economic historians characterize this period in the United States as one of profound transformation in the relationship between the state and capital.[4] Technological changes had developed systems of mass commodity production in the United States by the end of the nineteenth century. Through these expanding economies (prefigured and enabled by global colonization), commodity production and transportation in the United States became increasingly consolidated in a few corporate trusts. These monopolies in oil, steel, and railroads grew so large that they rivaled the power of the federal government.[5] This power was concerning because, as Stephen Skowronek argues, up until post–Civil War Reconstruction, the US federal government was largely unrecognizable as a state in the European sense but was rather a loose configuration of "courts and parties" that organized political life under a laissez-faire legal doctrine.[6] Under laissez-faire, the US state was limited to a court system that settled contractual disputes, enforcing the so-called rules of the game that upheld the free market in the United States and ensuring private property rights for white men. Without a regulatory apparatus in place, the corporate trusts were not only completely unfettered by government interference but capitalists also began to directly control the government. Corporations seized control of municipal and state governments, paying retainers to municipal officials, legislators, judges, and lobbyists to enact policies that were preferential for business. The corporations also established political machines to ensure the election of their preferred candidates.

Meanwhile, new threats to Anglo supremacy in California were brought on by the rapid industrialization and urbanization of the United States at the end of the nineteenth century. Industrialization and urbanization created new forms of sociality, bringing unmarried men and women into contact, as well as enabling homosocial gatherings of nonfamily members; both changes threatened to destabilize the Spanish colonial and Anglo moral orders in California.[7] Additionally, responding to the deadly, debilitating, and exploitative conditions of industrial labor and corporate agriculture, workers formed militant unions guided by the philosophies of Marxism and anarchism.[8] Labor organizing brought the working class into at times violent confrontation with the state, when law enforcement was developed to protect the private property interests of capitalists.

The Progressive Era at the turn of the twentieth century altered this arrangement of state, labor, and capital, including in California. In the first two decades of the twentieth century, a new administrative and social welfare state was developed, intended to intervene in the effects of industrial capitalism by regulating corporations and providing a social safety net for citizens.[9] An emergent, predominantly Anglo, middle class of college educated professionals formulated a new vision of social good growing out of the Protestant gospel.[10] A reaction to the social and economic dislocations caused by the industrial revolution of the late nineteenth century, the Progressives proposed building a regulatory state that could intervene to guide the market and protect society from capitalist externalities. Progressivism was also a reaction to the specter of organized labor and to an imagined future where a multiethnic, multiracial, and multigendered proletariat would be empowered to recreate the political economic order. Progressives promoted scientific rationality, professionalism, and faith in the state to rationally manage social problems in a way that preserved existing white supremacy and heteropatriarchy.[11]

While the Progressives are well known for challenging capitalist control of the government, they also went after labor unions. Instead of identifying the problems of the era as rooted in capitalism, Progressives were troubled by the behavior of poor and working-class people. For Progressives, solutions would not come through the theory of labor exploitation but through the discourse of social problems. They were thus susceptible to repeating racist and sexist tropes about labor.[12] Their scientific solutions targeted working-class morality, such as the growth of the commercial sex industry, resulting in theories of deviance and criminality that conflated biological threats with moral ones. They enacted a series of reform projects designed to build a modern state that could respond to criminality, insanity, poverty, vagrancy, venereal disease, commercial sex, gambling, child labor, child abandonment, and the growth of urban vice districts. Newly educated middle-class women played key roles in promoting social reform projects, extending their mothering work to children, disabled people, and their fallen sisters.[13]

Progressives envisioned an administrative state that would replace the corporate and monopolized political machines with efficient, scientific bureaucracies. They established a professional government with a political class and civil service that was designed to be immune from direct control by capitalist interests. Early twentieth-century reforms in the United States separated state managers from capital managers by passing antitrust legislation that reduced the power of corporate monopolies.[14] In California, Progressive Era reformers built an administrative state that removed the courts and parties from the specific grip of the railroad and public utility trusts that had gained a chokehold on state and municipal governments.

However progressive this project was, the regulatory and social welfare state was not revolutionary. Instead, the administrative state offered an alternative to monopoly capitalism by undermining the radical critique of capitalism offered by labor unionists, socialists, and anarchists. US Progressive reforms insisted on a statist approach to regulating wages and conditions, and, as a result, in addition to new relationships between capital and state, new relationships between labor and the state were created. Rather than dismantling capitalism itself, the transition from laissez-faire to the administrative state reestablished capitalism as the economic structure of California. Instead of competing with the interests of capitalism, the administrative state constructed new circuits for capital to flow. Capital now had new managers: a political class empowered to channel money through the collection of taxes, the financing of state works, and the regulation of labor.

American political development scholars have described the specifically racialized and gendered effects of the state built by Progressive reformers. For example, although welfare programs were enacted in the name of care, these programs were used throughout the twentieth century to increase the surveillance of the intimate lives of marginalized women.[15] In another example, strategies of direct democracy designed to increase public empowerment were quickly used to exclude racialized groups from full citizenship.[16] A third example is described by economic historian Thomas Leonard, wherein Progressive labor regulations created new categories of people who were construed as unable to labor, or at least whose labor was constructed as undeserving of a minimum wage, with the purpose of regulating labor costs.[17] Eugenics played a key role in this imaginary. Reformers insisted social problems were caused by the unchecked breeding of the poor, wherein the inherent weakness of the parents caused undesirable traits to appear in their children. Eugenics offered scientifically guided solutions that promised mastery over disease, illness, and impairment through the regulation of marriage and reproduction. Using eugenics and racial science, one of the groups that Progressives constructed as unable to labor was the defective class. One of the strategies for removing the defective class from the labor force was through commitment to carceral eugenics institutions. Many people in disability institutions of confinement spent most of their time idle, in no small part because they were conceived as incapable of being productive in the world outside of the institution.

However, scholars of critical disability studies and queer-of-color critique argue that surplus value is also extracted from surplus populations, specifically through the use of detention and confinement.[18] Despite the use of institutionalization to construct some as unable to labor, segregation to the farm colonies did not mean that the defective class was removed entirely from the process of capital accumulation. As Natalie Lira and Susan Schweik show, the labor of institutionalized people, especially women made to do domestic and care work, was instrumental to the operation of institutions for disability confinement.[19] I argue that the administrative state in California used state institutions to extract surplus value from the defective class, creating new pathways for both disciplining gendered and racialized laborers, as well as extracting value from nonlaboring surplus populations. Carceral eugenics played a role in extracting forms of value from people constructed as disabled, and specifically from those disabled people assigned to the category of women.

By theorizing carceral eugenics, this chapter adds to the analysis of the political economic shifts of the Progressive Era. To flesh out the political economic conditions in California in the early twentieth century, I start with two sources: the first is a novel by Frank Norris titled *The Octopus: A California Story*, published in 1901. A romanticized version of a real-life struggle in Central California between Anglo settler farmers and the railroad industry, I use the novel to describe the integration of corporate trusts into all levels of governance during the end of the nineteenth century. My second source is a collection of newspaper columns attributed to Alice Smith in the 1910s, a commercial sex worker who lived in San Francisco.[20] Smith's account, undoubtedly sensationalized and the identity of the actual author questionable, nevertheless is a useful description of the second industry that dominated the political economy of California at the turn of the twentieth century—namely, commercial sex and the supporting industries of alcohol and gambling. While the corporate trusts of railroad and public utilities extracted surplus value from the male workforce, it was the vice industries that targeted women by offering (limited) economic options for paid labor. Smith's description of labor in the vice industries shows the ways that the emergent administrative state in the Progressive Era colluded with the vice industries to discipline women workers through institutionalization, further driving down gendered labor costs.

I also return to the annual reports sent to the state legislature, this time focusing on appropriations requests, operating budgets, and especially the cost-cutting strategies used by institutional administrators. The daily economic operation of carceral eugenics institutions illustrates the excruciating financial details that had to be worked out in the transition from unfettered monopoly capitalism to the administrative state. The financing of eugenics institutions was a site for the administrative state to test strategies for channeling capital and regulating surplus populations. I dive deeper into the archive of the League of Women Voters of San Francisco to tell the story of the short-lived Industrial Farm for Women, a case that illustrates the tension between purely financial economy and the moral economy demanded by eugenics. Through struggles like the one over the farm, an administrative state was birthed that could extract forms of surplus value from disabled people and people assigned to the category of women. This archive illuminates how carceral eugenics operated to channel capital into new flows as the scientific, moralistic administrative state replaced laissez-faire in California.

From Trusts and the Underworld to the Administrative State

According to women reformers at the turn of the twentieth century, California was ruled by two dominant groups: corporate trusts—specifically railroad and utility industries—and underworld industries of commercial sex, gambling, and alcohol distribution.[21] Both corporate trusts and the vice industries sustained their economic weight by investing in political control at the state and municipal levels, in all branches of government. In Progressive theory, it was political and economic control by both the corporate trusts and the vice industries that threatened the economic livelihoods, morality, and happiness of the good people of the middle class.

Although it is questionable whether Frank Norris can be considered a Progressive, his 1901 muckraking novel *The Octopus: A California Story* describes in extensive detail Progressive concerns about the political economic arrangement at the end of the nineteenth century. The villain of the novel is the railroad trust in California, integrated into the political system by employing and paying off elected officials and judges, who subsequently directed state and municipal government policy for the benefit of the railroad's shareholders. The novel fictionalizes a land dispute that occurred in 1880 between the Southern Pacific railroad (SP) and emergent agribusiness in the southern San Joaquin Valley.[22] In the mid-nineteenth century, SP was granted one square mile lots of land from the US Congress throughout the state of California, upon which they had the option to construct rail lines. Southern Pacific had planned to construct a rail line from San Jose to Southern California along the coast, but the company abandoned those plans in favor of an inland line through San Joaquin Valley, a move that Congress approved in 1866. In the interim, homesteaders—or squatters, depending on your point of view—had settled on the plots that were legally owned by SP and started to farm the land. SP exercised the option to change the path of the rail line and came to the homesteaders asking them to either vacate or to pay an inflated price for the real estate—up to four to twenty times the value estimated by Congress at the time of the original land grant. Deadly conflict ensued between the farmers and the agents of the railroad.

Norris's description of the railroad industry from the perception of the homesteaders is evocative of Progressive horror at the political economic arrangements of the late nineteenth century. Early in the novel, a flock of sheep wanders onto the railroad tracks and is killed by a regularly scheduled train:

> It was a slaughter, a massacre of innocents. The iron monster had charged full into the midst, merciless, inexorable. To the right and left, all the width of the right of way, the little bodies had been flung; backs were snapped against the fence posts; brains knocked out. Caught in the barbs of the wire, wedged in, the bodies hung suspended. Under foot it was terrible. The black blood, winking in the starlight, seeped down into the clinkers between the ties with a

prolonged sucking murmur. . . . Presley saw again, in his imagination, the galloping monster, the terror of steel and steam, with its single eye, cyclopean, red, shooting from horizon to horizon; but saw it now as the symbol of a vast power, huge, terrible, flinging the echo of its thunder over all the reaches of the valley, leaving blood and destruction in its path; the leviathan, with tentacles of steel clutching into the soil, the soulless Force, the iron-hearted Power, the monster, the Colossus, the Octopus.[23]

The slaughter of the sheep is a metaphor for the destruction the railroad industry caused the hardworking middle-class families in the valley and a foreshadowing of the death the corporate trust justified to continue hoarding profits.

The highest drama of the novel takes place when the farmers fight to keep from being evicted from the land. They first conspire to covertly take over the state railway commission. It is here that readers learn just how tightly the SP political machine was entrenched in municipal and state government—entangling legislators, judges, commissioners, and even newspapermen in industrial profit-making above all else. Tragically, the efforts of the farmers to fight this machine are thoroughly subverted. When the railroad company proceeds to physically evict farmers from the land with the aid of a US marshal, the novel fictionalizes the armed standoff during which several farmers were shot and killed.

In the last section of the novel, Norris elaborates on the tragic fallout of the shootout and in so doing creates an allegory for the consequences of unchecked monopoly capitalism. The novel starkly depicts the social ruin that Progressives understood to result from corporate trusts and their political machines. As a result of the tragedy, widowed women and their children come to ruin through starvation and premature death. A lurid passage juxtaposes a luxurious dinner at the mansion of the vice president of the SP railroad with the wandering of a widowed woman and her small child lost in the streets of San Francisco. As the guests at the dinner gorge themselves, the mother dies from hunger and cold. Norris insists: "They fattened on the blood of the People, on the blood of the men who had been killed at the ditch. It was a half-ludicrous, half-horrible 'dog eat dog,' an unspeakable cannibalism."[24] In Norris's view, corporate forces impoverished and killed men, women, and children so that others could be rich. While the greed of the railroad trust caused ruin to women indirectly through the death of their husbands, Norris also depicts the direct exploitation of women by the underworld exploiters of the vice industries. Minna, the daughter of a farmer who is killed in the shootout, is left without financial resources and is forced to flee to San Francisco. Short on money and without a resumé to establish employment, she is quickly recruited into the commercial sex industry. In Norris's representation, the corporate trusts financially desta-bilized the middle-class family, and the vice industries were there to profit off of the destruction that resulted.

Another publication from the time period that explores the role of the vice industries in the exploitation of women's labor is the newspaper col-umn "A Voice from the Underworld." Published between 1913 and 1915 in the *San Francisco Bulletin*, and recently republished in a book titled *Alice: Memoirs of a Barbary Coast Prostitute*, the column elaborates on the strug-gles of the real-life versions of Norris's character Minna.[25] Although the column is attributed to a sex worker named Alice Smith, the authors of the book note there are serious questions as to the identity of the author, given that newspapers of the time offered sensationalistic accounts of so-called white slavery. Yet the details presented in the text suggest that it is possi-ble it is a ghostwritten amalgamation of the accounts of multiple women involved in the commercial sex industry. This means that the stories in the columns are relevant descriptions of the general experiences of early twentieth-century sex workers.

The columns analyze the push-and-pull factors that likely landed women and girls in the commercial sex industry at the turn of the century. The narrator, Alice, tells the story of being raised by her maternal grand-parents in a small Midwestern town. She discusses the lack of economic opportunity and explains that when her family hit hard economic times, she went to work as a teenager in two of the few jobs available to women in rural areas: first as a domestic and then as a restaurant server. Conse-quently, she was vulnerable to being recruited by a family member to live in an unnamed metro area out west with the promise of economic op-portunity. There Alice got a job as a nanny, where she experienced sexual harassment and the threat of rape by her employer. She later worked as a telephone operator and, most miserably, at a laundry. Throughout, Alice's goal of sending money back to her poor grandparents was stymied by the cost of living in the city. After a fight with her relative, she ran away from home and entered the commercial sex industry.

Alice shows through her own experience, as well as through the stories of friends and comrades, that women of the early twentieth century were pushed into commercial sex through a combination of poverty, limited job prospects, low pay, high cost of living, and restrictive expectations on the moral behavior of women. She indicates that once women entered commercial sex work it was difficult to leave due to systems of debt that were created by the industry and the respectability politics of a society who treated women like Alice as "fallen" and morally irredeemable.[26] Alice's columns importantly counter the patriarchy inherent in Norris's novel, which depicts the ruin of women and children coming after the loss of the male breadwinner. Alice points out that the heteropatriarchal nuclear family ideal of the male breadwinner and female wife and mother was always economically unsustainable. Any women who stepped outside of this ideal, or who were forced outside of it, were threatened with poverty. Alice insists instead: "It seems to me that about half the women I know in this life are divorced women; who are not getting any money from their former husbands, and who have a child or parent to support."[27] Divorced women, single parents, and women caring for aging parents without a safety net were easy targets for the vice industries.

In Norris's novel, the hardworking and morally upright middle class are the clear protagonists who will save the day from the vice industries and the corporate trusts. According to Thomas Leonard, the new middle class formed the core of the Progressive movement, and their strategy was to build an administrative state that could respond to social, economic, and political problems caused by vice industries and corporate trusts. Progressives sought to supplement what Adam Smith called the "invisible hand" of the market with "the visible hand of a powerful administrative state."[28] The administrative state was to be run by a highly educated, professional class of experts: social engineers, who "worked outside politics (or, better, above it), proceeded rationally and scientifically, and pursued neither political power nor pecuniary gain but only the public good, which the engineer could identify and enact."[29] The Progressive solution to the corporate trusts and vice industries was to build a regulatory apparatus, tax industry, and social welfare system designed to protect good society from the corruption of greed.

However, Leonard calls the Progressives "illiberal reformers" because they overcame the problems of the laissez-faire system by building an administrative state rather than supporting mass democracy movements. As Leonard details, racial science and eugenics played a key role in imagining and enacting the new political economy of the early twentieth century. One of the ways this played out was in Progressive economic strategies for identifying the surplus classes and driving them out of the labor market with the purpose of keeping wages high for white male nonimmigrant workers. Discussing the real purpose of Progressive support for minimum wage, Leonard describes how the policy "identified inferior workers by idling them. So identified, they could be dealt with. The unemployable would be removed to institutions, or to celibate labor colonies. The inferior immigrant would be removed back to the old country or to retirement. The woman . . . would be removed to the home, where she could meet her obligations to family and race."[30] While the Progressive Era is celebrated for wrangling the political machines of the corporate trusts and taming the energy of the vice industries, it was also a period of introducing new disciplinary power over bodies. Leonard's account emphasizes the ways that Progressive economists sought to remove disabled people, immigrants, and women from the labor market so that they could no longer compete with white, able-bodied men for work. These actions also created new technologies for extracting surplus value from the defective class.

The Burden of Carceral Eugenics

Removing the unemployable to eugenics institutions cost the state of California money, because the state's carceral infrastructure had to be built and maintained. The problem of paying for the carceral infrastructure preceded the Progressive Era, dating back to the establishment of California as a US state in 1850. Indeed, because some of the first acts of the new state of California were carceral in nature (most notably the "Act for the Government and Protection of Indians," which legalized the enslavement of Indigenous children and women in Anglo homes), one of the first conflicts among California's political leaders was how to pay for imprisonment. Shelly Bookspan's fascinating history of the first ninety-two years of California's prison system describes early experiments with private leasing and private prison construction at the current site of San Quentin State Prison. As Bookspan puts it, "Clearly California was eager to transfer the financial burden of the prison to someone else."[31]

Less controversy seems to have shaped the disability institution. Margaret H. Smyth, the first woman superintendent of a state hospital in California, describes the establishment of the "State of California Insane Asylum" in the same year as San Quentin State Prison.[32] The land for the asylum was gifted to the state by Captain Charles M. Weber, who had purchased it from the Mexican government (who had inherited it from the Spanish Crown, who had stolen it from Indigenous Californians). Coinciding roughly with the legislature's acceptance of responsibility for San Quentin after failed attempts at contracting out both prison construction and maintenance, the state legislature in 1863 also took on the responsibility of paying for construction at the state asylum. According to Smyth, the legislature passed a modest five-cent land tax on every $100 of land valuation "for the purpose of erecting buildings for the care of the insane."[33]

After the initial struggle to fund construction came an even deeper ambivalence about paying for the daily operations or "maintenance" of state institutions. As the philosophy of eugenics seeped into governance at the turn of the century, the cost of maintaining carceral institutions increased. Concern about the growing populations at each facility was the focus of an oversight report to the legislature in 1900:

> A charity that continuously creates a demand for its support of three quarters of a million dollars a year, and which promises not only to keep up this expense but to increase it year by year, is certainly one that cannot be looked at from any narrow point of view.... From a charitable standpoint we might wish to maintain it more liberally, to hold people to save them from themselves, and to open its doors to more extended classes of defectives... but of paramount importance to a community is the ever recurring, ever increasing expense of maintenance.... We must accept the conclusion that this great expense will continue and increase, and we must be prepared to make provision for the insane as they are sent to the Hospitals, bearing in mind that we are maintaining them now as economically as it can safely be done under the present conditions.[34]

Net annual expenditures for state hospitals, state homes, state reform schools, the Pacific Colony, and the Industrial Home for the Adult Blind had exploded from the "three quarters of a million" described by the commission to $2,809,011.16 by 1924. That nearly three-million-dollar price tag came after administrators worked diligently to save the state nearly $1.2 million in in-kind production and revenue-generating schemes. Eugenics institutions cost the state less than 1 percent of the annual budget, but only because by 1923, the overall state budget had ballooned to nearly $80 million across two years, more than double the budget of just eight years prior.

The price tag of carceral eugenics grew for several reasons. One was the increasing per-capita cost of maintenance. At the time of the 1900 report, the Commission in Lunacy noted, "The cost of maintaining one patient one year is $139.94."[35] However, by 1924, the State Board of Institutions calculated that the cost for caring for one patient had doubled to $277.10.[36] Another factor in the cost equation was the ever-growing population inside of institutions. In 1900, the Commission in Lunacy pleaded with the state to expand accommodations across the state, given that institutions like Napa State Hospital, which was at almost 200 percent capacity, had patients sleeping on hallway floors and in the tailor shop.[37] Things had not improved by 1920, when the State Board of Charities and Corrections reiterated the need for "increased facilities for the care of the feeble-minded," writing to the state legislature that "the Sonoma State Home has a waiting list of over 800 and the Pacific Colony is available for only forty boys having institutional training."[38] The situation only marginally improved with the construction of new institutions, including Norwalk State Hospital in 1915 and the Pacific Colony in 1927. A display at the Patton State Hospital Museum includes photographs from the 1940s and 1950s depicting rooms and hallways crowded with beds and cots and other furniture piled in the corner teetering over narrow walkways. Included in the display is a reproduction of a newsletter clipping dated February 27, 1951, explaining that the then statewide director of the Department of Mental Hygiene inspected the facility and was "so impressed" by the crowded conditions that he took these photographs back with him to Sacramento to seek more appropriations to expand facilities.

Throughout the early twentieth century, speculation was rampant that overcrowding was a problem particular to California.[39] The Commission in Lunacy observed at the turn of the century that the state was committing more defective people per capita than New York or Iowa.[40] According to figures provided by the commission, at the turn of the century, California was committing three more people per ten thousand than Illinois and almost two more people per ten thousand than New York. In the report, the commissioners argued that California had this higher per-capita ratio of institutionalized people because there was a higher percentage of state residents born in other countries or other US states. Dr. Asa Clark explained: "Considering the matter from a practical standpoint, it must be borne in mind that California is situated at the terminus of several transcontinental railroads; that upon these roads are constantly coming great numbers of people, many of them of roving dispositions with unstable nerve organizations and with barely sufficient money to land them in California. Necessarily disappointment awaits many, and when the crushing influence of poverty overtakes them, the mind gives way and they inevitably become wards of the State."[41] So-called native Californians (those who were born in the state) were assumed to be less inclined to defectiveness than those born elsewhere. A 1917 survey of mental defectives in California's institutions and schools, for example, argued, "The ratio of feeble-minded among foreign born prisoners is twice as high as that of feeble-minded among American born prisoners."[42] The inherent instability of so-called nonnative Californians combined with the geography of California conspired to make the removal of the defective class from the labor market an endless endeavor for the new administrative state.

Good Economy

Confronting the cost of removing the unemployable from normal society was one among many growing pains faced by the new administrative state. By the early 1920s, managers of the state were determined to reign it in, experimenting with how to operate carceral eugenics institutions as economically as possible. The director of the new Board of Institutions declared: "In conducting this department, I have endeavored to do so in an economical manner, but careful that it should be constructive economy and not destructive."[43] The director's concept of "constructive economy," or what others called "good economy," attempted to hold together the eugenics goal of containing the defective class while doing so at the least financial cost to the state. The director's report shows some of the tactics deployed to reduce the cost of detaining the defective class, including building farm-colony-style institutions that strove to be economically self-sufficient; supporting deportation efforts; and engaging in efficiency campaigns that reduced employment costs.

Several eugenics institutions in the state of California were built on the farm-colony model, one that Dr. Leonard Stocking, the superintendent of Agnews State Hospital, imagined "could be made nearly, if not quite, self-supporting by horticulture and agriculture."[44] From a financial point of view, the promotion of the farm-colony model takes on an additional valence—not just as a way of removing the defective class from normal society but also as a strategy of economization. This philosophy is evident in the rise of the reorganized Board of Institutions, which replaced the Board of Charities and Corrections in 1921. In a 1924 report to the legislature, W. D. Wagner, the director of the Board of Institutions, lamented that many of the state's institutions had become "merely custodial" rather than actual farming colonies that could be self-sufficient.[45] Ideally, according to Wagner, eugenics colonies would be placed on specific plots of land that could be made agriculturally productive, starting with providing their own water supply drawn from wells, springs, or rivers. (In this way the defective class would not need to be included in the state's massive water infrastructure projects, such as the diversion of the Colorado River in Southern California.[46]) In Wagner's estimation, colonists would use drilled or river water to raise poultry and hogs, operate dairies, and grow grains, vegetables, and fruit. Good economy was created when institutions could sustain their populations off the land. Wagner declared that the failure of institutions like the Industrial Farm for Women (IFW) could be attributed to the land selection process. In the case of the IFW, it was not actually capable of hosting a farm that could employ institutionalized people in providing for their own needs.

Wagner's report also discusses other cost-cutting strategies beyond self-sufficiency, including the deportation of nonresidents and aliens to their respective states and countries. Deportation directly from institutions facilitated the removal of another one of the Progressive's unemployable groups: racialized immigrants. Wagner insisted that decreasing the rate of population growth in institutions was "the result of increased vigilance on the part of the hospital authorities and the deportation bureau of this department in returning to their respective states and countries nonresidents and aliens who have no legal residence in California."[47] Efforts to deport racialized, foreign-born defectives from state institutions began as early as 1891 and initially targeted Chinese nationals (who could not become naturalized citizens due to federal legislation). The practice of deportation from state institutions was codified in the (later overturned) 1897 Insanity Act. While the law was still in effect, the state Commission in Lunacy called for the deportation of all foreign-born and nonresident patients: "We would suggest . . . that inasmuch as the work of deporting patients to their respective countries has been inaugurated, it be continued, and that the insane natives of other countries be returned to their respective governments, as there is no reason why the taxpayers of California should support the paupers of other countries as well as those from other States of the Union."[48] The commission claimed that this practice of deportation directly from institutions would save Californian taxpayers thousands of dollars per year, noting in 1900 that "five Japanese were deported to their own country, at a savings to the State of $1,000 per year."[49] By 1924, the state deportation agent reported that 498 people had been deported from state institutions, split between 181 "aliens" (over fifty of whom had lived in the United States for over three years) and 317 "non-residents" returned to their states of origin. He estimated that this practice was saving California over $400,000 that year alone, and that in the past twenty years, deportation had provided the state a net savings of $2.5 million.[50] By the 1924 report, the national groups that were deported in the largest numbers by far were Mexicans and Italians, although dozens of countries were the recipients of deportees.

Finally, Wagner's 1924 report discusses a third strategy of good economy: efficiency practices, borrowed from corporate managers, including reductions in institutional staff and reducing the wages for staff. Wagner pointed out that "it will be seen that the per capita cost of the total maintenance of each institution has been materially reduced, the greatest reduction being in the cost of salaries and wages."[51] He went on to claim that these cuts had not materially reduced the standard of living for patients because "they have been better housed, have been given more comforts and amusements, have been as well clothed and fed, and have been given as good medical care and attention—perhaps better, for much new equipment has been purchased." Instead of cuts to quality, Wagner claimed that the lower cost of per-capita maintenance could be attributed in part to "the elimination of many unnecessary positions." Using the language of industrial factory management, Wagner declared that the board had been able to reduce the per-person cost of custodial care by simultaneously laying off staff and increasing production. As all good industrial factory managers must, Wagner was careful to note that these efforts at efficiency had not in any way reduced the quality of the product—in this case, the quality of custodial care.

Through these practices of good economy—moving the farm colonies toward self-sufficiency, a deportation program, and cutting staff and reducing wages—the administrators of carceral eugenics sought to come as close to a zero-cost program as possible. Yet permanent custodial care continued to extract millions of dollars from the state per year. The most obvious way to reduce the cost would have been to decrease the overall population in eugenics institutions. However, this idea did not become popular for decades. Did the necessity for carceral eugenics overcome the push for good economy? Or was the struggle for good economy just a growing pain as state-managed capitalism grew into a force that could discipline labor and extract surplus value from surplus populations?

Spiritual Economy

There is some evidence that the necessity for carceral eugenics simply overcame the desires for good economy. According to Dr. Asa Clark, the superintendent of Stockton State Hospital, the humanitarian impulse of the modern era had created the problem of the defective class: "Consequent upon a discontinuance of the atrocious cruelties which, to a certain extent, eliminated the insane, has appeared perhaps the most appalling phenomenon in the history of our race: thousands upon thousands of dangerous lunatics are with us, and millions upon millions of money [sic] are required for the protection of society and for the support of these more than useless unfortunates."[52] This theory rested on the core premise of eugenics—namely, that defective people passed on weakness to their children, which predisposed those children to poverty, delinquency, criminality, insanity, and immorality. Because modern society had, in the eugenics imaginary of the past, stopped outright killing people part of the defective class, the state was stuck with paying "millions upon millions," as Dr. Clark put it, to implement more humane versions of reproductive control.

In 1918 the State Board of Charities and Corrections concurred with Dr. Clark: "Failure to prevent the reproduction of defectives is now entailing upon society an economic loss amounting to billions of dollars and misery beyond calculation, first, to the unfortunates themselves, second, to their families, and, finally, to society at large."[53] Both Clark's and the board's dim views prefigured a solution: if the state could construct programs that got rid of the defective class by limiting their unchecked reproduction, the state would eventually save money in the long run. Carceral eugenics strategies could help reduce the population of the defective class that would require state intervention in the future. The financial investment now would be rewarded with eventual relief through the slow genocide that would occur through eugenics segregation and sterilization programs. Investments in controlling "the reproduction of defectives" now in the present would save "billions of dollars" in the future, according to the Board of Charities and Corrections.

The board's use of the phrase "misery beyond calculation" is an indication that something beyond good economy was factored into state spending. The threat of defectiveness to the futurity of the human race was so egregious that the cost of not intervening was incalculable in financial terms—human misery could not be weighed against the purely financial costs of containment. The superintendent of the California School for

Girls repeated this phrase in her report, also dated in 1918: "The ultimate expense to society of allowing these [feebleminded] girls to reproduce and to spread disease is beyond calculation."[54] The "ultimate expense" of failing to build eugenics intervention programs was "beyond calculation" because the moral, racial, and civilizational threats could not be fully accounted for in conventional cost-benefit analysis. The concept of spiritual economy, a balance of moral order, used by reformers in the struggle to rebuild the Industrial Farm for Women, offered a counterweight. A state guided by spiritual economy could consider the moral imperative to protect the body politic from degradation, as much as the capitalist imperative to preserve profits in the marketplace.

This biopolitical calculation is nowhere more evident than the historical moments when carceral eugenics coincided with external wars. At first glance, World War I and the subsequent spread of the global influenza pandemic had a negative impact on the operations of carceral eugenics, straining the limits of good economy until the system threatened to collapse:

> The past two years have been rather hard ones in the state hospitals, and have not been free from trouble. Although we have increased the wages of attendants and nurses, our force has been considerably reduced owing to the high wages prevailing in factories and shipyards, and business generally, on the outside. Too, our expenses have been materially increased, in spite of considerable effort at economy. Many of our people enlisted for war service, still further crippling us, and within the two fiscal years ending June 30, 1920, we were unfortunate in having a very considerable epidemic of influenza in most of the hospitals.[55]

Yet the interests of eugenics collided with World War I so that the internal biopolitical war against the enemy within aligned with the war against the enemy outside. In 1918, the Board of Charities and Corrections, for example, argued that the need for containing defective adult women in a reformatory "[had] been forcibly shown in the last two years of the war when prostitutes have been temporarily detained in the counties, released, and floated on to the next community with no attempt of any kind of their social, mental, and physical rehabilitation."[56] In the same year, the state was asked by the Commission in Lunacy to appropriate $15,000 toward the building of a special cottage at Sonoma State Home for "delinquent and defective females who had been venereally affected."[57] The appropriation was secured despite the scarce resources in the state because "the construction of a cottage for the housing of delinquent feeble-minded females from around the army and navy camps [was] a protection to enlisted men. This change in the use of the appropriation was made as an urgent war measure supported by the state government and the federal government."[58] Articulating eugenics institutions "as an urgent war measure," reformers capitalized on the war economy and consequently heightened the sense of the defective class as an internal threat. To face the enemy over there on the war front, the menace of the defective class demanded limited state resources be invested here at home.

Michel Foucault argues that the racialized other against whom modern war is waged is not an external foreign enemy but is produced on the domestic front.[59] California Progressives illustrate how this could be so even during times when there is an external enemy—even during wartime, a low-grade, peaceful war was conducted against internal domestic enemies, also known as the defective class. The discursive production of the defective class as a threat to the social order, and the insistence that their menace required a modern state apparatus that could deploy technologies of containment over bodies and collectivities, justified state spending on carceral eugenics beyond the limits of strictly good economy.

The California Industrial Farm for Women

The Industrial Farm for Women (IFW) is only a footnote in carceral history, but as a case study of the debate over good economy and spiritual economy in California, the story is compelling.[60] The IFW was the result of advocacy by the Board of Charities and Corrections and campaigning by California clubwomen organized under the banner of the Women's Legislative Council of California.[61] It was the penultimate achievement of the latter's Progressive focus on criminal justice reforms that were perceived to benefit the lives of women and girls. Reformers from some of the council's member organizations, such as the Women's Political League of California (later the League of Women Voters), had prioritized criminal justice reforms on their agendas since before the turn of the century. The San Francisco chapter of the Women's Political League of California, for example, monitored conditions for women at the San Francisco County Ingleside Jail and promoted the hiring of woman police officers, prosecutors, and judges, arguing that women were better equipped to provide justice to other women.

The Women's Legislative Council of California spearheaded the state-wide effort to lobby for a reformatory for women, with the argument that women engaged in vice activities could be rehabilitated through the care and protection of their moral sisters. This argument happened to align with military concerns about venereal disease spreading among US troops through rampant prostitution during World War I.[62] With the memory of World War I still fresh, the reformatory was established in 1919 by the passage of a state law that promised "an institution for the confinement, care, and reformation of delinquent women."[63] The California legislature also authorized an initial appropriation of $150,000 to purchase land and begin construction on the facility. It was the first corrective institution operated by the state solely for adult women, and specifically for women convicted of repeated vice misdemeanors, primarily vagrancy (a euphemism for a combination of prostitution and drug addiction). Women convicted of felonies were to serve time in the extremely overcrowded women's quarters at San Quentin State Prison.

The IFW was sited in Sonoma County, about fifty miles north of San Francisco, on a 645-acre piece of property near the existing Sonoma State Home, accepting its first thirty-five inmates in January 1922. Immediately practices of good economy were implemented, especially self-sufficiency and occupational therapy. According to the superintendent of the IFW: "They [the wards] have a large share in running the place, their activities consisting in housework, laundering, dining-room service, nursing, small animal husbandry, goat dairying, vegetable gardening, fruit picking and preserving, care of the two acres of lawn and ornamental gardens, sewing, needlework, weaving, and office work involving typewriting and stenography."[64] Further, the superintendent noted that a "handicraft department" was being organized, which would employ people in making weaving and embroideries that could bring in income to support the facility.

World War I had ended in 1918. While the memory of commercial sex workers with venereal disease threatening the troops played a key role in support for carceral eugenics funding during the 1919 legislative session, by the next session war was no longer a useful discursive strategy against the demand of good economy. In 1921, Governor William Stephens overhauled the administration of the state's "charities and corrections" institutions to develop "an intelligent plan of reorganizing our state government along lines of efficiency and economy."[65] The reorganization consolidated power in the hands of one powerful director of institutions rather than multiple boards of trustees. In this postwar political economic context, women reformers with their biopolitical calls for spiritual and moral economy faced an uphill battle against the masculinist discourse of strict economy.

In the year prior to its opening, the IFW became a symbol of government overreach and overspending in the debate over the 1921 King tax bill (SB 855). The King tax bill proposed to increase the annual property tax on public service utilities, banks, insurance companies, and other corporations. It was strongly opposed by the railroad and utilities corporations. According to a pamphlet signed by several presidents of women's reform organizations, the very entities that Progressives opposed—namely, the corporate trusts of public utilities and railroads and the vice underworld—argued that instead of increasing taxes the state should cut spending. These forces named the IFW as a specific example of the kind of spending that should be cut. At a legislative hearing regarding the proposed tax, legal counsel for San Francisco-Oakland Terminal Railways spoke against the IFW, as did the "president of the Pacific Gas and Electric Company, [who] told the Senate that he 'did not believe this is a time for embarking on new fads or fancies or social experiments.'"[66]

Women reformers took the Progressive stance that the state should exert the power of taxation over these corporate entities that had dominated California politics for decades, because the need of women for state supervision was so acute. Women reformers such as Mrs. Aaron Schloss, the president of the California Federation of Women's Clubs, countered the corporate call for economy by proclaiming, "We will not have so many feeble-minded, perhaps, in the future to take so much money from the state, if we begin at the beginning."[67] The feebleminded—coded as reproducing women—were presumed to be the source, or the "beginning," of social problems. Reformers argued that building a reformatory for adult women was good "spiritual economy" in the face of a "too expensive" "physical and moral menace."[68] Women reformers characterized strict economic arguments against the IFW as hiding what they deemed to be "forces of evil," that they could only challenge through the practice of "moral efficiency."[69] Reformers derided those who could not see beyond financial cost, standing on the side of "the Federal military authorities, the American Social Association and Captain Matheson" of the San Francisco Police Department who they argued "are in a position to speak more authoritatively on it than the underworld exploiters, corporate lobbyists, and other agents intent upon reducing their taxes."[70] By putting commercial sex and vice industries in the same category as public utilities, reformers positioned themselves against all those who thought in terms of economic calculation only. Reformers pointed to social welfare groups, the military, and policing organizations that conceptualized eugenics programs in terms of necessary protection to the body politic. The women in favor of the IFW concluded, "A properly conducted institution that protects society from the twin evils of immorality and disease cannot be an extravagance."[71]

Unfortunately, the legislature's support for the IFW never rematerialized, and the state declined to appropriate sufficient funds for an annual budget or for further construction on the site. The superintendent Blanche Morse lamented that the annual budget of less than $46,000 made it impossible to operate.[72] The governor initially allocated only $41,000 for the farm in 1923, taking a principled stance against the director of institutions and the director of the Board of Control, who argued that the IFW was sited on a piece of land that could not actually be farmed; the inability to farm made any state spending on the institution unjustifiable. Demonstrating how the state viewed eugenics institutions as interchangeable sites for containing the defective class, the directors' rationale was that all the women at the IFW were so-called narcotics, or drug addicts, who could be placed at state hospitals at a much lower cost of maintenance. Explaining his minimalist allocation to the farm, the governor noted that he was doing so despite how "the majority of people seem opposed to [the] purposes" of the farm, admitting that the original bill approving the farm was a mistake.[73]

In March 1923, just over a year after the IFW opened its doors, a fire burned down the main building. The few dozen people confined to the IFW were either moved into the campus's hospital building or transferred to other institutions including Sonoma State Home and Napa State Hospital. Concerned, members of the San Francisco branch of the League of Women Voters convened to ensure the continued operation of the IFW. At the meeting, the suggestion was raised that clubwomen themselves could supplement or replace state funds with a collection of private money that could be used to rebuild and maintain the institution. Meanwhile, the governor's revised April budget removed the already modest allocation for the IFW, noting the "burning of the women's home in Sonoma makes an appropriation unnecessary."[74] Despite approval of two pieces of legislation proposed by clubwomen to fund the IFW (one to authorize the board of trustees to accept donations and gifts, and the other to appropriate $80,000 to rebuild), the governor ultimately squashed the future of the IFW. Vetoing the appropriation of $80,000, Governor Stephens insisted that it was too small an amount to do any good and again referenced the director of the Board of Institutions who had claimed that the women could be sent to the state hospitals and there segregated in a more economical manner.

Though short-lived, the California Industrial Farm for Women is a discursive ground for examining how the demands of strict economy and spiritual economy played out as Progressives worked to build the administrative state. The discussion shows that both positions—those for and against the farm—were guided by eugenics. Women reformers agitated for institutions that could reform fallen women and give them a chance to reintegrate into society, no matter the financial cost, because it would, in the long run and in the spiritual sense, work out better economically. The government men who opposed women's reformatories on the grounds of strict economy never argued that carceral institutions should be closed entirely; rather, they insisted that women should be moved to cheaper institutions, presumably because they did not invest as heavily in rehabilitation. Yet both stances presumed the existence of a defective class that could be justifiably contained by the state.

The fact that the IFW was caught up in the debate about the King tax bill is important. Ultimately the tax raise was passed—I am sure to the dismay of the public utility and railroad corporations. Given that the appropriation for the farm was a drop in the bucket of the state's $90 million budget in 1921, the corporate argument for cutting the farm was not an adequate alternative to raising taxes, which was projected to contribute millions of dollars in state revenue. While critiquing state spending on the farm was not a successful strategy to oppose corporate tax raises, the discourse undoubtedly contributed to the early demise of the IFW. This would seem to be evidence that cost did impose limits on the impact of carceral eugenics. At the same time, the specter of eugenics continued to be a threat large enough to generate support for other costly carceral investments, ultimately compelling capital to submit to new political economic arrangements.

This is nowhere more evident than in what happened after the farm closed. After the legislature declined to rebuild the Industrial Farm for Women in 1923, women reformers regrouped. They pivoted on the suggestion of the lieutenant governor to advocate for building the state's first prison for women, dedicated as the California Institute for Women (CIW) in Tehachapi in 1935. It was the CIW that inaugurated a prison construction boom that would weigh down the state budget for nearly a century.

Disciplining Labor

Despite the failure of the Industrial Farm for Women, carceral infrastructure proved to be an enduring feature of both the California landscape and the state budget. I speculate that this is not just because the philosophy of eugenics prevailed over good economy, but because carceral eugenics was (and is) usable for capitalist accumulation. One way carceral eugenics was leveraged by capitalist forces was as a technology for extracting surplus labor. In a conventional Marxist sense, this possibility seems illogical because the system of capitalism requires the creation and reproduction of a docile labor force, and in theory, eugenics insists both on the slow genocide of a large class of people who could be potential workers and the prevention of the reproduction of another generation of workers. However, as Cedric Robinson theorizes in his formulation of racial capitalism, capitalism has always leveraged hierarchical difference to produce surplus populations who are then vulnerable to underpaid and unpaid labor exploitation.[75] Marxist feminists have elaborated how this works in relation to racialized gender, theorizing that those assigned to the category of women are sometimes exploited for unpaid reproductive labor instead of, or in addition to, productive labor, to ensure the regeneration of the worker and the next generation of workers.[76] Building from this theory, I argue that the state investment in early twentieth-century carceral eugenics paid off as an experiment in disciplining a racialized gendered labor force.

Kelly Lytle Hernández describes how the criminalization of vagrancy and begging was deployed as a strategy to forcibly convert boys and men into workers in early twentieth-century Los Angeles.[77] In a passage that is eerily reminiscent of Karl Marx's description of the process for forcing people into the labor market, the state Board of Charities and Corrections prescribed:[78]

> Vagrancy is an astonishing evil in California. Our mild winter climate, our bountiful orchards, and our hospitable people make this a tramps' paradise. Here this man of easy life can sleep in the winter season often out of doors, and in the morning throw his shoe into a friendly orange tree and bring down a breakfast. By a little exertion he can beg from our homes almost anything he may wish to eat. This tramp population during the winter months is a large one and composed of all classes. There are old criminals knocked out by too much imprisonment, young criminals hiding under the garb of a vagrant,

yegg-men who have sworn never to do any work, gay cats who will work occasionally for drink money, blanket-men who tramp with their sleeping blankets through the State in summer, working a day or two here and there and who return to the lower dives along the city's water front for winter and live on what they can beg or the refuse picked from garbage cans.... This State at this time is harboring more of the vagrant class than ever before.... What shall be done with them?... There is but one thing that will solve the tramp problem—long imprisonment at hard labor.... It would pay this State to establish at least three workhouses or farms...located so as to be convenient to the gateways of the State. Then arrest every vagrant and send him for from three to six months to the most convenient workhouse.... It will be far cheaper for the State to bear this burden now than a later and larger one in our State prison.[79]

A few months in the state reformatory for boys was imagined to discipline the "tramps," "gay cats," and "yegg-men" into productive workers. If rehabilitation did not succeed, at least the state extracted some surplus value from the labor of those men and boys during their incarceration.

A passage in one of Alice Smith's essays indicates that these strategies also worked for women and girls. Through a collaboration between vice and licit industries in California, state institutions were leveraged to keep women vulnerable to exploitation and to push gendered labor costs down.[80] Smith relates the story of a friend named Annabel who was forced to pay a protection bribe to a police officer to continue "working the streets"— one of the most dangerous forms of commercial sex due to the risk of violence and exposure to criminalizing forces. When Annabel was unable to pay the bribe, the officer set up a sting operation to trap her, and she was sent to court. Now criminalized, Annabel was sentenced to six months in a workhouse. The story of Annabel is just one piece of evidence to support Smith's overall materialist argument that women in the early twentieth century were pushed into commercial sex due to structural economic conditions. As Smith theorizes:

Evidently a prostitute was one who sold herself for money. Well, I wondered, was there anybody in the world, according to that, who didn't sell herself or himself for money? Didn't everybody supply some demand, in some more or less disagreeable way? And wasn't everything always for money? Everybody who does something that goes against his best self, just for money, is a prostitute, but sexual prostitution is lots worse than any other.... But the "demand" is there, and it's got to be supplied. Only, don't blame the women that supply it. Everybody supplies some demand—the demand that happened to hit them hardest when they were weakest.[81]

I add to Smith's analysis of gendered capitalism that the story of Annabel also illustrates the ongoing political economic functions of criminalization. Criminalization hurts workers, while capitalists have found ways to profit from criminalization. Smith's entire story arc drives toward her goal of leaving the commercial sex industry. Yet a combination of debt and moral judgment conspire against her. Made vulnerable by the threat of being locked up by the state, the characters in Smith's tale ironically have no choice but to remain in vice industries. The vulnerability that emerged from the risk of being incarcerated helped to drive down wages and put women at risk for lifelong debt and poor living conditions.

The story indicates that capitalist interests ultimately benefit from biopolitical technologies of governance because these enable the hyperexploitation of labor. As Foucault describes, the mode of modern governance that he calls "biopower" is "indispensable" to capitalism because "the rudiments of anatomo- and bio-politics ... [act] as factors of segregation and social hierarchization, exerting their influence on the respective forces of both these movements, guaranteeing relations of domination and effects of hegemony."[82] The administrative state built by the Progressives may have challenged the status quo of late nineteenth-century political economy, but only in response to the capitalist exploitation of labor as an insufficient technology for social control. While purporting to build a social welfare system, the state government also enforced social hierarchies through its unique mediums for disciplining workers, especially carcerality.

Because the name of the city is kept ambiguous in Alice Smith's columns, the reference to a workhouse for women raises questions. According to the comprehensive study of women's prisons by Nicole Hahn Rafter, California was the only state in the western United States to have a women's reformatory—the Industrial Farm for Women.[83] As recounted previously, the IFW did not open until 1922, several years after the newspaper column attributed to Smith was published. In lieu of an industrial farm, the most likely destination for a street sex worker in California would have been the county jail. San Francisco had a specific women's jail (the Ingleside Women's Jail, rebuilt after the 1906 earthquake) that housed those convicted of commercial sex. Calling it a workhouse could have been a reference to the building's former life as a juvenile reformatory, or the story could be the pure fiction of a ghostwriter, an embellishment of memory, or a reference to the East Coast, Midwest, or southern United States where workhouses for women were more established. The workhouse in the story could be a reference to a juvenile reformatory such as the one in Ventura, California, which under state law did accept women up to the age of twenty-one, or twenty-three in rare cases. Inmates at the reformatory were put to work at the orchards and vegetable gardens, and in other activities that promoted the subsistence of the institution.

If Annabel was sent either to the School for Girls or another California institution such as a state hospital or one of the homes for the feebleminded, then "workhouse" would have been an apt description. Patients raised livestock and cared for dairies; grew vegetables and harvested from orchards; produced clothing and furniture for the institution and for sale; laundered clothes, cooked and served meals, and cleaned; created handicrafts for sale; and even assisted in constructing new buildings on institutional sites. Touted as "vocational training," labor was offered as a "treatment and adjustment" for the insane, feebleminded, delinquent, and otherwise defective people.[84]

Vocational training served to funnel disabled, racialized, and gendered groups into low-paid industries. For example, a report by the Commission in Lunacy notes that toward the end of World War I, both men and women at Sonoma State Home were sent to work harvesting local agriculture and processing at a local tomato cannery. In the southern part of the state where the population of Mexican American youth was growing, the Board of Institutions continued agriculture loaner programs after the war: "The increase in population of the School, especially the Mexican population, can be very profitably placed at agricultural work . . . many of them derive valuable training in the kind of work they will follow after release from the School."[85] The defective class was disciplined into specifically racialized forms of work through vocational training.

Vocational training was also highly gendered. Institutions asserted a model of the nuclear family that encouraged girls and women to become housewives. For example, girls or women who could land a respectable husband would be considered for parole or release, whether they were at Sonoma State Home, the California School for Girls in Ventura, or the Pacific Colony. As the Board of Institutions explained, "With marriage and home life as a possible future before every girl and domestic service as the most available vocation, or source of income, the training in this department [of Household Arts] is of vital importance."[86] In preparation for this glorious future, institutionalized people assigned to the category of girls and women were taught gendered skills such laundering, cooking, cleaning, caring for other patients, vegetable gardening, and home-based manufacturing like sewing, garment-making, and producing linens, rugs, and baskets.

However, these skills were also instilled in girls and women who were not expected to land a husband; they were instead paroled out to local families where they worked as domestic help. According to administrators at Sonoma State Home, "During the past two years we have been allowing selected cases, mostly girls, to go out to work in families, where they make from $15 to $30 per month with maintenance. . . . We have more calls for girls than we have reliable girls to send out."[87] While there were some vocational programs in manicures, shampoos, and facial massages, or, for the select few, secretarial work and nursing, training to be domestic workers was by far the most common. Natalie Lira argues that it was through the myth that women and girls were going to become mothers and housewives that these vocational training programs funneled them into unpaid reproductive labor and care work inside of the institutions and into low-paid domestic work outside of the institutions.[88] This aligns with Marie Mies's explanation of how the two processes work hand in hand: the valorization of the housewife obscures the actual conditions of women's productive labor and drives down the pay in industries like domestic labor and home-based piece work.[89]

Given that many of the girls and women were institutionalized for violations of immorality—commercial sex or at least sexual looseness—the gendered occupational therapy offered in carceral eugenics institutions can be construed as an attempt at job retraining. In this instance, working-class girls and women who had strayed into the one form of prostitution for which demand was high—namely, commercial sex work—were disciplined back into unpaid or low-paid domestic labor. Through this job retraining, they were reformed by the benevolent hand of the state from a fallen woman into a gendered body that was trustworthy enough to be employed in low-paid domestic labor. In an examination of the Pacific Colony, Lira finds that Mexican-origin women were specifically targeted for these kinds of labor, through intersecting discourses of gender, race, and disability. Lira also underscores the irony of this dynamic, especially for Latinas, as it was often the same gendered and racialized persons who were "expected to care for other people's children after being prevented from having their own" through sterilization and confinement.[90] Channeling institutionalized women into low-paid reproductive labor while denying them control over their own reproduction was a core way that the new administrative state became involved in extracting surplus value.

Surplus Value and the Defective Class

The new administrative state of California also experimented with other strategies of extracting surplus value from the defective class. These experiments included occupational therapy as a strategy to justify unpaid labor, the commercialization of crafts, and forcing of families to pay out of pocket for institutionalization. The first of these, occupational therapy, marked a shift away from nineteenth-century asylum treatments that forged recovery through relaxation and contemplation in the quiet countryside. By the early twentieth century, the California State Commission in Lunacy argued that idleness produced insanity, and that occupation was therefore a therapeutic response: "Occupational therapy has attained an important position in the treatment of mental diseases. . . . Efforts are made to induce every patient who is physically able to work, to engage in some occupation. Idleness induces introspection, the brooding over troubles, the nursing of delusions. . . . Occupation fits a recoverable patient to return to civil life and helps him cope with the difficulties that have to be met with in the struggle for existence."[91] The philosophy of occupational therapy insisted that treatment and recovery would come not through rest but through active participation in work.

However, occupational therapy was treated in a bifurcated way according to disability. Noncustodial cases, especially those housed in the reformatories, were more likely to become wage earners in society. For custodial cases, however, the goal of rehabilitation was always in tension with the understanding that the defective class would be segregated in institutions for their entire lives. Disability scholars theorize that capitalism profits by dictating who can and cannot work, or whose labor is "skilled" or "unskilled" and therefore deserving of little to no pay, and by invoking biological or mental impairment as the natural cause of this inequality.[92] James I. Charlton describes disabled people as a "surplus" population, who are excluded from definitions of employment/unemployment, alongside undocumented migrants, retired people (who often wish to work), and women (who do unpaid labor).[93] This theory can be used to examine how the labor of disabled people was obscured under the guise of therapy.

By creating the concept of occupational therapy, the administrative state could put patients to work without pay, having them perform labor that saved state institutions money.

As the Board of Institutions described it, labor was not only "one of the most valuable therapeutic agencies in the treatment of the insane," but "all of these various activities serve to materially reduce the cost of operation."[94] Just as important as the therapeutic function of work, then, was the understanding that such work could provide for the daily needs of patients and inmates, thereby reducing the state's financial investment in the enterprise of carceral eugenics. The most ambitious understandings of occupational therapy at the state's juvenile reform schools went even further beyond subsistence and entered the realm of commercial activity. For example, the objectives of the Department of Household Arts at the California School for Girls were, "first, Educational. Training in technique and appreciation of such work as tends to promote interest and efficiency in home making. Development of speed and accuracy in work which may serve as a basis for a vocation. Second, Utilitarian. The making of all garments, household linens, rugs and baskets used in the institution. Third, Commercial Value. Adding to contingent fund receipts from work of the various branches of the department."[95] At other institutions where the defective class was thought to be less curable, the emphasis on the utilitarian value of producing necessary materials for the daily needs of the farm colony remained. Administrators at these other institutions also experimented with capitalizing on labor, selling for cash the crafts that institutionalized people created.

The proceeds of these sales were not returned to institutionalized people as a wage but were deposited directly into the accounts of the institution as income. However small the receipts were for this kind of occupational therapy, this practice extracted surplus value from institutionalized people, especially egregious when those people were categorized as custodial cases. The construction of the defective class as unable to compete in the modern workforce, and instead benefiting from living on farm colonies (and later sheltered workspaces), kept this system of value extraction in place.[96] Just as the idealization of the housewife masks gendered surplus value extraction, the concept of occupational therapy masked the extraction of value from disabled people.

Another innovative way that the state extracted surplus value from disabled people was by collecting cash payments from their families. The 1897 insanity law allowed the state to charge the estates of patients and their family members for their detention, euphemized as care. Although the commitment process of the 1897 insanity law was overturned, the state continued to bill and collect monies for full or partial payment of the cost of institutionalization. Any property or money in the bank owned by a patient, including Civil War pensions owed either to a patient or their husbands, was fair game. For the fiscal year that ended in 1924, the Department of Institutions reported that payments from the trust funds of inmates for their care contributed $150,412.04 to the state.[97] At some institutions, such as Napa State Hospital, trust fund collections totaled 5 percent of the yearly budget. The possibility of collecting more from the families of patients kept the state paying administrative collections staff to travel and pursue legal recourse against those who refused to pay. The accounting records show that staff incurred expenses totaling thousands of dollars in the quest to enforce collections.

Charging families for the institutionalization of their kin meant that value was extracted from the nonlaboring defective class as an "existentially surplus population," which Grace Hong and Neferti Tadiar separately theorize is never considered potential labor but is still a valuable source of capital extraction.[98] Elaborating on this concept, Hong writes, "Today's populations are not only surplus labor but are also merely surplus: existentially surplus. In other words, currently, certain populations are not necessary to capital as potential sources of labor, but instead are useful for their intrinsic lack of value."[99] Hong's example of an existentially surplus population is US prisoners. She theorizes that their existence is not productive as hyperexploitable labor (although a small percentage of prisoners are highly exploited laborers), but productive as another kind of capital for corporations, including state-run industries. These businesses earn profit in ways that Marx never envisioned, such as from the construction of new prison cells and the provisioning of food and other necessities to the populations that fill the institutions.

In conceptualizing the eugenics institution as a site of capital extraction beyond labor exploitation, I am drawing mostly from theories of late capitalism and post-deinstitutionalization. Ruth Wilson Gilmore, for example, describes shifts in political economy that led to groups of laborers in the United States being made surplus in the 1960s and 1970s due to the offshoring and outsourcing of manufacturing.[100] While Gilmore describes how these conditions were ripe for carceral solutions in the form of California state prisons, this period coincided with deinstitutionalization without community infrastructure-building, which arguably created an additional pool of existentially surplus people. In addition to the expansion of the prison industrial complex, other neoliberal solutions that were equally carceral were developed in the 1980s in response to the problem of unproductive disabled people who could not be put to work as unskilled laborers. Consequently, the carceral treatment of disablement became big business in the second half of the twentieth century.[101] Johnnie Tuitel's concept of handicapitalism is an apt descriptor here; it describes the corporate profits made by charging insurance companies and the government exorbitant amounts to house disabled people in private nursing homes, boarding homes, for-profit psychiatric hospitals, and group homes.[102] As Marta Russell and Jean Stewart argue, disabled people are in the late twentieth and twenty-first centuries worth more to the gross domestic product when occupying these institutional beds than they are in their own homes.[103]

While the theorizations of the existentially surplus and handicapitalism are grounded in an analysis of post-1970s neoliberalism and financialization, I use these concepts to gesture toward the ways that surplus value was extracted from the defective class as early as the turn of the twentieth century. Well before the economic restructuring of the 1970s, the state experimented in extracting value, developing strategies that were later deployed in collaboration with private corporations during the expansion of the carceral industrial complex in the mid-twentieth century.

My analysis of the political economy of carceral eugenics insists that the administrative state that replaced laissez-faire was not designed to compete with capital but to manage it. The process of building the administrative state did not diminish the power of capital but instead wrestled capital into new collaborations and circuits. The Progressive's administrative state used the ideology of carceral eugenics to justify channeling money in new flows under the guise of containing the defective class. Through the entire process, the administrative state sought to comply with the logics of capitalism, ranging from developing practices of good economy to strategies of extracting unpaid labor from disabled, gendered, and racialized populations.

Contrary to the depiction of the Progressive Era as one of broad-based social welfare, this rechanneling of money did not redistribute it equitably but directed it back toward the elite and an emergent middle class. These new flows of money provided income for Anglo private landowners who had been granted deeds from land stolen from Indigenous peoples, facilities construction contracts, and even income for utilities and railroad corporations in the form of infrastructure development contracts. After a period of mostly voluntary work, the new administrative state brought good-paying professional jobs for the middle class.

Conceiving of the political economic shifts of the era in this way challenges the consensus about the period as progressive, in the general sense of the word. Instead, I argue that carceral eugenics allowed the administrative state to virtually launder money. The state collected taxes from the public and from corporations, used it to build the carceral state, and then used that money to pay the middle class to discipline labor, and otherwise extract surplus value from the defective class. The political economic model of carceral eugenics then served the state when California started a massive expansion of the prison system in the 1970s.[104]

4

From Maternalist Care
to Anti-eugenics

Next to the display of ceramics, drawings, and paintings by patients at Patton State Hospital Museum is a mostly empty wooden display case with a plexiglass window. At the bottom of the case in a haphazard arrangement are a handful of letters and newspaper clippings slipped into plastic sleeves (see figure 4.1). In the corner is a stack of burlap sugar bags. The placard for the display explains the correlation: these letters addressed to or written by patients dated to 1925 were found stuffed in a sugar sack in an attic of the cottage that now houses the Human Resources Department.

When visiting the museum, I lingered over this display as long as my tour guide would allow. She was not an archivist or a historian, just a staff member at the state hospital not usually assigned to give tours. She could not have known how I longed to break the plexiglass and liberate the letters from their imprisonment. These were items that must have been loved, treasured, and cried over. I thought the letters should be rematriated, and I wondered if any effort had been put into finding the writers or the intended recipients. Although now any survivors would almost certainly be very old, deceased patients may have relatives alive who would treasure a memory of their ancestor. Those that could not be rematriated I certainly longed to read, as the state archives contain little written from the perspective of institutionalized people. All that was available to me was a glimpse through glass, where I could hardly make out the words to the first page of one letter.

This encounter with the letters reminded me of my very first trip to the California State Archives in Sacramento. As an overly eager researcher, I requested the item titled "Correspondence Files—Stockton State Hospital." All my hopes deflated as I watched the archivist return to my table (the one she had assigned so she could keep an eye on me) with just four manila folders. One slim folder was titled "Letters of Gratitude 1933–1940." Among all the records I examined at the state archives, this first request turned out to be the only section that contained the actual words of patients at institutions for disability confinement in the early twentieth century. This is not just due to poor record-keeping practices but also because, as Zosha Stuckey argues, disabled people were denied literacy well into the twentieth century.[1]

The irony that I, a committed abolitionist and critical disability scholar, could only find written words from institutionalized people in a folder labeled "Gratitude" was somewhat mediated upon deeper inspection of the letters. The feeling of gratitude must have been in some cases performative and in others just one of a complicated set of feelings. Even legitimate feelings of gratitude for helpful staff did not necessarily suppress the desire for freedom outside of the institution.

My encounter with these letters is a starting place for an undertheorized dimension of the eugenics policy of segregation—namely, opposition to eugenics among institutionalized people in the early twentieth century. Similar to Natalie Lira's investigation of resistance at the Pacific Colony, I seek out moments in the archive when institutionalized people resisted eugenics through acts, embodiments, and expressions that asserted their right to live and, further, their right to live outside of the institution.[2] I fantasize about rewriting the history of eugenics from below, from the perspective of those categorized as defective. This speculative practice

4.1   Personal letters and newspaper clippings on display at Patton State
Hospital Museum. Photograph by the author, 2019.

calls to me because a critical disability history of resistance to eugenics
institutions is still incomplete.[3] Although Kim E. Nielsen's *A Disability
History of the United States* identifies the 1930s and 1940s as formative of the
disability rights movement, even in her book, state hospitals and homes
for the feebleminded remain underexamined as sites where resistance to
eugenics took place.[4] In this chapter, I piece together traces of noncompliance to maternal eugenics authority in California. I highlight the practices
of institutionalized people that indicate a yearning for something different. These acts include using legal and formal means to seek freedom and
extrajudicial strategies of escape. Institutionalized people also used their
bodies to refuse to comply with the demands of the maternalist eugenics
state. They refused to answer questions, get out of bed, or eat. Refusal was
on a spectrum of unruliness that dysgenic people practiced, and the effect
was to claim value for oneself in the face of eugenicist devaluation of the
defective class. I read the archive for places where the epistemologies, emotions, and motivations of patients shined through eugenicist obscuration,
and so I work toward developing an alternative history of anti-eugenics.

By examining the few pieces of writing from patients stored in the California State Archive, reading this archive against the grain, and interpreting newspaper accounts, I recount practices of nonacquiescence that can be interpreted as crip practices of anti-eugenics.

To understand exactly how revolutionary these practices were, I start the chapter by describing the maternalist eugenics imaginaries of middle-class and elite activist women. Women reformers imagined a caring, maternalist state that could detect the difference between those who could be properly developed into normal humanity and those who needed to be humanely sacrificed. One of the places this fantasy of the maternalist eugenics state is described is in the feminist utopian novel *Herland* written by Charlotte Perkins Gilman.[5] After describing the fictional nation of Herland as the ideal that reformers sought, I return to state archival documents, and specifically the annual reports sent to the state legislature. I describe how elite women working in institutions sought to cultivate in institutionalized women a shared desire for a caring version of eugenics. Through their practices of refusal, institutionalized people rejected this version of freedom and asserted the possibility of other futures.

Reading the archive as what M. Jacqui Alexander calls a "palimpsest," I identify the maternalist eugenics imaginary as it was cocreated through and against crip practices of anti-eugenics.[6] This dual method of reading exposes that it was queer and crip futurity that was at stake in every act of refusal to the logic of eugenics.

Imagining a Maternalist Utopia

In the early twentieth century, Progressive reformers captured the governing apparatus in California, attempting to build a state that was genuinely interested in the lives of citizens. This new caring state envisioned modes of intimacy between the government and its citizens by extending the responsibility of mothering out of the home, away from the exclusive privilege of the family, and into the hands of a scientific state apparatus operated by women. This is exemplified by the California State Board of Charities and Corrections in a report that insisted: "More and more the necessity of caring for the future citizen by the best possible method is becoming a national necessity, and duty."[7] The vision for the maternalist state is the context within which I treat resistance to eugenics that would otherwise appear to be nothing more than the acts of ungrateful children.

The fictional nation of Herland described by Charlotte Perkins Gilman is a distillation of the efforts of women reformers in the early twentieth century to build a maternalist state that cared for its citizens, especially women, children, and disabled people. Gilman's 1915 novel was recuperated by white feminists in the 1970s, celebrated as a depiction of the utopian benefits of matriarchal society and a full manifestation of the politics laid out in Gilman's nonfiction books, including *Women and Economics* and *The Home: Its Work and Influence*.[8] *Herland* is the story of three male explorers who encounter an entirely female society cut off from the rest of the world for centuries. The biological explanation for the society being exclusively female is spontaneous parthenogenesis, with natural selection for only female children. Combined with generations of adaptive social learning, the "race of women" have engineered a harmonious utopia without disease, disability, criminality, poverty, fatness, or vice. These were the very same goals of elite and middle-class activist women throughout the Progressive Era, including in California. Gilman accomplished it by parthenogenesis while the maternalists of the Progressive Era had to resort to innovations in public policy.

As others have assessed, Gilman's fantasy of female society is, like many of the strategies adopted by women reformers of the era, eugenicist to its core.[9] Both Gilman's fiction and nonfiction writing on behalf of women's equality espouse social Darwinist and nativist ideas. Like many other elite women of the time, Gilman also argued that culture was adaptable and could be used to improve the race. This view is compatible with a Lamarckian version of eugenics, mobilizing culture in the project of self-directed human evolution. Herland is a society that has achieved the pinnacle of civilization through centuries of cultural adaptation that shapes the society's breeding program. In recounting the origin story of Herland, one of the discoverers describes "a period of 'negative eugenics'" in which "unfit" women chose not to conceive if they knew they were not going to pass on the best stock.[10] These women would, in other words, decline motherhood for the good of the country. Here Gilman neatly solves the problem of genocide by making eugenics consensual. Every citizen of Herland devotes her life to the improvement of the race. As the male explorers in the novel recount, "Very early they recognized the need of improvement as well as of mere repetition, and they devoted their combined intelligence to that problem—how to make the best kind of people. First this was merely the hope of bearing better ones, and then they recognized that however the children differed at birth, the real growth lay latter—through education."[11]

In addition to consensual negative eugenics, the society enacts a specifically maternalist eugenics, integrating both nature and nurture toward the goal of human perfection. The male explorers marvel that through this art of consensual eugenics, "sickness was almost wholly unknown among them, so much so that a previously high development in what we call the 'science of medicine' had become practically a lost art"; "they lacked all morbid or excessive types"; "it is—yes, quite six hundred years since we have had what you call a 'criminal.'"[12] Having gotten rid of sick people, fat people, and criminals, the society is also able to dispense with immoral women and queers: "There was no sex-feeling to appeal to, or practically none. Two thousand years' disuse had left very little of the instinct; also we must remember that those who had at times manifested it as atavistic exceptions were often, by that very fact, denied motherhood."[13] Any sexual feelings, which we must presume in a women's-only utopia would be expressed as same-sex desire toward another female or as self-pleasure, are construed as threatening to slide the nation backward in time and women who experience them are consequently disciplined with reproductive control.

However, as this passage reveals, not all citizens of Herland were so patriotic as to deny themselves queer sex or the fruits of crime—hence the continued need, even after hundreds of years, for subtle but persistent forms of social control by the state. The maternalist fantasy of an educated and rehabilitated womanhood, where women would thoughtfully and consensually choose to act in the best interest of the race, was ultimately enforced by the teeth of the caring state. *Herland* illustrates the vision of national, societal, and human perfection as well as the strategies for change adopted by maternalist reformers in the late nineteenth and early twentieth centuries. Consensual, voluntary reproductive control was preferred, and reformers built a state that provided educational and rehabilitative programs for women to learn such self-control. As in the novel, reformers hoped to resort to state force only in those extreme cases of "atavistic exceptions," where women were so backward in hereditary stock that they could not make good by controlling themselves.[14]

Although Gilman's ideology drew on national influences, she was specifically connected to California. Born in Connecticut and living much of her life in New York, she moved to Southern California from 1888 into the 1890s and later returned to Pasadena (where her daughter lived) a year before her death in 1935. Not uncoincidentally, maternalists in California sought to create a state similar to Herland during the Progressive Era. Maternalists sought to build a state that could inculcate the values of self-government that were bred into Herland citizens and that could intervene whenever atavistic unruliness appeared.

The comprehensive social structure of the imaginary Herland, which had been perfected over centuries, became so advanced that state institutions were all but absent. However, the real maternalist state in California was conflated with—almost a euphemism for—state custody in state psychiatric hospitals, state homes for the feebleminded, and adult and youth reformatories. The concept of state care for reformers came to mean care within an institution. Reformers imagined "an institution . . . which shall, by its watchful and wise care and training, turn back into the world citizens who shall maintain themselves honorably and usefully when they reenter society."[15]

State care was gendered, targeting those assigned to the category of women and girls because this was the portion of the population over whom elite women had jurisdiction. Shortly after opening the School for Girls, women reformers were instrumental in passing AB 685, which established the California Industrial Farm for Women. AB 685 was "an act to establish an institution for the confinement, care and reformation of delinquent women. . . . The purpose of said institution shall be to provide custody, care, protection, . . . training and reformatory help for delinquent women." Later, the law establishing the California Institute for Women copied AB 685 almost word for word, articulating the state's first prison for women as a site not for punishment but for state care.

As if in an attempt to replicate Herland, state care was imagined as the jurisdiction of newly educated women professionals. Elite women in the early twentieth century had recently benefited from access to higher education and were increasingly seeking roles for themselves in the fields of law, public policy, medicine, social work, and education. As observed by Nichole Hahn Rafter and others, new professionals generally did not attempt to alter conventional European colonial views about women's natural roles as wife, mother, and sister, but instead worked within and expanded on those roles from moral compass for the family to moral compass for the nation.[16] However, this discursive strategy limited women to having moral authority only over children or adults who could be infantilized, such as disabled people or other women. Women reformers theorized that building sex segregated facilities created opportunities so that "adult female offender[s] might receive that more intimate and understanding care of women for women."[17] Women police officers, penal staff, attorneys, judges, and social workers were envisioned not as general public servants but as those who would specifically care for other women, children, and disabled people.

One such maternalist public servant is illustrated by the career of Grace Maxwell Fernald, who in 1911 landed in the Psychological Department and Laboratory at the State Normal School in Los Angeles (which became the University of California, Los Angeles).[18] Fernald is known most widely for her contributions to theories of learning and in developing remedial reading techniques. However, Fernald's early career started in the research of juvenile delinquency. Through an arrangement with the California School for Girls, Fernald conducted an extensive psychological examination of at least one hundred juveniles (up to the age of twenty-one).[19] Using the Binet-Simon IQ test and the Stanford revision, Fernald worked to classify people according to mental age, using the categories "moron," "borderline," and "normal." Her solution to preventing juvenile delinquency and adult criminality was for early IQ testing for defectiveness in public schools to determine which students should be permanently segregated from the "normal," which she determined would have "saved the state incalculable expense and disorder, as well as securing greater happiness for the unfortunate individuals themselves."[20] Fernald's efforts show how maternalists introduced humane reforms to the practice of state care in part through the language of eugenics.

This commitment to eugenics allowed a few women to break out of patriarchal limitations, with a few achieving enough status to serve at high levels in state institutions. The best example is the formidable Margaret H. Smyth. Smyth graduated from Stanford University's Cooper Medical School in 1898, and shortly after was among thirty women who participated in the first examination in California for women medical professionals to work in state hospitals.[21] She was appointed an assistant physician for what was then Stockton State Mental Asylum. She worked as an assistant physician, overseeing the female ward at the hospital until 1929, when she became the first woman superintendent of a state hospital in the entire United States. Upon her retirement, Mary Jo Gohlke reports that it was said that Smyth was "one of the biggest MEN in state service," and that even Governor Earl Warren attended her retirement reception. Smyth was nationally recognized for "perfect[ing] the technique for sterilization surgery," as well as for her "progressive" policies against "striking or harming a patient."[22] Like Fernald, Smyth's success was based on her simultaneous commitment to Progressivism, maternalism, and eugenics. These women used eugenics institutions to try to bring about the maternalist state, acting as a vanguard for the kind of Progressive revolution articulated in *Herland*.

The Impossibility of Making Good

The vanguard of the maternalist state led a valiant effort to cultivate among their charges a willingness to defer pregnancy if it was in the best interest of the nation. Like the fictional Herland matriarchs, the maternalists intended to establish a practice of self-government among institutionalized people in California. Self-government was a prophylactic of restrained desire that would reduce socially undesirable reproduction without further state intervention. The citizen who desired to make good in the eyes of the state was a core component of the maternalist utopia.

In addition to the corporate monopolies and vice industries, the enemy of the maternalist state was ungoverned instinct. The feminized members of the defective class who resisted self-government were perceived to be clinging to an instinctual desire for freedom. Reformers conceived of this instinct for freedom as anachronistic, even though it ironically was enabled by modern changes in urban living and global movement.[23] As Fernald argued in a 1916 report to the state legislature, "In the case of most of our girls, as would be expected, ungoverned instinct is a part of the problem which confronts us. . . . Civilized life requires the control, though not the complete suppression, of practically all forms of instinctive action. The only way in which such control can be exercised is through the force of ideas which direct the activity along the line opposed to the instinct. When ideational activities become habit, a permanent control over instinct is established."[24] The desire to be ungoverned by society and family marked the defective class as a threat to civilization. Administrators needed to suppress instinct and replace it with self-government and deference to authority. Suppressing instinct became the goal of rehabilitation under state care. Progress required the inculcation of habits, discernments, and behaviors that exhibited internalized restraint and resistance to ungoverned instinct.

Administrators of state institutions in early twentieth-century California referred to the practice of disciplining people into civilized life as "making good." In addition to undergoing sterilization surgery, defective women and girls were expected to "make good" in order to be released on parole from institutions. Making good was a particular goal for juvenile delinquents and dependents in the reform schools, as well as for sex workers and other women "in the life."[25] A seven-point plan for making good included, first, undergoing medical treatment of the body, curing venereal disease, and learning to enact proper personal hygiene.[26] Second, it included training in women's work, such as cooking, cleaning, and serving. Third, women needed to complete schoolwork in the domestic sciences, the household arts, and secretarial skills. Fourth, women had to learn how to engage in wholesome recreation. Fifth, they must adopt "respect for the law" and participate appropriately in collective self-government. Sixth, regular attendance at religious services was required. And finally, they must cultivate of a sense of beauty. As the superintendent of the State School for Girls described, "This purpose [of the school] ... is to set the girls' feet on the road to right citizenship. . . . Into the texture of this life enter the threads which enter into the life of the good citizen everywhere. Some of these are the building and maintaining of sound bodies, useful work, vital schooling, wholesome play, respect for law, practical religion, beauty, hope, vision."[27] Elements of this comprehensive program developed at the State School for Girls are also evident in the treatment offered to the mad, the blind, those with physical impairments, and the so-called feebleminded in institutions for disability confinement. For example, in the state hospitals, patients were treated to reorder their mad thinking, by reintroducing executive control functions over the subconscious and wild instincts run amok. A report from Agnews State Hospital discussed such strategies for the "re-education" of patients though military drills, calisthenics, pretend "battles," dances, basketball games, camping in the mountains, basket weaving and fancy work, and job retraining (see figure 4.2).[28] The Board of Institutions later pontificated that the purpose of these rehabilitative activities was that they worked at "stimulating functioning on right lines, by surroundings that appeal to the higher consciousness through the senses. . . . Much of the physician's direct mental treatment in all cases must be made along the line of suggestion aiming at self-control in physical, mental and moral actions."[29]

The first step toward self-control was to learn to defer to the judgment of institutional administrators. According to the medical superintendent at Agnews State Hospital, the policy of an "open hospital, depending, not on barriers and too curtailed liberty" rested on the belief that it was possible to cultivate among patients "self-control and an understanding of why here."[30] Further, by offering occupational therapy, on-campus jobs, "diversions and amusements," it was possible to create "a general good feeling and contented atmosphere among patients and employees," wherein "a large proportion of our patients are reached and made, if not contented, at least

4.2   Class in gymnastics, Sonoma State Home. Photographer unknown. Published by California State Printing Office, 1921.

willing to await our judgment about going out."[31] Making good was an affective reorientation that required relinquishing resistance to being locked up. Patients learned to await the decisions made by administrators content in the knowledge that there was a reason why they were institutionalized.

This deference to administrators is related to the "respect for law" cultivated at the School for Girls by an experiment in which inmates could be elected to a council where they proposed measures for action that represented their interests: "Pupils who have been a month on the honor roll of the School... constitute the voting body of the School.... This voting body elects a delegate from each cottage community to represent it on a central council.... Its delegates report to their respective cottages the proceedings of the council and, at need, bring before the voting body measures for action."[32] Of course, as the report goes on to remind the legislature, this council offered only nominal power because the superintendent of the school would override any decisions that did not conform to the overall vision of rehabilitation into good citizenship. Through this exercise in self-government, the girls were also practicing deference to state power.

Relinquishing resistance was assumed to eventually turn into cheerfulness and happiness about being institutionalized: "Our work in reeducation has been very satisfactory—patients who were stupid and untidy before entering the class are now cheerful, showing marked improvements in mental condition and habits."³³ Later, the Board of Institutions insisted that this contentment showed up in the institutional practice of occupational therapy, explaining that "a normal person likes employment that is interesting and agreeable or that brings remuneration or produces something beautiful or elicits commendation. We are using these psychological facts to incite in the abnormal the normal feeling and attitude toward life."³⁴ The same passage notes that normal feeling was measured by whether patients showed up to their on-campus jobs and "engaged in [them] cheerfully and with interest." Any person who did not express enjoyment at the chance to have a job would have been categorized as resistant to treatment. Making good was established through the "stability and industry of the girl"— that is, by eagerly allowing surplus value to be extracted from one's labor.³⁵

Ultimately administrators attempted to cultivate within assigned females a recognition that they had been offered an opportunity for which they should be appreciative. The Board of Institutions insisted that because "inmates are given the best of scientific care and treatment," eventually they became "apparently happy and decidedly grateful to the state for what is being done for them."³⁶ Making good was demonstrated by a person's "appreciation of the justice and fair play of the school in directing her conduct."³⁷ Making good meant relinquishing the yearning for freedom in favor of gratitude for the protection offered by the state. The Board of Institutions memorably described the achievement this way: "Slowly, but effectively, the feeling of hostility and rebellion at being deprived of what they are pleased to term 'freedom' is being replaced by a sense of gratitude and appreciation for the protection and opportunities offered by the state. This must of necessity result in a higher type of citizenship. . . . To this end all efforts must bend toward raising the status of the school from that of custodial care to one of *protective opportunity*."³⁸ As administrators refashioned the carceral eugenics policy of segregation into an opportunity, deep gratitude for the state was expected to replace any previous desires that institutionalized people had for alternative versions of freedom.

Despite the insistence on the possibility of achieving gratitude for state care, there were no illusions among reformers that this process was not extremely painful. As a report by the California Board of Prison Directors insisted:

> The discipline which saves a man imposes upon him a greater amount of suffering than that which is purely retaliatory. It is easier for a prisoner to adapt himself to the ordinary rules and regulations

of a prison, and perform a certain amount of labor, than to submit to the discipline of institutions which make a constant draft upon his mental, moral, and physical powers; and prisoners who have served time in both classes of institutions almost invariably so testify. The old system said to the prisoner, "Be good"; [it] merely asked [him to] be submissive. The new system says "be good," but also "be good for something."[39]

The board revealed that it intended for state rehabilitation, treatment, and care to cause mental and physical suffering that would force institutionalized people to assimilate to the normative demands of modern citizenship. This is strikingly similar to Foucault's theorization that the disciplinary power exerted on the individual in state institutions of correction transforms the soul into "the prison of the body."[40]

An institutionalized person was only fully rehabilitated to citizenship if she aspired to marriage. This was a heteronormatively gendered understanding of good citizenship: "The girls are constantly taught that, having been sent to the School by the courts of California, they are at the School to be trained into good citizens; that honorable self-support is required of them by the state; that service goes hand in hand with joy; and that happy marriage is one of the noblest means to these ends."[41] Those who truly desired to make good were to learn to desire able-bodied, middle-class, and white supremacist conjugal marriage.

This illustrates a paradox of the role of institutions in the Progressive project to craft a new relationship between citizens and the state: institutions were "not so much places of detention from freedom as places in preparation for freedom."[42] The feminized defective class had to become inmates of the state's institutions, relinquishing their autonomy and submitting to a program of discipline, in order to learn how to live as free citizens. People in the state's institutions were denied autonomy in the process of becoming "inmates," submitting to a program of coercion to teach them to adopt the practices of good citizenship. The ultimate measurement of preparation for citizenship was whether the person adopted a desire for a statist version of freedom, one that exceeded her anachronistic instinct for the wrong kind of nonstatist freedom. Statist freedom challenged the specifically American desires for freedom practiced by capitalists (centered on unrestricted profit) and enclosed on the radical practices of freedom being developed by the underclass (centered on unrestricted movement and relationships).[43] This eugenicist conceptualization of freedom hinged instead on the practice of self-government and deference to authority, and it required a state.

The violence of inclusion into the bourgeois moral order has been theorized by Saidiya Hartman, who traces the extension of legal rights to Black subjects during the Reconstruction of the US South.[44] Hartman describes the process as one that facilitated "relations of domination, the new forms of bondage enabled by proprietorial notions of the self, and the pedagogical and legislative efforts aimed at transforming the formerly enslaved into rational, acquisitive, and responsible individuals."[45] In these instances, legal power was deployed to recognize the humanity and individuality of Black subjects, not in order to free them, she argues, but rather to "tether, bind, and oppress" them within the reconstituted racial order.[46] Gayatri Spivak describes the resulting existence as a violent shuttling between subject and object status.[47] Those who are included for strategic purposes of re-forming the social order are never full subjects with agency and sovereignty over the self but are only temporarily afforded subject status in the eyes of the law when it is convenient for the exercise of bourgeois state power. Frantz Fanon called this existence a form of "peaceful violence."[48]

Extending this framework of analysis to the eugenics era, I argue that the caring state tethered (to borrow Hartman's term) so-called inmates in a part-subject, part-object status. This occurred through the process of attempting to grow within the defective class a desire for the caring state but without a concrete promise that the embodiment of such a desire would lead to their freedom from the institution. Eugenics was a genocidal campaign against the defective class, but at the same time maternalism was focused on intervening on the feminized body to turn it into a gendered citizen—one who loved the state with a maternalist patriotism.

The effort to inculcate within institutionalized people a desire for the carceral state is another example of the violence of liberal inclusion. Through this intimate relationship of care and desire between the feminized defective class and the state, reformers crafted a new kind of defective subjectivity. In the process, institutional administrators worked to suppress any instinctual desires for freedom, in the process curtailing the experimental practices of sociality, kinship, and imagination that blossomed in the early twentieth-century period of urbanization and globalization.[49] Instead, the defective class was coerced into replacing their desires for life and life outside of the institution with practices of self-government and deference to authority. State care disciplined into the patient the skills and training to provide the self-care appropriate to normative citizenship, including suppressing desires for sex and socially undesirable reproduction.

At the same time, the goal of self-governance was in a recursive loop with the logic of eugenics. Under the discourse of eugenics, once a body was determined to be defective, the development of an individual was permanently stunted because "mental defectiveness is not a disease that can be medically treated. It is due to hereditary defect that results in a defect of development. We find a brain development very much like that of an infant. Feeble-mindedness in the parents brings about the same condition in the progeny. The untrained mental defectives are incapable of self-support and must be pensioners on their more intelligent fellows. A cure cannot be expected."[50] Denied a cure, the defective class was seemingly excluded from the possibility of reconstruction and the opportunity to catch up with their normal peers. Eugenics was a practice of temporal distancing, through which the other is permanently deferred from the promise of liberalism yet subjected to unrelenting demands that they continue to strive for inclusion. In particular, so-called borderline cases of defectiveness exasperated staff and administrators, because girls and women resisted self-discipline: "It is practically, if not actually, impossible to develop enough resistance within her [the high-grade defective] so that it is ever safe for her to become a free member of society."[51]

Feminist scholarship has described how many populations were excluded from the promise of care by the state, such as women of color who have been routinely denied access to forms of social welfare.[52] Yet to understand the simultaneity of inclusion and exclusion, I find Mimi Thi Nguyen's discussion of the diagnosis of trauma among refugees to be most apt, in that it helps to explain the temporal distancing that occurs through diagnosis.[53] As Nguyen argues about Southeast Asian refugees, the traumatized body experiencing symptoms of dislocation in time is incapable of claiming the rational individuality assumed in liberal political theorizing. The temporally wandering, split, emotional body does not perform in the ways that the liberal state and neoliberal capital need. For Nguyen, the diagnosis of trauma works to reposition the refugee as an incoherent subject incapable of self-possession and instead invites biomedical interventions and criminalization. It is through such a process that those who have been placed at a temporal distance from the center of empire and the pinnacle of human achievement are never able to progress fast enough to catch up. The temporal other is relegated to a perpetual state of transition, to a time-space of never-not-quite-here-and-now.

This perpetual state of transitology (to borrow a phrase from post-socialist scholarship) keeps in place the illusion that through discipline the defective body can be made to catch up to the normal present; however, the moment of achieving normality is endlessly deferred.[54] Despite the constant exercises toward self-government, the inmate was stuck between subject (who could claim bodily autonomy) and object (needing to be intervened on because she could not be trusted). In this liminal space, any person categorized as defective who claimed autonomy over themselves, even if it was through means that may not have been recognizable as political, challenged the foundations of carceral eugenics.

Toward a History of Anti-eugenics

Records left by institutionalized people are rare, especially prior to World War II. The problem of locating the records of institutionalized people is a continuation of eugenics: it disappears those labeled as dysgenic, and obliterates the other possible futures that disabled and queerly bodied people could have created. This did not become clear to me until the end of my research, when I realized that I had been so caught up in telling the story of eugenics, I had not been diligent enough in tracking how institutionalized people resisted eugenics. Revisiting my notes and materials, I observed a pattern of acts, embodiments, and expressions that asserted the right to live and, further, the right to live outside of the institution. Almost too late for this book, I realize that the next history to be told is the history of eugenics from below.

Eugenicist versions of the future were a dominant ideology in the late nineteenth and early twentieth centuries in the United States, but alternatives were articulated. Perhaps most well-documented is the resistance to eugenics sterilization by those who worried that access to birth control would lead to immoral sexual behavior.[55] Yet as scholars are now discussing, antisterilization activities were not necessarily inherently anti-eugenics, and antisterilization was not necessarily an alternative vision of freedom for dysgenic people.[56] Institutionalization was often promised as the appropriate alternative to sterilization. Carceral eugenics—the physical containment of the defective class in the name of a healthy body politic—was still accepted by those who opposed sterilization.

I seek instead anti-eugenics from below, traces of possible oppositional consciousness by those who were targeted by state-sponsored eugenics programs. In Merri Lisa Johnson and Robert McRuer's definition of cripistemology, disabled people generate knowledge that emanates from their position as a "surplus" class whose presence threatens the political and economic order.[57] If eugenics is the ideology that the defective class is a menace to the future, then anti-eugenics is the cripistemology of dysgenic people who articulate a will to live; counter the social devaluation of their lives, families, and communities; insist on having children, parenting, and creating networks of care; and express desires for freedom beyond institutionalization.

I understand my effort as indebted to the antipsychiatry and self-advocacy movements, which began in the 1960s, as recorded by Paul Williams and Bonnie Shoultz, Gunnar Dybwad and Hank Bersani Jr., and Roland Johnson, among others.[58] Although the decades leading up to the 1960s must have been formative for the disability rights movement, locating written articulations of the politics of institutionalized people in this period presents several challenges. One challenge is that the records stored by the state archives continue to narrate institutionalized people through ableist rhetoric. Returning to the example at the beginning of this chapter, the one place I encountered the written words of patients in the state archives was in a manila folder labeled "Letters of Gratitude." Initially disturbed, I did find that the letters offer insight into much more complicated analysis of confinement than the concept of gratitude. One letter, written by someone I call Katherine and dated April 26, 1937, explains that she was voluntarily admitted to the hospital but had asked that she be released several days prior. Katherine wrote, "Any more of this 'prison' existence will stifle me—I thought I could take it—But now I want to get out. . . . I hold the highest regard for you and doctor Paine and most of your staff—I think you have a wonderful hospital (but many things needed) but I beg of you to please release me." What to make of the letter-writer calling the hospital a prison and later describing it as wonderful? I interpret it as a rhetorical strategy, couching Katherine's plea for freedom in a compliment that demonstrated her normal status that required esteem for medical professionals and state supported treatment. The letter-writer deftly places the blame for needing to leave on herself, noting that she thought she "could take it." This letter affirms ambivalence about eugenics institutions, consciousness of institutions as spaces that seem idyllic from the outside but are experienced as sites of horror. Further, the letter suggests that some patients both felt and interpreted the eugenics institution as a carceral space, one that was not only prisonlike but an actual site of imprisonment, from which they could not escape. This letter is an indication that the performance of gratitude for incarceration cultivated by the maternalists did not entirely suppress desires for other kinds of freedom.

The limited number of letters in the state archive is evidence of the ways that many disabled, mad, and neurodivergent people were actively denied literacy or access to the materials to write.[59] Others would have been nonliterate or nonspeaking, relying on forms of nonverbal communication to express their thoughts, emotions, and motivations. Nonverbal communication includes hand signs, stimming, behavior, sounds that do not form words, and, in the present, the use of augmentative and alternative communication (AAC) technologies. These forms of communication do not leave written records, making it challenging but not impossible to locate desires for freedom among people confined to carceral disability institutions, desires which were not fully articulated as a political platform until later decades.

Given the dearth of ephemera created by institutionalized people available in the state archive, I instead read the official archive "against the grain"—a method developed by postcolonial subaltern studies—for traces of anti-eugenics cripistemologies.[60] Following this method most closely, there is evidence of anti-eugenics among those who used the legal system to exit the institution. An example is an assigned-female person at the Sonoma State Home who was successful at using the court system to escape, indicated by the short note in her record that she had been "discharged September 1920 by writ of habeas corpus." William Blackstone declared in the mid-eighteenth century that habeas corpus was the proper strategy for challenging "all manner of illegal confinement."[61] Under the short-lived 1897 insanity law, the US constitutional right to a writ of habeas corpus was reiterated as applicable to confinement in eugenics institutions. Habeas corpus was the counter to parens patriae, the legal doctrine that indicated it was the state's duty to see that those who are incapable of self-care receive care. Writs of habeas corpus could challenge confinement on the grounds of jurisdiction, due process, or improper proceedings, yet these claims might not lead to freedom as the state could then rectify these problems and maintain custody of the institutionalized person. The person who escaped via habeas corpus in September 1920 probably instead claimed that she was not feebleminded as the state asserted, and therefore her detention was illegal. On one level this claim is a form of anti-eugenics because it countered the state's determination of truth in this individual case. On another level, such a claim reinforced the philosophy that some people did deserve to be institutionalized for eugenics purposes. The only legal question in that case would be whether the state erred in its determination that one single individual belonged to the defective class.

Given the great difficulties that patients must have faced in seeking a writ and mounting the burden of proof required, some instead pursued public inquiry. Local newspapers reported on cases where former inmates and family members appealed to state oversight agencies to investigate abuse inside the state's eugenics institutions. One such case was a 1903 investigation into allegations of abuse at what was then Southern California State Hospital (now Patton State Hospital). One former patient on parole named Rev. J. S. Matthews reported that he had seen another man named Rev. E. E. Plannette "choked, jumped upon and abused."[62] Unfortunately, the abused man's wife, friends, and current inmates did not substantiate the claims of abuse, leading to the conclusion that the staff's physical restraint of Plannette was appropriate given his tendencies toward "excitability and violence." Other patients also failed to substantiate any other charge of "ill-treatment." However, from my experience in human rights monitoring at California state prisons, many imprisoned people have expressed fear of speaking out against abuse lest they invite staff retaliation. It is possible that those who testified in the 1903 case could not be assured of their safety, especially given that other charges in the case regarded the use of drugs like apomorphia to discipline unruly patients. The reporters of the story dismissed any testimony given by patients, arguing, "Many of these rumors of ill-treatment were traced to patients and to former employees, who, in most cases, were discharged for cause.... The testimony of patients was taken in several cases and given such credence as seemed warranted by the mental condition and the corroborative circumstances in the case under consideration."[63] In later cases, investigators determined that those who reported abuse were seeking fame that comes from being involved in scandal.[64] Given the many strategies for undermining the credibility of those who reported abuse, the attempt by Rev. Matthews to bring these complaints can be interpreted as an incredible act of solidarity with his friend Rev. Plannette. It was also a radical reformulation of what was appropriate treatment of people held captive at eugenics institutions and a courageous move that articulated an alternative conception of justice.

However, despite some cases of successful writs and public hearings, the means most available to institutionalized people for expressing anti-eugenics were not legal or formal. Cripistemologies of anti-eugenics can primarily be found in evidence of daily practice. This is specific to crip epistemologies because of the reliance on forms of nonspeaking communication to express thoughts, emotions, and motivations. For the purpose of seeking anti-eugenics in the past, I identified in the archive forms of behavior that were noncompliant with the care provided by the maternal state. I speculate that at least some of these acts of noncompliance were practices of anti-eugenics. They are not articulated forms of protest, such as seeking formal rights or access to employment. The daily practice of anti-eugenics by institutionalized people was instead an unarticulated structure of feeling that was at times messy, dirty, sexually explicit, violent, and self-sabotaging.

Consider that inmates at the California School for Girls were caught during the 1916–18 reporting period systematically cheating the IQ tests that determined placement in the school's housing units, classrooms, and training programs. As the superintendent of the school recounted:

> If the test is done satisfactorily it is necessary that the subjects get the idea of doubling the last number given. The final answer will be the doubling of 16, or will be 32. After several months work we began to get the answer 32 even from some of our defectives. We immediately carried the test one step farther and obtained the most peculiar answers . . . showing that they had simply learned the answer to the test from other girls, usually in the detention home or in some other institution where these tests had been given as a part of the Stanford Series.[65]

In short, the administration uncovered a widespread effort to teach other girls how to pass the IQ test, cheating the state of the right to diagnose and categorize an individual as part of the defective class. That this cheating effort took place across state institutions reiterates the point that people in the defective class circulated among the variety of facilities. This means that a network of people conscious of how the state was trying to categorize them as defective was at least partially formulated, and that a collective effort by those categorized as defective intended to cheat the state out of the satisfaction of a defective diagnosis. This example could be interpreted as a practice of anti-eugenics because the participants challenged the notion that status should be determined on the basis of IQ testing.

Another nonlegal and nonformal practice was that of physical escape from state institutions.[66] According to annual reports to the legislature, dozens of institutionalized people each year attempted escape from various institutions. Escape was taken seriously, and sheriffs were called upon to return inmates. According to the Commission in Lunacy, a segment of the defective class—"criminal drunkards or drug habit [cases]"—were particularly inclined to seek opportunities for escape: "Seldom desiring treatment they look upon their detention in a hospital as an outrage, and, therefore, are constantly desiring to escape. Conspiring against attendants or nurses they are a source of constant anxiety."[67] While administrators took pride in the number of escapees who voluntarily returned, I submit that permanent escape was not always the goal of a person, and that a voluntary return should not always be read as acquiescence. A person may have wanted to connect with a date, have a night on the town, or visit with friends and family outside of the institution. They may have voluntarily returned to avoid being tracked down by the authorities and forcibly returned. Temporary escape also signaled a thumb to the nose of the carceral state, showing that the state did not have complete control over defective bodyminds. Escape was not a practice available to all, such as nonambulatory people or people restricted to locked wards. However, family and friends sometimes were able to assist, such as the case of a woman from Sonoma State Home in 1915 who "escaped with her husband who had come to visit her."[68]

Another example of resistance that can be read as anti-eugenics is organized property destruction. The State Board of Charities and Corrections recalled a riot that took place in the girls' quarters at Whittier reform school: "At Whittier we surround our girls' department with a high board fence. We have women on watch all night in the dormitories, a man on watch in the yard, guards on the windows and locks on the doors, and even then we had a riot last year, in which the girls held possession of the premises for several hours, smashed windows and raised trouble generally. We keep the girls from getting away by force."[69] An organized riot also took place in 1921, described in the *Los Angeles Times* as a "conspiracy to destroy by fire all the buildings at the California School for Girls here and then stage a wholesale escape of the 160 inmates of the institution." When the sheriff was called to quell the riots, the inmates reportedly bashed him over the head with a chair. The reporter for the *Times* called the incident "one of the most sensational riots ever witnessed in any State institution."[70] The property damage and the general trouble recounted here can be interpreted as a practice of both anticarcerality and anti-eugenics. Jessica Calvanico argues that cases of arson in state homes and reform schools is evidence of political resistance to incarceration and to carcerality more broadly.[71] Calvanico's account of fire at the Samarcand Manor State Home and Industrial Training School for Girls in North Carolina, and the subsequent arson case against twelve of the girls, makes me curious about the fire that burned down the main building of California's Industrial Farm for Women in 1923. Just a year after the institution opened and accepted its first inmates on misdemeanor and vice crimes, the main administration building burned completely beyond repair. The state legislature, already refusing to appropriate enough funds to maintain the institution, declined to appropriate any money to rebuild the main building, and the institution was closed. I have been unable to locate records on the suspected cause of the fire, and I wonder: Could it have been arson? Were there attempts to put out the fire? Could this have been a bid to secure individual or collective freedom? Fires and riots refused confinement and the ways that carceral eugenics diminished individual life chances in favor of the collective good.

Along these lines, I interpret violence against the agents of the state as another possible form of anti-eugenics practice. Examples of violence at the hands of patients are pervasive in the archive. A Stockton State Hospital patient was observed: "Restless at night, attacks nurses, threatens to kill them."[72] An inmate at the California School for Girls was returned after parole because she "threatened to kill [the] boarding mother," while another was in a runaway plot that involved "attacking [a] matron."[73] Dr. Margaret Smyth's history of the psychiatric system in California tells the story of one of the first women admitted to Stockton State Hospital in 1852. The woman named Mary Anna came from France and is described by the superintendent this way: "She is engaged most of the time in prayer. August 2, talkative, violent. October 10, quiet and disposed to work. March 10, 1853, perfectly rational. July 20, 1854, fought all the attendants." [74] Violence against the agents of the state both destroyed and created. It led to injury among institutional staff, who did not necessarily deserve it in the course of doing their job. On-the-ground staff were not those who created the institution or maintained it. While some institutional staff may have used the opportunity to abuse patients, others may have just needed a job or even had good intent in helping others. Violence against the agents of the state was not necessarily fair, but it was one of the few means available to patients to create an alternative valuation of their lives, one that prioritized the life of the patient over those that the state had privileged as good stock.

Perhaps even more difficult to grapple with are instances of public exposure and other violations of sexual regulations. Staff at Sonoma State Home repeatedly reported that certain people were "addicted to masturbation."[75] The definition of addiction in the present emphasizes that a behavior must interfere with the other functions of a person's life. There is no way of discerning whether the behavior that staff at Sonoma observed was truly an addiction over which patients had no control or whether attempts at discrete masturbation would have been counted as against policy. The latter seems most likely at the School for Girls when administrators noted: "The girls are not here through lack of knowledge of sex hygiene—they know everything. . . . It seems wiser to encourage modesty under the supervision of the night dormitory watch, than to permit them to continue wrong practices alone in single rooms."[76] This note suggests that because such sex was reserved for a time when the defective girl was alone, that it was likely not an addiction but rather an act of defiance against the gendered norms of sexual propriety. However, it is much harder to interpret accounts of masturbation in the state home for the feebleminded and the state hospitals given the almost complete lack of privacy in those facilities. Almost all masturbation would have been public and therefore could have been documented by staff as addictive. That some patients found pleasure in their own bodies under these conditions is defiant and miraculous, a form of anti-eugenics that insists on pleasure for those whose bodies were disposable.

On the other end of the spectrum of anti-eugenics are examples of what could be called nonaction. I draw on what Audra Simpson and Ruha Benjamin have separately named as a "politics of refusal"—refusal to speak on demand or to cooperate in a medical exam, even if cooperation is considered by authorities to be good for the person.[77] José Esteban Muñoz might consider such refusals as semideliberate acts of "misrecognition"—failures to be interpellated into hegemonic discourses, in this case the discourse of eugenics.[78] One example of refusal or misrecognition that I have written about elsewhere is the case of Elise, who was committed to Sonoma State Home in 1914.[79] What is known about Elise comes from a casebook entry completed by a staff member upon Elise's arrival. This staff member guessed that Elise was approximately twenty years old, clarifying that "little is known about [Elise]. She came from Los Angeles County Hospital. They received her from Whittier Reform School. . . . Was then tried twice for insanity and both times dismissed."[80] Failing to acquire a legal ruling of insanity, Elise was quickly diagnosed a "moral imbecile" to justify her placement at the institution. The lack of information about patients like Elise is frustrating as a researcher invested in learning more about the kind of people incarcerated in eugenics institutions. However, I also wonder if Elise was a nonspeaking person or, even more intriguingly, if she was exercising her agency by refusing to answer questions. Either way, her failure to respond to questions prevented the staff at Sonoma State Home from completing the eugenicist practice of the family history. Elise could not or would not comply and could not or would not give away any information through which the state could claim to know the truth about her. Instead, the institution was forced to admit that "little is known about [Elise]," putting limitations on the state's capacity to determine eugenics difference.

Another example of refusal to perform good biocitizenship was practiced by those who refused to give consent to sterilization surgery. Though their consent was explicitly not required by state law, and therefore the denial of consent did not guarantee that surgery would not proceed, administrators did often ask for family member consent to sterilize a person as a kind of courtesy. Although the correspondence records from Stockton State Hospital contain numerous examples of family members giving consent to sterilize a patient, what is missing are those letters from family members who did not give consent. The letters must have existed at some point because notes in the record of operations of Stockton State Hospital indicate: "Rec'd letter June 29, 1919, stating did not want him sterilized"; or: "Brother in Law Mr. B proved that relatives did not give their consent." To register such a refusal is a notable example of a practice of anti-eugenics. It served notice to the state that one would not comply with the apparatus of eugenics.

Daily refusal was the means to practice anti-eugenics most available to the defective class. Some may have consciously chosen to resist while for others it was an unconscious refusal, or the mere fact of living in a body that was simply not capable of complying. The records of these bodies serve as evidence of ways of being in the world that rejected the terms of making good and being grateful to the state for one's confinement. For example, the state archive records one woman who "refuses to eat" and another "lying on the floor[;] would not stay in bed." Documents from Sonoma State Home and Stockton State Hospital noted those who showed other types of refusals or rejections:

> Resists very actively throughout examination.
> Girl smokes and uses alcohol.
> Moral irresponsibility + general inefficiency + unreliability.
> Desires to run away and drown herself. . . . Unmanageable.[81]

While these refusals to eat, lie in a bed, or take direction were pathologized by state administrators as evidence of defectiveness, these refusals are also forms of civil disobedience against the strictures of carceral eugenics, demonstrating an anti-eugenics "structure of feeling," to borrow from Raymond Williams.[82]

The practice of anti-eugenics preceded institutionalization and continued afterward. Many, particularly women and girls, were institutionalized as a result of engaging in refusal outside of the institution:

> Refuses to obey orders or directions of parents.
> Runaway—stole uncle's car—ven[ereal] infection.
> Running away from home many times.
> Hitchhiked to LA.
> Vagrancy.
> Been wandering for 3 months.
> Has been having immoral relations with Joe Banauto + others.
> Girl married Filipino.
> Child paroled to do housework. Found soliciting among Chinamen.
> Counterfeiting.[83]

These people stole from their families, printed fake money, ran away, hitchhiked, refused to settle down, and engaged in interracial nonmonogamous and commercial sex. These refusals to be interpellated into gendered norms of propriety are nascent forms of anti-eugenics, whether or not they were consciously articulated as part of a political platform.

These acts of refusal in the archive gesture toward ways of being in a body, forms of intimacy and kinship, desires, affects, and temporalities that persistently exceeded the efforts to contain them under the terms of eugenics. I therefore interpret them as evidence that a cripistemology of anti-eugenics existed among institutionalized people in the decades prior to the political articulation of a disability rights movement. Although I focus on institutionalized people, there are brief mentions that the wider defective class shared these practices of anti-eugenics. Public distrust of state institutions in the form of reluctance to cooperate in the commitment of defective people is recorded by the State Board of Charities and Corrections in a 1916 report: "There is a great need in the state of making some systematic efforts at popular education . . . for combatting prejudices and erroneous ideas, which are widely held concerning state institutions. . . . The horror with which people look upon treatment in state institutions is amazing. Even public officials, judges, and others often feel that in sending a patient to a state hospital for treatment, they are almost guilty of an irreparable injury to the patient, and of stigmatizing forever the family. In one locality an open and organized effort to discredit the state hospitals was encountered."[84] Natalie Lira's case study of the Pacific

Colony in Southern California uncovers more of these "rebel archives" (to borrow from Kelly Lytle Hernández), specifically against the sterilization of institutionalized people.[85] Lira describes how Mexican-origin families reached out to religious leaders and the Mexican consulate in attempts to stop sterilization surgeries on institutionalized family members. This example suggests there was a nascent politics among institutionalized people, former inmates, family, friends, and community leaders that challenged reproductive control by the state. This politics prefigured and created the grounds for the 1960s antisterilization movements that were successful at eventually toppling many state eugenics policies.

Queer and Crip Kinship beyond Respectability

Kinship has been and remains one of the core strategies of survival for institutionalized and incarcerated people, as Susan Burch explains in her wonderful history of the Canton Asylum in South Dakota.[86] Recovering practices of anti-eugenics creates the possibility for a political kinship that claims as ancestors these ghosts from eugenics' past. It is kinship in the "chosen family" sense, wherein queers are liberated to create their own structures of care and build connections with elders of their choosing, creating new lineages after having been rejected and cast out from one's blood family of origin. I imagine a lineage traced to those defectives who were targeted for assimilation, segregated from normal society, and, in some cases, prematurely killed by the state. This is a kinship based not on identity but on ways of being that exceeded what the state construed as normal. It is a form of political kinship that is informed by queer and crip, but that in the most radical sense rejects any attempts to police the boundaries of these formations.

This kinship-building is informed by what Lisa Marie Cacho takes up as "disremembering value" through the work of "re-member[ing] the other."[87] Cacho calls for re-membering "the populations who are most frequently and most easily disavowed, those who are regularly regarded with contempt, those whose interests are bracketed at best because to address their needs in meaningful ways requires taking a step beyond what is palatable, practical, and possible."[88] For Cacho, this practice of re-membering the disavowed is necessary for rejecting the politics of respectability that attach social value only to those subjects who assimilate to dominant norms of respectable behavior. Elsewhere I have proposed "re-membering the other" as a practice of politicized historical research that seeks to tell the story of radical experiments in embodiment and sociality.[89] Re-membering these pasts is a practice of resistance that challenges current social hierarchies and expands the possible futures yet to come.

Building kinship with those disavowed through eugenics requires pushing against the politics of respectability and of recognition that have in the past structured historical accounts of queer and disabled people. Who am I accountable to as a scholar of gender, sexuality, and disability history? It would certainly be easier to write a complete history of a woman like Dr. Smyth.[90] However, Dr. Smyth directly sterilized patients and was responsible for segregating thousands of disabled people at Stockton State Hospital. She actively participated in the attempted obliteration of dysgenic bodyminds. She is one of the ones who tried to convert us queers and crips but acquiesced when the state instead tried to humanely kill us. In contrast to the official record left by Dr. Smyth, the defective class was an amorphous collectivity of unruly bodies. They were working-class and poor people, assigned to the category of women, who were involved in radical experiments in desire and sociality, people who did not have the means or even perhaps the desire to leave extensive records. Given the difficulties of locating their perspectives, scholars of eugenics and eugenics institutions must be more vigilant to avoid an arc of history that continues to center middle-class white men and women professionals.

How can we build more accountability to people I have mentioned in this chapter, including Katherine (the woman who wrote a letter equating a hospital with a prison), Rev. Matthews (the man who tried to hold authorities accountable for beating his friend), and Elise (who refused to answer questions about herself), or others who were targeted for institutionalization in the early twentieth century? Identifying their refusals and interpreting them as affirmative desires for life, kinship, justice, and freedom is an essential practice toward abolishing carceral eugenics. I call on scholars to continue to craft a "rebel archive" (to again borrow from Hernández) of oppositional consciousness that can challenge the eugenicist logic that disabled and mad people are destined to disappear.[91] Let us lovingly seek the epistemologies, emotions, and practices of freedom of institutionalized people in both conventional and speculative archives. Let us emphasize the evidence of oppositional consciousness, traces of resistance and refusal, ways of being in a body, forms of intimacy and kinship, desires, affects, and temporalities that exceeded eugenicist efforts of containment. It is through the practices of freedom of the defective class that we can enact our own anti-eugenics and imagine abolishing carceral eugenics.

Reviewing the history of carceral eugenics illuminates the forms of enclosure and the future queer and crip trajectories foreclosed in days past. I mourn the loss of these other futures, and I also mobilize this affect as a challenge to the perception of present conditions as normal, natural, inevitable, timeless, or teleological. The state violence recounted in this book has always been shared with a healthy dose of what José Esteban Muñoz calls "critical hope."[92] Re-membering opens the door for us to imagine possibilities for an otherwise and to change how we organize political, social, economic, and cultural life. These imaginaries are necessary to challenge eugenicist utopianisms that write disabled people out of the future.[93] I offer this history of eugenics to invite us to dream queer and crip futures into matter.

5

Menacing the Present

In 2003, officials in California formally apologized for the state's past eugenics programs. California senators declared, "The 'science' of eugenics has since been discredited; now . . . the Senate of the State of California . . . hereby expresses its profound regret over the state's past role in the eugenics movement and the injustice done to thousands of California men and women."[1] While historic, the apology narrowed the scope of the state's responsibility for eugenics in several ways. For one, the apology equated eugenics with the state's asexualization law and sterilization program, obscuring other policies that officials implemented or tacitly supported. Additionally, the timeline created by the apology cast eugenics solely as a movement of the past. Depicting eugenics philosophy as having already been rejected by the state, the California Senate avoided taking responsibility for addressing eugenics in the present.

Another way the apology was limited is that it failed to promise justice for survivors of eugenics. But due to continued campaigning by advocates, in 2021 the California legislature authorized the Forced or Involuntary Sterilization Compensation Program.[2] The program provided monetary compensation for an (at the time) estimated 831 survivors of forced sterilization alive in the state and allocated $1 million to establish historical markers acknowledging the history of sterilization.[3] Notably, the program offered compensation not only to survivors of the asexualization law but also to survivors of sterilization surgeries that violated informed consent procedures in California state prisons after 1979. Therefore, one important aspect of the reparations program was that it acknowledged that reproductive control continued in state institutions into the twenty-first century.

A lesser-known acknowledgment of the state's eugenics history took place in 2002, with the passage of Senate Bill (SB) 1448, sadly titled "Deceased residents of state hospitals and developmental centers." In the bill, the California Senate found that at least twenty thousand (since revised to upward of forty-five thousand) people died while living at a state hospital, state home, or developmental center between 1851 and 1960. The bill states that many were buried in unmarked or mass grave sites with no identifying information. The bill authorized a public partnership with three disability rights organizations—Disability Rights California's Peer Self-Advocacy Program, People First of California, and the California Network of Mental Health Clients—to inventory state records in an attempt to identify and memorialize those who died. These organizations started hosting an annual Remembrance Day ceremony and have erected monuments at several of the cemetery grounds (see figure 5.1), some of which demand "Let no person ever again be removed from the community by reason of disability."

Significantly, the project recognizes that disabled people are still experiencing long-term confinement. SB 1448 acknowledges this as well, but only for the distressing purpose of developing a plan "for the future interment of patients who die while residing at a state hospital or developmental center and are unclaimed by a family member." Disability Rights California's Peer Self-Advocacy Program (PSAP) more broadly observes: "We still house people involuntarily for years on end, they still die away from their loved ones, and they are still being held against their will for 'treatment.'"[4]

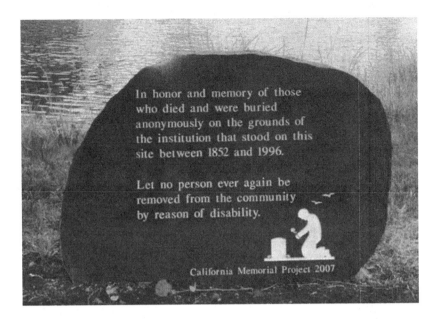

5.1 Memorial created by the California Memorial Project in 2007 on the former grounds of Stockton State Hospital. Photograph from the Disability Rights California website, 2023.

The program has conducted oral histories with currently institutionalized people, some of whom are noted to have been confined for over thirty years and who will probably die while institutionalized. One of the stories posted on the PSAP website is of a man named Greg, who tells about several people who died from COVID-19 while confined. The one change between past deaths in institutions and present deaths is that there are memorials with "music and talking."[5]

Liat Ben-Moshe observes that attitudes toward institutionalization for what has come to be called "mental illness" began to differ from the confinement of intellectually or developmentally disabled (I/DD) people in the later part of the twentieth century.[6] In addition, despite the early connections between disability confinement and the juvenile and women's reformatory movement, most people today hold different opinions about what are now considered to be distinct institutions. While there is currently broad sentiment against segregating children and transition-age youth in large state institutions, there continues to be widespread acceptance of hospitalization for so-called mental illness.

Given the continued acceptance of some forms of institutionalization, the decline of state hospitals is often narrated with regret, as if the changes that have taken place over the second half of the twentieth century were a mistake. The narrative that Ben-Moshe calls "the new asylum" thesis obscures the ongoing operations of institutions of disability confinement and offers only a simplistic and reductionist account of the ways that the logic and practice of carceral eugenics has moved into jails and prisons.[7] In this chapter, I offer a compressed history of California's institutions during the second half of the twentieth and early twenty-first centuries. Countering the state's claim that eugenics is now "discredited," my purpose is to theorize the ways that carcerality continues to be a form of state-sponsored eugenics in the present.

First, although the populations of state hospitals and other institutions for disability confinement have declined since the 1970s, the state of California still operates some institutions that were built in the eugenics era. State hospitals and developmental centers confine a small population of people primarily through an integration of disability with the criminal legal system. As the oral histories collected by the California Memorial Project note, some of these individuals will spend decades confined, and others will die in confinement.[8] Whether intentional or not, institutionalization still functions to control the reproduction of criminalized disabled people and to deny them other possible futures. Despite changes in institutional naming and treatment philosophies that purportedly transition these facilities away from their eugenicist past, institutions for disability confinement continue to segregate a now criminalized defective class, tightly controlling their participation in social reproduction. This control has become explicitly racialized, as the institutionalization of Black Californians far outstrips their representation in the community as a whole.

Second, despite the decline of populations in state hospitals and developmental centers, reproductive control through state confinement has actually expanded through the growth of the state's prisons, which, at the end of 2022, incarcerated 97,179 people (down from the height of 131,260 in 2017).[9] Early twentieth-century eugenicists did include prisons as sites that could be used for the purpose of segregation, because so-called criminals were viewed as an especially troubling component of the defective class. Until the 1960s, however, people labeled defective were far more likely to end up in an institution for disability confinement. This changed in the second half of the twentieth century. In the 1970s, California governor Ronald Reagan slashed social spending, having derisively equated it to a "fat man"; prisons escaped these cuts and instead became viewed as legitimate investments for the neoliberal state.[10] Prisons disproportionately confine Black people in men's prisons compared to their overall population, and, although less egregiously, they also disproportionately confine Black people in women's prisons, as well as Latines, Pacific Islanders, Indigenous people, and some Asian groups.[11] Although a small fraction of the total population of imprisoned people are held in women's facilities, those labeled as white women make up the fastest growing demographic across the prison system.[12]

Prison administrators have further promoted prisons as appropriate sites for disability confinement, through a discourse that James Kilgore calls "carceral humanism."[13] Through claims that so-called mentally ill prisoners can and should remain incarcerated to receive treatment and to protect society from danger, the logic of segregation is perpetuated. However, despite this discourse of carcerality as care, disabled prisoners experience premature aging, disablement, and premature death inside of jails and prisons. The juxtaposition of the promise of care and the lived reality of violence and death is eerily reminiscent of early twentieth-century state institutions. Prisons are the new "parallel worlds" that limit the opportunity of the defective class to reproduce both physically and socially.

I challenge the idea that eugenics is a philosophy and practice that is safely locked in the past, instead demonstrating how carceral eugenics lingers in multiple state policies governing a variety of institutions. Carceral eugenics persists, grows, and has adapted to the twenty-first century. Through the functional control of reproduction, the relegation of populations to social death, and the disruption of life-giving and life-affirming care networks, carceral eugenics in California menaces not only the past but also the present.

Still Confining Disability

Carceral eugenics continues at sites that were established over one hundred years ago for the purpose of segregating disabled, gendered, and racialized populations. On the very plots of land that were devoted to segregation in the eugenics era, the state of California maintains psychiatric hospitals and developmental centers. That these state institutions remain operational surprises even me, given that there have been over fifty years of state and federal policies limiting the cases in which disability confinement can occur. After peaking in the 1960s, the number of medium- and long-term disabled residents of institutions has dramatically declined, and in the past ten years, several more California institutions have been closed. While a comprehensive history of the fate of California's eugenics institutions is beyond the scope of this chapter, I briefly sketch what happened in the state's institutional landscape starting in the 1950s and how the state arrived in a policy environment where some of California's original eugenics institutions continue to detain residents.

Ben-Moshe describes how declines in state hospital admissions started in the late 1950s nationwide, aided by the spread of new professional paradigms toward community integration of people with physical and mental disabilities.[14] In California, parent groups and professionals lobbied policymakers to transition away from custodial care of the feebleminded toward the medical and psychiatric treatment of I/DD children. The transition toward treatment affected the Pacific Colony and Sonoma State Home in specific ways. Although I have shown that these institutions held a wide variety of people in the early twentieth century, the Pacific Colony and Sonoma State Home were not designed primarily for psychiatric treatment. Curiously, in 1953 these two institutions were renamed as state hospitals— Pacific State Hospital and Sonoma State Hospital, respectively. Two similar institutions also opened in the 1950s: Porterville State Hospital in 1953 and Fairview State Hospital in 1959. Although the intention was to push away from warehousing disabled people and toward treatment and rehabilitation, the renaming arguably reinforced a cultural conflation of physical, mental, and psychiatric disabilities.

Meanwhile, according to those involved in parents groups, the strategy against institutionalization was to invest in regional centers that could provide care while disabled children remained with their families.[15] State legislation passed in 1965 established two regional centers, one in Northern California and one in Southern California. The centers were effective, according to those involved, at decreasing the number of children sent to state hospitals for long-term institutionalization.[16] Hope for change diminished when Governor Reagan took office in 1967. At the time, the number of patients in state hospitals had fallen to twenty-two thousand. Reagan's platform was simple: to cut the state budget. The descendent of previous oversight boards, the Department of Mental Hygiene had their budget slashed by 10 percent.[17] The promise of further reduced budgets, combined with his close political relationship with California assemblyman Frank D. Lanterman, explains Governor Reagan's support for the passage of the 1967 Lanterman-Petris-Short (LPS) Act.[18] The purpose of the LPS Act was to end "the inappropriate, indefinite, and involuntary commitment of persons with mental health disorders" by establishing a series of time limits for civil confinement and a set of due-process rights when each limit was reached.[19] The LPS Act narrowed the state's ability to commit individuals to institutions, but it notably did not prohibit long-term institutionalization.

The problem with the LPS Act was that it did not promise any kind of replacement services for people with disabilities. Parents groups who had lobbied for regional centers and community-based supports had done so by highlighting the horrendous conditions inside of institutions, and cuts without replacement community supports were untenable. Assemblyman Lanterman used his leverage with Reagan to pressure the governor to increase spending on the Department of Mental Hygiene in the 1969 budget, a move that helped to fund AB 225, the so-called Lanterman Mental Retardation Services Act.[20] The act guaranteed one regional center for every one million residents of the state. The goal, according to parent groups, was to replace the long-term hospitalization of I/DD children and adults.

Both Lanterman acts undid the conflation of various types of disabilities by distinguishing between I/DD people and people with psychiatric disorders. However, the second Lanterman act guaranteed state provided care to I/DD people but not people with mental illness. As a result, it became easier for the state to keep developmental centers open while closing state hospitals focused on psychiatric disorders without investing money in alternative community supports. As a result, the state closed several psychiatric hospitals after the LPS Act went into effect in 1969 and repurposed others as institutions for the care of I/DD adults. However, some institutions for I/DD children and adults remained operational well into the twenty-first century.

Within five years of the 1967 legislation, the state had closed four psychiatric hospitals, and the number of patients confined to state hospitals fell to seven thousand. The state first closed two of the newest institutions—DeWitt State Hospital and Modesto State Hospital—both of which had originally been built as military hospitals during World War II and converted only after the war was over. After closing in the early 1970s, both properties were turned over to county governments and now house juvenile halls, government offices, and a junior college. More significant were the closures of two of the state's oldest institutions, originally built in the nineteenth century. Mendocino State Hospital and portions of Agnews State Hospital were sold to a Buddhist monastery and a computer technology company, respectively. However, Agnews had started a program for I/DD adults in 1965, and this program continued past the 1972 closure of the state hospital.

The rest of the closures that occurred as a result of the LPS Act did not happen without years of sustained self-advocacy on the part of disabled people and their families. It took another twenty-five years for the next hospital to close: in the 1990s, Camarillo State Hospital emptied. Originally slated to be converted into a prison, it was instead turned into the campus for the newest California State University, Channel Islands, after community outcry. Shortly thereafter came perhaps the most important victory of deinstitutionalization in California: the state's oldest state hospital at Stockton closed in 1996 after one hundred forty continuous years of operation. Ten years earlier, the state had tried to breathe new life into it by converting it to a developmental center, shifting the facility to the rehabilitation of I/DD adults. With the shuttering of the Stockton campus after decades of organizing by the psychiatric survivors and self-advocacy movements, the institution where hundreds of thousands of people had been confined, thousands reproductively sterilized, and thousands had died abandoned by their families and communities was finally just a memory.

Despite this massive victory, the 1967 LPS Act targeting psychiatric hospitals ran its course with the closure of Stockton State Hospital. However, the movement to close large state institutions gained momentum again in 1999 with the US Supreme Court decision in *Olmstead v. LC*, which narrowed the circumstances under which institutionalization as a form of care for people with disabilities could be used, and confirmed the right to community supports for independent living. Over the next several years, state and federal funding policies collaborated to drastically limit the number of state-operated beds for I/DD adults and children. In 2003, the governor of California directed the state's Department of Developmental Services to close Agnews Developmental Center (the program that remained after the hospital was closed), which was completed in 2009. Then, during the 2012 California budgeting process, a trailer bill (AB 1472) placed a moratorium on new admissions to the state's three remaining developmental centers. The only exceptions were for people involved in the criminal justice system and for acute crisis stabilization. In 2014, the federal Centers for Medicare and Medicaid Services passed the Home and Community-Based Services Final Rule. Compliance with the rule, which was supposed to conclude in March 2023, requires the state of California to transition almost all people living in state-operated residential institutions to community settings.

Motivating these policies was a series of horrific allegations of physical and sexual abuse against residents by employees at the state's developmental centers. The Centers for Medicare and Medicaid Services threatened enforcement action and decertification as early as 2012.[21] The state of California signed a series of settlements with the Centers for Medicare and Medicaid Services. As a result, the state's second home for the feebleminded, what started as the Pacific Colony and later rebranded as the Frank Lanterman Developmental Center, was completely closed in 2015. The property was transferred to California State Polytechnic University of Pomona. Notably, this namesake institution of Frank Lanterman, the legislative force behind California's deinstitutionalization legislation, did not succumb to closure until fifty years after the LPS Act. The Sonoma Developmental Center, still on the site of the Sonoma State Home for the Feeble-minded, remained open as a residential facility until 2018, when the last long-term resident was moved to a smaller "community-based" facility.[22] Despite the so-called closure, some people still live at Sonoma, even if the terms are not intended to be long. That is because the state still operates a nursing facility for "acute or chronic medical conditions" and an "Intermediate Care Facility," which includes five residences working to transition adults to independent living.[23]

The promise to move *all* people out of large state institutions and into community-based settings where they can live independently has not yet been realized. While the closure of any institution of disability confinement is a success against mass institutionalization, it has also meant in practice an overreliance on private families to provide care. Those families that have financial resources and health insurance can hire low-paid, mostly immigrant women; otherwise, the care work must be done by families themselves, and given gendered inequalities in care work, that usually means by women.[24] For families unable to provide direct care, the only other alternatives are county or privately run nursing homes and group homes that accept Medicare funding. Many disabled people have expressed that they experience nursing and group homes as miniature versions of state institutions, given that residents have little to no control over their environments or movements.[25]

Further, California still operates five large state hospitals: three institutions that are each over one hundred years old, including Napa (opened in 1875), Patton (1893), and Metropolitan (1916); one facility that opened in 1954 called Atascadero State Hospital; and one new institution that opened in 2005 called Coalinga State Hospital.[26] Together these state hospitals have a total bed capacity of just over six thousand, and at the end of 2020 (the last year for which I could find information), they were about 87 percent full.[27] Operating under a different division, the state also has two developmental centers that were built in the 1950s: Porterville and Fairview. Most of the state hospitals and developmental centers are located in the Central Valley (Coalinga, Porterville) and the southern part of California (Atascadero, Fairview, Metropolitan, Patton), with only one institution located in the north near the San Francisco Bay Area and Sacramento (Napa). This geography is important because the Central Valley and Southern California have high concentrations of Black, Latine, and Asian communities.

The state hospitals continue to house civilly committed patients under the narrowed rubrics of the LPS Act. The act allows for conservatorships in limited cases of "severely disabled individuals who represent a danger to themselves or others."[28] LPS commitments make up only a tiny fraction of the patient population in the state's hospitals. The one exception is the Metropolitan State Hospital in Los Angeles County, where civil commitments made up 39 percent of the population in 2016.[29]

If not for LPS Act commitments, what justifies the continued operation of state institutions for disability confinement in the post-deinstitutionalization era? The reason these institutions are still operating is that state hospitals now house patients committed through the penal code rather than civil commitments. State hospital populations are those found "incompetent to stand trial," "offenders with mental health disorders," "mentally ill prisoners transferred from California Department of Corrections and Rehabilitation," "not guilty by reason of insanity," and "sexually violent predators."[30] This emphasis on committing those at the intersection of criminality and mental illness began at least as early as the 1950s with the opening of the state hospital in Atascadero. While many state hospitals up to this point had secure wings, Atascadero State Hospital was the first to be built exclusively for the so-called criminally insane, with high security technology, especially at the perimeter. The establishment of Atascadero at the intersection of disability confinement and incarceration in the middle of the 1950s marked a new form of carceral eugenics, one where the defective body began to be identified primarily through its pathologically criminal behavior or potentiality for crime. Atascadero gained notoriety in the 1970s when activists in the gay liberation movement decried the use of conversion therapy for homosexuality.[31]

One consequence of the criminalization of the defective class is that the same pattern of racial disproportionality that is found in the criminal legal system is found in California's state hospitals. According to population counts for 2020 (the last year they are available), patients at the state hospitals were classified as 42 percent white, 25 percent Black, 25 percent

Hispanic, and 4.5 percent Asian.[32] These counts are made by the state and do not consider individuals who identify as belonging to one or more race or ethnicity. Yet comparing to the US Census data collected in 2020, only 6.5 percent of Californians identified as Black or African American alone. Even accounting for those who may identify as Black plus one or more other races, the disproportionate representation of Black people in the state hospitals is a very clear mirroring of the racialization of the prison and jail systems in the United States. The integration of disability confinement and the criminal legal system has also impacted people assigned as female. While women were much more likely to be institutionalized in the early twentieth century, they now make up just 14 percent of the total population in California state hospitals.

After federal decertification due to cases of abuse was threatened, closure plans for the state of California's two remaining developmental centers, Fairview and Porterville, were put in place in 2016. Over the course of five years, both facilities closed their long-term residential programs. As of 2023, people are still living on site in short- or medium-term programs. Fairview Developmental Center has an acute nursing and medical facility and a by-court-order-only residence program for "severe behavioral challenges" that require "short-term crisis stabilization."[33] Porterville Developmental Center's ninety-six-bed Secure Treatment Program locks up people with "multiple maladaptive behaviors, including sexual and/or other criminal offenses, assaults, self-abuse, property destruction, drug abuse and other socially undesirable and antisocial behaviors."[34] The Secure Treatment Program remains an exception to the process of closing long-term residential programs by focusing on the confinement of criminalized I/DD adults. The prisonification of disability institutions is further evidenced by the existence of the Office of Protective Services, a full-blown police force tasked with policing the state's developmental centers and regional community centers.

This survey of California's institutions for disability confinement shows that despite decades of self-advocacy by disabled people and their families, state-operated institutions that were invented to segregate the defective class are still here. Large state-operated institutions have survived in part by integrating in new ways with the criminal legal system; now most people are institutionalized directly through the criminal system. Although beyond the scope of this study, this suggests that institutions for disability confinement survived deinstitutionalization by adapting to a neoliberal policy environment wherein criminal detention is viewed as a legitimate function of the state (or perhaps the only legitimate function of the state). By collaborating with the criminal legal system, California's institutions for disability confinement justify their continued necessity even with a mountain of state and federal policy designed to close them.

State hospitals and homes for the feebleminded operated in the early twentieth century to segregate the defective class from society in part for the purpose of reproductive control. The genocidal impulse of segregation was in some ways overridden by reforms that transitioned institutions toward treatment and care in the mid-twentieth century. However, in crip theory, treatment and care are still forms of ableism, emblematic of what Eli Clare calls the "ideology of cure," wherein the disabled bodymind becomes understood as a problem that needs fixing.[35] The state institution that is designed for treatment is still a part of the carceral eugenicist pendulum, one that swings between a strict segregation of all those deemed disposable on the one side and, on the other side, a drive to treat and rehabilitate the redeemable among the defective class. Both sides of the pendulum construct groups of people as "problem bodies"—to again borrow from Clare Sears—who need to be solved in some way in the name of protecting the body politic.[36] Like disability, criminality has its own eugenicist history of being theorized as a heritable trait. Some modern neurobiology and evolutionary biology reproduces the idea that a propensity toward criminality could be part of one's genetic makeup.[37] Disabled criminals consequently have a double legacy of eugenicist ideology against them, confronting genetic determinism on two fronts.

Both warehousing institutions and institutions designed for treatment, rehabilitation, and care can operate through fear of the sexuality of disabled people and their potential reproduction and are part of a spectrum of social controls of disabled sex through means that range from the overt to subtle. The intent of securely segregating criminalized disabled people need not be explicitly for the purpose of reproductive control to have the effect of reproductive injustice. That is, no state actor needs to say aloud that persons confined at state hospitals or secure developmental centers are there for the purpose of preventing them from socially reproducing. The effect of state confinement in disability institutions is the same: it controls a population's ability to parent when, where, and how they choose and limits their engagement with other aspects of social reproduction. Twenty-first century institutions of disability confinement passively continue the eugenicist mission of throwing away groups of people deemed too defective to be free. While the confinement of disabled people at the state level occurs at a smaller scale than in the past, it remains one tool among many to hinder the physical and social reproduction of disabled bodies, menacing possible crip futures.

Carceral Humanism and the New Rehabilitation

The closure of many institutions for disability confinement during the second half of the twentieth century coincided with the state of California investing massive resources into the prison system. Ben-Moshe argues the connection between the two processes is often narrated through what she calls the "new asylum thesis."[38] This thesis in part places the blame for the rise of the prison industrial complex in the 1980s on the closure of institutions for disability confinement. In California, the narrative goes like this: the Lanterman-Petris-Short Act of 1967 so dramatically reduced judicial commitments to state hospitals that long-term custodial care was all but ended. As a consequence, there has since been no other way for the state to deal with so-called mentally ill people. As homelessness and street crime inevitably exploded, more and more people who would have previously been institutionalized now became incarcerated, leading to an explosion of the prison population and jail cells full of people in dire need of treatment, rehabilitation, and care.

Building on Ben-Moshe's incisive analysis, I am interested in the ways that the new asylum thesis has been used to expand the California Department of Corrections into the business of rehabilitation (the abbreviation changed to CDCR in 2004). Coinciding with the closure of state hospitals, the California Department of Corrections innovated new facilities for the confinement of disability, creating prisons promoted as sites for the treatment of disabled adults, including those with physical disabilities, chronic illness, psychiatric disorders, and substance abuse disorders. These facilities also contain disabled and nondisabled transgender prisoners. Treatment, rehabilitation, and care may seem like a move away from the eugenicist policy of segregation, in that these practices promise the future return of criminalized individuals to their communities as healthy, mentally well, contributing members of society. This is a false promise on many levels, including because, as I discuss in the next section, prisons are disabling and death-dealing institutions. Before discussing the red herring, however, I ask how these fantasies of treatment, rehabilitation, and care move the CDCR into the business of disability confinement in ways that are more complicated than the new asylum thesis suggests.

For the first eighty years of California, from 1852 until 1932, the state operated only two prisons: the first was San Quentin State Prison, just north of the city of San Francisco; the second was Folsom State Prison, about twenty miles northeast of the capital, near Sacramento.[39] Starting with the construction of the California Institute for Women in Tehachapi in 1932 (although a protracted legal struggle delayed the transfer of prisoners there), the state built another ten prisons in a thirty-three-year span that ended in 1965. Reaganomics austerity ground both conventional prison and innovative carceral construction to a halt in the 1970s. However, in 1984, under Republican governor George Deukmejian, the state kicked off an even more intensive thirteen-year construction boom that included at least twenty-three new major prisons, plus additional community corrections facilities, prison camps, and mother-prisoner centers.[40] As of 2023, the CDCR operates thirty-five prisons of varying security levels and populations, plus smaller fire and conservation camps.

California's first prison boom, the one that started in the late 1930s and lasted until the mid-1960s, included several experiments that were intended to separate low-level offenders from more so-called hardened criminals, providing programming that could help the redeemable make good and parole back into society.[41] One innovation in prisoner classification was the opening of the California Medical Facility (CMF) in 1955, just outside Vacaville, about halfway between the Bay Area and Sacramento. It was imagined by then governor Earl Warren as a "psychopathic hospital," a mission later translated by the state legislature as a "facility for psychiatric and diagnostic male felons."[42] The facility was a mirror to Atascadero State Hospital, which opened the year prior. Each facility was designed to contain a similar population of criminalized mentally ill patients, but they were administered by two separate state bureaucracies. Also mirroring the accusations that Atascadero was used specifically to target homosexual men for painful conversion therapies, CMF received prisoners with the disease that came to be known as AIDS in the 1980s. Incarcerated people and researchers have since charged that the prison became the site for quarantining prisoners with HIV/AIDS from general prison population.[43]

The first prison hospital in the country, CMF currently incarcerates around four thousand people for the purpose of intensive outpatient health care, inpatient psychiatric care, or twenty-four-hour nursing care and hospice care.[44] CMF innovated the first hospice in a California prison for dying prisoners, legitimating the refusal to release even those on their deathbeds and replicating the practice of segregation until death. Most recently, CMF established an administrative segregation unit for transgender prisoners, who say they faced violence from other prisoners and harassment from guards while in general population.[45] *Administrative segregation* is prison-speak for protection through isolation—a variety of incarcerated people who are at risk of violence from other prisoners and prison staff are placed in solitary confinement or special locked units with the rationale that this is the only way that prison administrators can increase their safety. What the state ignores is that isolation can also make imprisoned people vulnerable to violence and contributes to mental and physical unwellness.

Another experiment in medicalizing the prison took place in the early 1960s, when the state of California was gifted a federal military hospital that had repurposed the Lake Norconian Resort, once a site for the recreation of wealthy elite and Hollywood stars.[46] The state turned it into a narcotics center, opened as the California Rehabilitation Center (CRC) in 1963. The CRC was at one point the world's biggest substance abuse treatment program for in-custody prisoners. Today it continues to offer a substance abuse treatment program while also housing other prisoners. Imprisoned people needing substance abuse treatment may also be sent to the California Health Care Facility (CHCF), opened in 2013 to provide both intensive mental health treatment and substance abuse treatment for almost three thousand prisoners on a 1.4 million-square-foot site east of the San Francisco Bay Area.[47]

These programs repackage prisons, to paraphrase James Kilgore, as sites appropriate for providing psychiatric care, mental health treatment, substance abuse treatment, HIV/AIDS care, and hospice.[48] Kilgore names this "carceral humanism." Carceral humanism is the response to bipartisan concern about a variety of problems with incarceration in the United States, including overcrowding, racial disproportionality, recidivism, and a reliance on solitary confinement. Government-provided or government-funded treatment is touted as both the more humane and the more cost-saving alternative to incarceration. Kilgore calls such programs that continue to incarcerate people, this time in the name of care, as "non-alternative alternatives," a way to further entrench the carceral infrastructure as the best way of dealing with social, economic, and political problems.[49]

I connect this modern repackaging of jails and prisons as sites of care and treatment to the history of eugenics. The very existence of medical prisons perpetuates the idea that some people must be separated from society at any cost, even if they are disabled, experiencing dementia, or dying.

This separation functions to limit bodily autonomy, including the choice to have children; to parent when, where, and how they choose; and to be part of life-giving and life-affirming-care networks. There is significant data that suggests that aging prisoners are at an incredibly low risk of recidivism, yet innovations like the geriatric prison unit or prison hospice imply that people must serve their original prison terms to protect society even if it means dying while in confinement. The prison hospice continues the practice of relegating a population to segregation until death, continuing to do so under the guise of humanitarian care. California governors since the late 1990s have been incredibly unwilling to entertain the main alternative to prison hospice—namely, granting so-called compassionate releases for dying prisoners.[50] The risk of death in congregate living settings during the COVID-19 pandemic brought renewed attention to the limitations of the compassionate release law, spurring advocates to pass changes in the California legislature.[51] However, compassionate releases are only increasingly necessary because of the dramatic increase of the number of people serving life without parole due to sentencing enhancements created in the 1990s such as the three-strikes law. As many aging lifers have argued, "life without parole" is often a death sentence in disguise.[52] There is a market perversity here that care in prison may be the best medical service that some individuals can receive given the reliance in the United States on private medical insurance. Yet many dying incarcerated people are insistent that they would still rather be released to the custody of family and friends.

The use of medical prisons for administrative segregation perpetuates eugenics. Although the justification is that removal is for the good of those who are at risk of violence in prison general population, ad seg contains the word *segregation*, rhetorically and practically connecting it to the eugenics policy of the same name. As prisoners with HIV/AIDS have pointed out, these units historically functioned to quarantine them in the name of preventing them from infecting the prison general population.[53] Medical prisons and medicalized administrative segregation were part of a wider practice of criminalizing people with HIV/AIDS in the 1980s—a form of queer and crip pathologization that had roots in eugenicist logic. Arguably, this continues with trans prisoners in the present. Although many trans prisoners request transfers to the CMF trans unit, where they express feeling safer and have access to gender-affirming medical care, they miss out on living closer to their families, as well as losing access to life-giving and life-affirming support systems and prison programming that may not be offered at CMF. Further, trans prison units do nothing to challenge the rampant homophobia and transphobia within prisons that puts at risk those who are not given permission to transfer.

This homophobia and transphobia spreads out from the prison, and the infiltration of carceral logics into all social institutions means that many people who have served time have difficulty integrating back into society, even if they have completed substance abuse or mental health treatment programs. This cycle replicates the endless loop of carceral eugenics, where the criminalized defective class, although subjected to some rehabilitation programs, is considered biologically tainted and therefore never quite safe enough to restore full citizenship. Even more troubling, as I discuss in a bit, is that the possibility of rehabilitation under carceral humanist models is undermined by endemic mental neglect and medical abuse that cause and exacerbate illness, injury, premature aging, and premature death.

As in the mental and so-called behavioral health systems, the past decades have seen a transfer of carceral power from the state to the county level. The state of California was forced to reduce prison populations through a court-ordered realignment process that began in 2011, transferring thousands of prisoners back to the jurisdiction of county sheriffs, who are the operators of county jails.[54] Designed for short-term (less than one year) incarceration, jails historically have offered very little by way of programming, treatment, or medical care. Seizing on the opportunity to entrench their power, jail operators have subsequently been keen to follow state trends and to repackage jails as mental health and substance abuse treatment facilities. These repurposing proposals have come as a direct response to pressure to reform. For example, in 2018, the Alameda County Sheriff's Office (across the bay from San Francisco) started coming under fire for the deaths of over thirty people in custody since 2014, causing it to have one of the highest in-custody death rates in the country.[55] Advocates alleged that many of those deaths were preventable and were the result of callous disregard for people experiencing substance abuse and mental health crises. Rather than respond to activists' calls to close the jail, the sheriff's office tried to garner support for the construction of new carceral facilities that would leverage state mental health care funds, promising to redesign the jail to best serve prisoners requiring mental health treatment.[56] Like the state's medical prisons, county jails purporting to offer treatment imply that some people must be confined by the government rather than be provided care in their own communities.

Ruth Wilson Gilmore warns that decarceration projects like the state's 2011 realignment process generate surplus state funds, state institutional space, and state labor that will need to be put to work and could very well develop novel forms of state surveillance, intervention, and violence.[57] The time is ripe for public-private partnerships between the state and carceral corporations to innovate forms of carcerality that target disabled people. What to do with criminalized disabled people if not secure them in institutions or incarcerate them in prisons and jails? Advocates warn about proposed government surveillance of disabled and mad people that includes nonconsensual medication, forced in-patient treatment programs, and the expansive use of conservatorships.[58] In March 2022, California governor Gavin Newsom announced a new policy called CARE (Community Assistance, Recovery, and Empowerment), which will force individuals with mental health and substance use disorders into court-ordered treatment programs, which may include required medication and/or in-patient treatment.[59] Although Newsom emphasizes that CARE treatment is a "diversion from more restrictive conservatorships or incarceration" and will be community based and "self-directed," individuals who do not comply or meet treatment benchmarks can be put under conservatorship. As is clear from the statements of supportive mayors, county supervisors, and judges, the program is specifically designed to deal with the explosive growth in the number of homeless people in state. This is yet another example of the "new asylum thesis," which interprets the Lanterman-Petris-Short (LPS) Act and deinstitutionalization as a mistake.[60] Rather than confront the role of neoliberal economic restructuring and wealth inequality in creating homelessness, proponents of this narrative also conveniently ignore that the promised community-based supports for independent living never materialized during deinstitutionalization, especially adequate funds for housing vouchers. Newsom's CARE Act poses as an alternative to racialized mass incarceration while reaffirming the commitment of the state to carceral solutions. Newsom's plan continues the practice of carceral eugenics through new technologies diffused into community-based settings that allow for the continued control of reproduction among disabled people.

A critical disability methodology demands skepticism of discourses that the state is capable of providing the kind of care, treatment, and rehabilitation that allows disabled people to live and to flourish. Some forms of treatment used in the past were invasive and ineffective or caused new injuries, exacerbated illnesses, and traumatized patients. Even evidenced-based, effective treatments could operate as disciplinary technologies in the Foucauldian sense when they attempt to cure the body and mind into a state of normality that is abnormal for that particular bodymind. Further, nonconsensual treatment, even if effective, is always a form of violence in the sense that it ruptures a person's bodily autonomy and must be carefully considered against the possible benefit of the treatment.

The history of treatment has implications for the present push of carceral humanism. It is politically urgent to understand the ways that carceral logics can manifest in caring guises as treatment and rehabilitation. This is especially true in the current moment of bipartisan acceptance of prison reform, which is yet again turning to claims of care, treatment, and rehabilitation to legitimate incarceration. Care, such as that which is imagined as occurring in institutions, is almost articulated as racialized privilege in the current discourse of reform. Calls for reform that grow out of this analysis demand investments in state treatment as a supposedly noncarceral investment in communities of color. However, what will likely occur is more of the same: people of color are more likely to be incarcerated in the new caring prisons and in the criminalized state hospitals. Investment in carceral infrastructure takes resources away from community-based mental health supports that allow disabled people to have children, parent, and participate in life-affirming networks of care.

Death-Making in Confinement

The repackaging, as Kilgore calls it, of prisons and jails as sites of medical care and psychological treatment is undermined by conditions that cause chronic illness, disablement, premature aging, and premature death.[61] Eugenicist logics blame incarcerated people for their choices to engage in risky activities, displacing attention away from structural conditions that cause or exacerbate illness, injury, and death. For example, the rampant spread of viruses like hepatitis or HIV in prisons is often assumed to be the fault of prisoners who have chosen to engage in sexual activity or intravenous drug use. This blame detracts from the systematic denial of harm reduction tools like condoms and clean needles that could reduce the spread of viruses.

Not only are carceral conditions debilitating and even deadly, but imprisoned people are also routinely prevented from accessing adequate medical and mental health care that can save lives. When health care for incarcerated people is mentioned at all in popular discourse, it is often to emphasize scandalous cases of medical abuse. For example, medical providers performed reproductive sterilization surgeries on people in California women's prisons at least between 2006 and 2010, doing so in ways that the state legislature later found skirted informed consent laws.[62] One doctor invoked eugenicist logic to justify the surgeries when he told an investigative journalist that without sterilization, the children of incarcerated people would overrun and destroy the state's scarce resources.[63] However, the same doctor insisted that people incarcerated in women's prisons all wanted to be sterilized and had leveraged their time in prison to access this form of medical care. This was a reference to the legal fact that imprisoned people are guaranteed the right to state-provided medical, dental, and health care through court decisions based on interpretations of the Eighth Amendment to the US Constitution, which prohibits cruel and unusual punishments. The lack of access to medical care outside of the prison due to neoliberal reliance on the private insurance system in the United States makes care difficult to access for low-income, noninsured, homeless, and rural people. This combination of conditions makes it possible for some people to position incarceration as a benefit because of the care that prisoners are supposedly able to access. As a consequence, incarcerated, institutionalized, and detained people are resented for receiving any resources from the state, especially things that might keep them alive and healthy such as comprehensive medical and mental health care. This resentment is a legacy of eugenics, one that contributes to the blame placed on the criminalized defective class for the increased likelihood of illness and injury.

What is hidden by this logic is that incarcerated people are completely reliant on the state and private corporations to provide all medical and psychological services. Incarcerated people are even more constricted than people on the outside who also have limited options due to the privatization of medical care in the United States. Incarcerated people are constantly working to access the most basic medical and mental health care, all the while being resented for taking resources they are assumed to not deserve. Further, what is missing from this discourse is that carceral systems are notorious for withholding medical treatments, especially preventative care, for exacerbating existing conditions, and for creating new illnesses, injuries, disabilities, and premature aging.

In the example of sterilizations in California prisons, the media coverage and legislative outcry focused on how nonconsensual tubal ligations were justified by at least one attending physician using eugenicist logic.[64] However, for decades, incarcerated and formerly incarcerated people in California's prisons have organized around a much more intractable problem of pervasive medical neglect.[65] Incarcerated and detained people report that they are frequently denied care beyond basic first aid distributed by unlicensed or entry-level medical workers, waiting to see licensed medical professionals and specialists until it is too late to do anything but the most radical (and cheapest) medical interventions. Medical problems are left to fester until there is nothing to be done but the most invasive procedure. One example of the problem is dental care inside of prisons. Many people enter prison with untreated dental problems, such as dying teeth. Although dental care is among the constitutional rights to care for imprisoned people, reports indicate that many imprisoned people can wait months to receive services beyond a routine cleaning. Working on overload and under pressure to provide cheap care, dentists working inside jails, prisons, and detention centers are far more likely to pull a tooth than try to save it with a root canal.[66] This can have a cascading effect on an imprisoned person's health, as not having enough teeth to eat solid foods can lead to malnutrition and digestive problems or can exacerbate existing conditions like heart disease and diabetes.

For reproductive health, incarcerated and formerly incarcerated people reported earlier in the twenty-first century that they waited months to years to be seen by doctors, had symptoms ignored or downplayed, and then finally underwent hysterectomies and oophorectomies for medical issues that could have been solved with much less invasive procedures, especially if they had access to preventative health care or had been able to see a doctor with earlier symptoms.[67] As both the dental and reproductive health examples illustrate, there is slippage between medical neglect and medical abuse, raising questions about when such invasive procedures are absolutely necessary and when the most invasive procedure has become a carceral standard of care. It is perhaps easiest to connect unnecessary reproductive system surgeries leading to sterilization to the concept of eugenics, as a pattern of such surgeries indicts the CDCR in a practice of direct reproductive control. However, all forms of medical neglect are legitimated, whether consciously or not, by the devaluation of the lives of detained people.

Carceral systems create new medical conditions in a variety of ways. One is by increasing exposure to infectious diseases and denying incarcerated people access to personal protective equipment (PPE). As has become abundantly evident with the COVID-19 pandemic, congregate living settings are especially vulnerable to contagious respiratory diseases that spread through aerosols or droplets. This is a problem when institutions do not give prisoners adequate PPE such as effective face masks. Blood-borne pathogens and sexually transmitted infections (STIs) are also a problem in carceral settings because of a long history of denying incarcerated people access to harm reductive PPE such as clean needles for intravenous drug use or condoms for sexual activity. There are consequently high rates of hepatitis and HIV/AIDS among incarcerated populations.[68] I argue that the refusal to provide access to harm reduction PPE is a form of carceral eugenics harkening back to the early twentieth-century policy of segregation and the goal of killing off the defective class while blaming them for their own weakness.

Additionally, people in congregate living settings are at high risk of physical injury due to violence from other prisoners and from guards who are authorized to use physical force in a variety of circumstances. Both the experience of violence, which can cause long-term injury, and the constant exposure to violence are debilitating; exposure to violence can contribute to high levels of chronic stress, which creates and exacerbates medical conditions such as cancer, heart conditions, digestion issues, and back pain. Further, the very tools that could assist with chronic stress are denied to detained people, who are offered virtually no nutritious food, limited access to exercise space or equipment, or time in nature. The poor food and lack of exercise exacerbates and leads to illnesses, including diabetes, heart disease, and digestive conditions.

Carceral settings also expose detained people to environmental injury. In California, prison siting in less populated areas, including deserts, has exposed imprisoned people to the fungal infection that causes valley fever.[69] Occupational health and safety standards are often relaxed in carceral settings, and those prisoners who are fortunate to have hyper-low-wage jobs have been exposed to carcinogenic chemicals and materials and unmaintained equipment. California and other states also employ prisoners in dangerous careers like wildland firefighting. As climate chaos deepens, wildland firefighters are increasingly exposed to hotter, faster-moving, and more unpredictable fires, as well as toxic levels of smoke inhalation. Even relatively safer forestry jobs like trail maintenance have to be performed in an unprecedented era of extreme heat conditions and unpredictable storm patterns due to climate chaos. Extreme heat conditions also affect people inside of prisons, which almost always lack air-conditioning or any tools for imprisoned people to cool themselves. Heat conditions "exacerbate chronic diseases, counteract medications, and increase the risk of dehydration and heat stroke among even the healthiest people," according to the Prison Policy Institute.[70] Climate change–caused disasters have also impacted imprisoned people, who have been denied the opportunity to evacuate in the past. From experiencing flooding in cells caused by hurricanes to smoke inhalation caused by supercharged wildfires, incarcerated people are often the last to be considered in climate emergencies.

Due to all of these factors, Mariame Kaba names prisons as "death-making institutions," because they expose incarcerated people to premature death.[71] In addition to all of the factors above, what the Bureau of Justice Statistics designates as "unnatural" deaths, including rates of suicide, homicide, and drug and alcohol overdoses, are higher in jails and prisons than in the general population. If the project of eugenics segregation was to kill off the defective class in the spirit of improving the heredity of the overall population, then prisons are also sites for carceral eugenics. Further, this version of carceral eugenics has a disproportionate impact on people of color. Black people are highly overrepresented in jails and prisons, significantly so in men's prisons.[72] Studies also show that Latine people, Indigenous people, and some Asian and Pacific Islander communities are also disproportionately locked up compared to whites, including in women's prisons.[73] This means that these racialized populations disproportionately only have access to care via detention medicine and, alarmingly, may otherwise lack access to medical care.

One commonly cited definition credited to Ruth Wilson Gilmore defines racism as "state-sanctioned or extralegal production and exploitation of group-differentiated vulnerability to premature death."[74] Disablement, premature aging, and premature death of criminalized populations is therefore one of the most pressing racial justice issues of our time. I add that incarceration is also one of the most important reproductive justice issues of our time, not just because of instances of sterilization surgeries but also because of the death-making conditions that deny criminalized disabled populations a future.

One campaign that can be understood as both a reproductive justice and racial justice movement is Close California Prisons, put forward by Californians United for a Responsible Budget (CURB),[75] which describes itself as a "Black-led statewide coalition of more than 80 grassroots organizations." Although the name says it all, the Close California Prisons campaign specifically demands that the state close ten prisons by 2025. Their list of priority closures includes some of the facilities I discuss in the chapter: California Rehabilitation Center, California Medical Facility, and California Substance Abuse Treatment Facility. These abolitionists are especially critical of carceral humanist solutions that allow the logics of eugenics to proliferate.

Abolishing Juvenile Prisons

CURB is working to build on the success of the rapid decommissioning of California's youth prisons—the descendants of the early twentieth-century state reform schools. Throughout this book I have considered institutions for the confinement of juvenile delinquents and dependents alongside state hospitals and state homes, arguing that the philosophy of eugenics guided the development of each institution and pointing out that individuals circulated among these institutions in the early twentieth century. Considering these institutions together also made sense because each were part of the same division of state bureaucracy in the early twentieth century. Even after the creation of the Department of Institutions in 1921, which separated the oversight of state institutions from the state prisons, youth reform schools remained under the same bureaucratic umbrella as state hospitals and state homes. However, this changed in 1941, when the state legislature created the Youth Corrections Authority (later California Youth Authority), becoming the first in the nation to implement the American Law Institute's model. The creation of a juvenile justice administration put the reform schools in a different policy environment than state hospitals and developmental centers. Yet, I argue that similar philosophical trajectories and reform efforts continued to guide each of these institutions for the rest of the twentieth century.

The formation of the Youth Corrections Authority followed on the heels of suspicious deaths of youth placed in solitary confinement at Whittier State School in 1939 and 1940, discussed further in Miroslava Chávez-García's essential account of the state's early juvenile justice system.[76] The public outcry that resulted led to many changes that, on the surface, appeared to move the institutions toward a treatment, education, and rehabilitative model inspired by former superintendent of Whittier State School Fred C. Nelles. Parallel to the movement toward treatment in the state hospitals and state prisons, in the 1950s and 1960s, the renamed California Youth Authority (CYA) opened several forestry camps, reception centers, and new state schools with the intention of treating, vocationally educating, and rehabilitating dependent and delinquent youth. Despite these aspirations, at least one personal account describes rampant violence that continued inside of the reform schools, where children as young as nine years old were sent.[77] Also problematically, the rehabilitative model legitimated the creation of more prisons for youth, even if some of them were smaller or in camp settings.

While state hospitals were being closed and regional centers being established, the juvenile justice pendulum swept decidedly away from rehabilitation in the 1980s and 1990s. Racist anti-youth ideologies such as the myth of the juvenile "superpredator" led to skyrocketing juvenile incarceration, peaking at more than ten thousand prisoners in the CYA in the mid-1990s, and hardening the schools into high security prisons. In 2000, this anti-youth backlash culminated in the passage of California's Proposition 21, the juvenile crime initiative statute, which required some youth as young as fourteen years old be tried in court as adults (a decision previously at the discretion of a juvenile court judge) and for some youth as young as age sixteen to be incarcerated in adult jails or prisons. At the height of Proposition 21 in 2008, 1,198 children under the age of eighteen were incarcerated through California's adult court system.[78]

Then, almost overnight, the pendulum quietly swung back toward rehabilitation. In 2004, the state closed the oldest reform school—the Fred C. Nelles Youth Correctional Facility on the site of the original Whittier State School. In 2007, state legislation SB 81 and AB 191 required all juveniles not convicted of serious felonies and/or requiring serious treatment to serve their time in county detention centers rather than in state youth prisons. Mirroring national trends, the new law, combined with reductions in crime levels, lowered the population under state custody in the renamed Department of Juvenile Justice (DJJ) to around just 1,700 in 2008 (from more than ten thousand just eight years prior).[79] In 2016, voters passed Proposition 57, which severely limited the filing of juvenile cases in adult criminal courts. More closures of youth prisons and camps followed. The final blow to the juvenile prison system came in 2020, when California governor Gavin Newsom signed SB 823 into law, directing the counties to retain all those convicted of crimes as juveniles and scheduling the remaining juvenile prisons for closure.

While the importance of the massive state disinvestment from juvenile incarceration cannot be emphasized enough, youth in the juvenile justice system continue to be locked up in the state's many county-level juvenile detention centers. This is a special problem for youth who are serving lengthy sentences or repeated confinement, because county centers may not have as many staff or resources to create programming, mental health treatment, or disability assessment to support youth.[80] Further, racially disproportionate incarceration of Latine and Black youth continues to be a problem, especially in counties with a history of relying on incarceration rather than other diversion programs or probation.[81] Numerous studies have shown that youth who come into contact with the juvenile justice system are dramatically more likely to come under state custody as adults. Further, although the most egregious aspects of Proposition 21 have been undone, some sixteen- and seventeen-year-old youth do continue to be tried as adults and can be sent to adult prisons if a judge warrants it. According to the Haywood Burns Institute, in 2019, there were sixty-four youth under the age of eighteen prosecuted in adult courts, the majority of whom were Latine and/or Black.[82]

Closures of all state-operated juvenile prisons in the state of California is an incredibly powerful example of how decarceration can be achieved fairly rapidly. The tale has some cautionary aspects too. One is that the process illustrates the danger of creating new lines between deserving and undeserving groups. For example, the closure of developmental centers, as Ben-Moshe points out, has leveraged the construction of I/DD adults as childlike and innocent (another form of ableism), which makes them undeserving of institutionalization and deserving of being at home with their families, receiving community supports.[83] This position is juxtaposed against the so-called mentally ill, who are identified as dangerous and violent and therefore deserving of institutionalization. A similar divide is made between juvenile offenders and those convicted of crimes as adults, wherein youth are more likely to be considered as reformable and given a second chance. Race and gender differences complicate these basic narrative frames, but the point I wish to make is that the closures are often accomplished by redrawing the line between those who deserve to be confined against those who are reimagined as deserving of bodily autonomy, family, and connection to networks of community care. People on both sides of the line suffer, as those determined to be undeserving of incarceration have their behavior constrained in new ways lest they cross the line back into the category of people needing confinement. Further, the integration of criminal and mental illness confinement that began in the 1950s has redrawn the line in such a way that makes remaining state institutions immune to decarceration.

The lesson from this tale is that we need an abolitionist vision to fully challenge carceral eugenics. Even as we dismantle parts of the carceral world, we must be vigilant against justifying other forms of detention. As we dismantle, we must also imagine, build, and create another world without borders, boundaries, bars, and cages.

Epilogue

Abolishing
Carceral Eugenics

Shortly after Carlos Escobar Mejia's death due to COVID-19 contracted while in Immigration and Customs Enforcement (ICE) detention in May of 2020, an ad hoc coalition began meeting in occupied Kumeyaay territory, also known as the San Diego-Tijuana metro area.[1] The goal was to streamline efforts to get as many people out of the local immigrant detention center as possible and to provide post-release support that would get detained people to their families and sponsors. Like other groups across the United States, this coalition adopted a name that started as a hashtag: Free Them All San Diego. The coalition continued to meet as the waves of COVID-19 ebbed and flowed inside the detention center. The population inside ICE-contracted detention centers across the United States was reduced to approximately fifteen thousand over the winter of 2020–21. Seizing the opportunity to close the detention centers completely, the coalition developed what we called the "Points of Unity," moving us from an ad hoc group responding to a crisis to a coalition demanding the closure of all immigrant detention centers in the United States. We declared:

> We are a coalition of organizations and activists based in the San Diego-Tijuana region who are committed to affirming migration as a human right. To achieve this, we are building for a world without cages, border walls, armed enforcers, and institutions built upon a foundation of white supremacy. Our work starts with closing the Otay Mesa Detention Center and freeing them all.
>
> We believe in the freedom of movement and that migration is a human right.
>
> We stand in solidarity with all migrants, refugees, and those seeking asylum, without condition.
>
> We struggle for abolition and for building a world without cages, borders, and armed enforcers.
>
> We support the decolonization of all occupied lands.
>
> We strive to build a democratic movement that is multi-racial, multi-ethnic, gender-inclusive, disability-inclusive, and welcoming of all faiths.
>
> We center the liberation of the oppressed in all aspects of our organizing.[2]

Our demands included shutting down Otay Mesa Detention Center (OMDC) and all other migrant detention facilities in California, releasing all detained migrant people without condition, stopping deportations of migrant people, defunding and abolishing the ICE department, and dismantling the border wall.

Free Them All San Diego organized a series of political education webinars where I and others developed a deeper understanding of the kinds of state violence occurring under COVID-19 that were part of a much longer arc of state violence against migrants. Building on my interest in understanding how detention centers impact the health of detained people, I organized a webinar titled "Resisting Medical Abuse and Neglect in Detention" featuring Free Them All San Diego coalition members, a collective member of Detention Resistance, and a senior organizer with the national Detention Watch Network.[3] After the presentations, a formerly detained asylum seeker who is a medical doctor specializing in infectious diseases detailed how detention itself causes injury and illness, in addition to exacerbating previously existing conditions. He described his own experiences of being a young man in prime health who, due to the stress of incarceration, the poor food, and lack of exercise, left detention with a new heart condition. Part of the central African diaspora, he detailed the particular stress of experiences of anti-Black racism at every step of his journey. His testimony illustrates how the lives of migrants inside of detention are devalued so dramatically that their suffering has become acceptable and normal, conducted in the erroneous name of protecting society.

This doctor's testimony was an act of resistance that has stayed with me in the years that followed. Indeed, it is the persistence of detained people to improve their conditions of confinement, to secure medical care, and to find freedom to reconnect with their families and care networks that drives me forward in accompaniment work. There are countless other stories of bravery in the face of carceral eugenics. In the early days of the pandemic, a person in the medical unit at OMDC banged on the doors for two hours until staff arrived to respond to another man who was having trouble breathing and could not stand. Several women enacted civil disobedience and threatened to hunger strike when staff tried to get them to sign a contract absolving CoreCivic of liability in exchange for access to face masks, persisting even when threatened by pepper spray. Detained people used their ability to write in English or Spanish to send letters to any advocacy organization they could find to plead for support—not only for themselves but for the strangers in their housing units. Dozens testified and participated in class-action lawsuits, enduring retaliation from guards, including verbal abuse and the use of solitary confinement. Detained people used grievance procedures and reported to ICE authorities; some endured retaliation, including being transferred hundreds of miles away or being put in solitary confinement. Many have resisted by refusing to sign voluntary deportation papers and by fighting for their right to stay in the United States near their family members, children, and care networks. These efforts have also gone beyond individual advocacy, as collectives of detained people have organized labor strikes and hunger strikes, using the limited tools at their disposal to decry forced labor conditions and medical neglect.

The self-advocacy of detained migrants to declare that they deserve to live, to be with their children and care networks, and to live freely is one of the most important anti-eugenics movements of the twenty-first century. This conclusion comes from identifying the continuities between early twentieth-century institutionalization with the ways that migrant detention centers continue to operate as forms of reproductive control by cutting off people from their children, families, and life-giving community networks of care. To dismantle eugenics our movements must tackle not just the forms of state-sponsored sterilization that crop up in detention centers but also the entire system of incarceration, institutionalization, and detention, which exposes migrants to illness, injury, premature aging, and premature death.

If state-sponsored eugenics includes the segregation of populations deemed to be a threat to the body politic, then in order to abolish eugenics, we must abolish prisons, jails, and migrant detention centers; all forms of bars, cages, and borders; and the carceral logics that grow out of fears of reproduction and social reproduction. Anti-eugenics requires a movement for carceral abolition. As scholars have demonstrated, it was through reforms that the current carceral system was created.[4] As I have shown in this book, early twentieth-century reforms invented carceral eugenics as a novel way to deal with problem bodies. Such reforms included medical work, social work, and psychological strategies for designating populations as defective; legal ways of removing and segregating problem bodies from the healthy population and the perpetual construction of new sites within which to contain them; innovative justifications for raising and spending state money on eugenics confinement; and deploying conceptions of freedom that were twisted into a desire for the carceral state. Because it is through reforms that carceral eugenics was created, anti-eugenics requires thinking beyond reforms, toward the abolition of the carceral system.

Abolition of the carceral system requires anti-eugenics and, specifically, anti-eugenics that is informed by queer and crip liberation. Carceral abolition requires disability justice and learning from disability justice organizers. This starts with identifying people in jails and prisons as disabled people and as people who have been disabled by the carceral system. It means fighting for their liberation, not just as racialized and gendered people but also as disabled people. This means identifying and pushing back on carceral humanist innovations in jails and prisons, ensuring that people receive care and treatment in their communities rather than perpetuating the notion that care is possible inside of a cell. It also means that abolitionists must call for the dismantling of all forms of carceral confinement, including jails, prisons, and institutions for disability confinement that are rooted in the history of eugenics.

The early usage of the term *free them all* applied equally to jails, nursing homes, psychiatric hospitals, and migrant detention centers. For those of us involved in both anti-carceral and disability justice work, there was never a distinction between any forced congregate living setting. When we say "Free them all," we mean free them all.

NOTES

Prologue

1   Bhatt et al., *Violence and Violation*.

2   American Friends Service Committee, Detention Resistance, and Pueblo Sin Fronteras, *Compounding Suffering during a Pandemic*; Langarica, Vakili, and Grano, *CoreCivic's Decades of Abuse*.

3   Kilgore, "COVID-19 Is Turning Prisons into 'Kill-Boxes.'"

4   Paik, *Bans, Walls, Raids, Sanctuary*; Ordaz, *The Shadow of El Centro*.

5   Langarica, Vakili, and Grano, *CoreCivic's Decades of Abuse*.

6   Langarica, Vakili, and Grano, *CoreCivic's Decades of Abuse*.

7   "The COVID Prison Project Tracks Data and Policy across the Country to Monitor COVID-19 in Prisons," COVID Prison Project.

8   "Patient & Staff Covid Tracking," California Department of State Hospitals.

9   Levin, "He Lived in the US for 40 Years."

10   The Spanish term *compa*, short for *compañero/a*, is a colloquialism for a friend, yet it also has a connotation of a comrade in revolutionary struggle. It is used within migrant justice organizations in San Diego to refer to people who are attempting to enter the United States or who have been targeted by US immigration enforcement.

11   American Friends Service Committee, Detention Resistance, and Pueblo Sin Fronteras, *Compounding Suffering During a Pandemic*; Langarica, Vakili, and Grano, *CoreCivic's Decades of Abuse*.

Introduction

1   At the point of incarceration or institutionalization, the state makes a determination of sex in order to place persons in sex-segregated facilities. This determination of sex does not always align with a person's sex or gender identity. I use the phrase "people in women's prisons" to observe this distinction. Elsewhere, I use terms such as "assigned female" to note that in most cases the only records available are based on the state's assignment of sex and gender.

2   Johnson, "Female Inmates Sterilized in California Prisons without Approval."

3   Chandler, "Female Offenders, Budget Issues Related to Conditions of Confinement and Illegal Sterilizations."

4   Ordover, *American Eugenics*; Stern, *Eugenic Nation*; Lombardo, *A Century of Eugenics in America*.

5   Stern, "From Legislation to Lived Experience."

6   Stern, "From Legislation to Lived Experience."

7   Russell and Stewart, "Disablement, Prison, and Historical Segregation."

8   Popenoe, *Applied Eugenics*.

9   Fox, *So Far Disordered in Mind*.

10   Brown and Schept, "New Abolition, Criminology and a Critical Carceral Studies."

11   Russell and Stewart, "Disablement, Prison, and Historical Segregation"; Ben-Moshe, Carey, and Chapman, *Disability Incarcerated*.

12   Ben-Moshe, "Disabling Incarceration."

13   Russell and Stewart, "Disablement, Prison, and Historical Segregation."

14   Sins Invalid, *Skin, Tooth, and Bone*.

15   Galton, *Inquiries into Human Faculty and Its Development*.

16   Galton, *English Men of Science*, 16.

17   Galton, *Hereditary Genius*, 64.

18   Roberts, *Killing the Black Body*.

19   Lombardo, *Three Generations, No Imbeciles*.

20 Ordover, *American Eugenics*.

21 Stepan, *The Hour of Eugenics*; Solomon, *Doing Medicine Together*; Kim, *Curative Violence*; Paul, Stenhouse, and Spencer, *Eugenics at the Edges of Empire*.

22 Roberts, *Killing the Black Body*.

23 Kline, *Building a Better Race*; Stern, *Eugenic Nation*.

24 Gohlke, *Remarkable Women of Stockton*.

25 Gosney and Popenoe, *Sterilization for Human Betterment*.

26 Black, "Eugenics and the Nazis."

27 California Senate Resolution 47: Relative to Eugenics.

28 Hernández, *Migra!*

29 "California Memorial Project," Disability Rights California.

30 Roberts, *Killing the Black Body*; Briggs, *Reproducing Empire*; Carpio, "The Lost Generation"; Schoen, *Choice & Coercion*; Tajima-Peña, *No Más Bebés*; Theobald, *Reproduction on the Reservation*; Villarosa, *Under the Skin*.

31 Ross et al., *Radical Reproductive Justice*.

32 Kline, *Building a Better Race*; Stern, *Eugenic Nation*; Stern, "From Legislation to Lived Experience"; Khanmalek, "Slavery"; Lira and Stern, "Mexican Americans and Eugenic Sterilization"; Novak et al., "Disproportionate Sterilization of Latinos under California's Eugenic Sterilization Program, 1920–1945"; Lira, *Laboratory of Deficiency*.

33 Kline, *Building a Better Race*.

34 "California Memorial Project," Disability Rights California.

35 Human Rights Program at Justice Now, "Prisons as a Tool of Reproductive Oppression."

36 Roth, "'She Doesn't Deserve to Be Treated like This.'"

37 Whatcott, "No Selves to Consent."

38 Bhattcharya, "What Is Social Reproduction Theory?"

39 Nishida, *Just Care*; Piepzna-Samarasinha, *Care Work*.

40 Bookspan, *A Germ of Goodness*; Faith, *Unruly Women*; Gilmore, *Golden Gulag*; Cairns, *Hard Time at Tehachapi*; Blue, *Doing Time in the Depression*; Hernández, *City of Inmates*.

41 Chávez-García, *States of Delinquency*.

42 Hernández, *City of Inmates*.

43 Ben-Moshe, "Disabling Incarceration."

44 Ben-Moshe, Carey, and Chapman, *Disability Incarcerated*.

45   Ben-Moshe, Carey, and Chapman, *Disability Incarcerated*, 10.

46   Ben-Moshe, "Disabling Incarceration."

47   Davis, *Are Prisons Obsolete?*, 66.

48   Fox, *So Far Disordered in Mind*.

49   Harcourt, "From the Asylum to the Prison."

50   Gilmore, *Golden Gulag*.

51   Fox, *So Far Disordered in Mind*.

52   Kline, *Building a Better Race*; Stern, *Eugenic Nation*; Lira, *Laboratory of Deficiency*.

53   Kline, *Building a Better Race*; Stern, *Eugenic Nation*.

54   Lira, *Laboratory of Deficiency*; Kaniecki et al., "Racialization and Reproduction."

55   Lira and Stern, "Mexican Americans and Eugenic Sterilization"; Novak et al., "Disproportionate Sterilization of Latinos under California's Eugenic Sterilization Program, 1920–1945."

56   Kaniecki et al., "Racialization and Reproduction."

57   Marie Kaniecki of the Sterilization and Social Justice Lab suggested to me that it could be possible to cross-reference US Census data on institutionalized people with county-level census data. Individual US census forms from the early twentieth century have been digitized by IPUMS and are available to researchers. IPUMS, "Home," Regents of the University of Minnesota, accessed November 10, 2023, https://www.ipums.org/.

58   Sentencing Project, *The Color of Justice*.

59   Rembis, *Defining Deviance*; Lira, *Laboratory of Deficiency*.

60   Lira, *Laboratory of Deficiency*.

61   Davis et al., *Abolition. Feminism. Now*; Kaba, *We Do This 'til We Free Us*; Bierria, Caruthers, and Lober, *Abolition Feminism*.

62   Davis, *Are Prisons Obsolete?*

63   Gilmore, *Golden Gulag*, 242.

64   Whatcott, "No Selves to Consent."

65   Ben-Moshe, *Decarcerating Disability*.

66   Ben-Moshe, "Dis-Epistemologies of Abolition."

67   Minich, "Enabling Whom?"

68   Kafer, *Feminist, Queer, Crip*.

69   Oliver, *The Politics of Disablement*.

70   Kafer, *Feminist, Queer, Crip*.

71   Baynton, "Disability and the Justification of Inequality in American History," 34.

72   Kafer, *Feminist, Queer, Crip*; Clare, *Brilliant Imperfection*; Sears, *Arresting Dress*.

73   Minich, "Enabling Whom?"

74   Lira, *Laboratory of Deficiency*.

75   Johnson and McRuer, "Cripistemologies," 130.

76   Clare, *Exile and Pride*; Kafer, *Feminist, Queer, Crip*; McRuer, *Crip Times*.

77   Throughout this book I default to identity-first language (*disabled person*, rather than *person with disability*) and, following that convention, default to the term "institutionalized people" to refer to persons confined to state institutions. This is not done out of disrespect for the People First movement, which began in the 1970s as part of the broader movement of self-advocacy by people who had been institutionalized. One of the demands of the movement was to recognize that they were people, not just their disability label. This has over time been distilled to a request to use so-called person-first language, such as "a person with Down syndrome." However, it is still within the spirit of the self-advocacy movement to promote the social model of disability and to make a political choice to start with disability as a form of identification. In this conception, to say "disabled person" is not to dehumanize or devalue but to draw attention to the ways that someone is materially debilitated through the structure of ableism. Other choices, such as the use of the term *patient*, are made to acknowledge common usage by the state to refer to institutionalized people, but with recognition that this term obscures the eugenicist function of institutionalization and dramatically overstates the amount of medical treatment that was available to institutionalized people. On a practical level, the overcrowded and understaffed conditions at eugenics institutions through much of the twentieth century meant that medical care was inadequate at best. The term *inmate* is used occasionally to acknowledge common usage by the state but also strategically to emphasize the discursive connections between carceral institutions and institutions of care. Throughout, I attempt to emphasize the humanity of people as much as possible while maintaining clarity of language.

78   Kim, "Toward a Crip-of-Color Critique."

79   Sins Invalid, *Skin, Tooth, and Bone*, 4.

80   Sins Invalid, *Skin, Tooth, and Bone*, 57.

81   Puar, *The Right to Maim*.

82   Forman, *One Flew Over the Cuckoo's Nest*.

83   Kafer, *Feminist, Queer, Crip*.

84   "Report of the California School for Girls, 1918–20," 8.

85   "Report of the State Board of Charities and Corrections, 1912–14," 19.

86   Benjamin, "Catching Our Breath."

87   Benjamin, "Catching Our Breath," 150.

88   Goeres-Gardner, *Inside Oregon State Hospital*.

89   Saidiya Hartman's scholarship, especially the book *Wayward Lives, Beautiful Experiments*, gave me the courage to write this paragraph. Although my subjects are very different from Hartman's, the care with which she treats those whose stories she attempts to recover, as well as the way she thoughtfully grapples with the impossibility of an unproblematic recovery, has heavily influenced my methods.

90   Haley, *No Mercy Here*, 88.

91   Cohen, "Punks, Bulldaggers, and Welfare Queens."

92   Whatcott, "Aiding and Abetting the Unruly Past."

93   Dinshaw, *Getting Medieval*, 47.

94   Hartman, "Venus in Two Acts," 11.

95   Foucault, "Nietzsche. Genealogy. History."

96   Benjamin, "Theses on the Concept of History"; Dinshaw, *Getting Medieval*, 140.

97   Muñoz, *Cruising Utopia*, 4.

98   Muñoz, *Cruising Utopia*.

99   "Days of Future Past" is the name of a storyline in the comic book series *The Uncanny X-Men*, spanning issues no. 141–42, originally published in 1981. In the storyline, X-Men from an apocalyptic future create technology to send a member of their team into the past with the goal of interrupting events to create an alternate timeline.

100   Norris, *The Octopus*; Gilman, *Herland*.

101   Smith, *Alice*.

102   Ben-Moshe, "Disabling Incarceration."

103   Davis, "Public Imprisonment and Private Violence."

104   Leonard, *Illiberal Reformers*.

105   Lira, *Laboratory of Deficiency*.

106   Gilman, *Herland*.

107 Whatcott, "No Selves to Consent."

108 Muñoz, *Cruising Utopia.*

Chapter 1. Making the Defective Class

1   "Report of the State Board of Charities and Corrections, 1916–18," 62.

2   "Report of the State Commission in Lunacy, 1910–1912," 22.

3   "Report of the State Board of Charities and Corrections, 1918–20," 10.

4   California Senate Resolution 47: Relative to Eugenics.

5   Ben-Moshe, Carey, and Chapman, *Disability Incarcerated.*

6   Clare, *Brilliant Imperfection.*

7   Fox, *So Far Disordered in Mind.*

8   Fox, *So Far Disordered in Mind.*

9   Abbott, *I Cried, You Didn't Listen.*

10   Williams et al., "Whittier Social Case History Manual."

11   Williams et al., "Whittier Social Case History Manual."

12   Miroslava Chávez-García, *States of Delinquency.*

13   "Report of the State Commission in Lunacy, 1906–8," 10–11.

14   "Report of the State Commission in Lunacy, 1906–8," 10.

15   Williams et al., "Whittier Social Case History Manual," 43.

16   Fernald, "Report of the Psychological Work in the California School for Girls"; Chávez-García, *States of Delinquency.*

17   Fernald, "Report of the Psychological Work in the California School for Girls."

18   "Report of the State Board of Charities and Corrections, 1912–14."

19   Fernald, "Report of the Psychological Work in the California School for Girls."

20   Fernald, "Report of the Psychological Work in the California School for Girls," 29, 32.

21   Fernald, "Report of the Psychological Work in the California School for Girls," 30.

22   "Report of the State Commission in Lunacy, 1898–1900," 93.

23   Erevelles, *Disability and Difference in Global Contexts,* 40.

24   Spillers, "Mama's Baby, Papa's Maybe."

25   Hong, "Existentially Surplus"; Tadiar, "Life-Times of Disposability within Global Neoliberalism."

26   Erevelles, *Disability and Difference in Global Contexts*; Bell, *Blackness and Disability*; Puar, *The Right to Maim*; Pickens, *Black Madness*; Bailey and Mobley, "Work in the Intersections."

27   Ben-Moshe, *Decarcerating Disability*, 5.

28   Roberts, *Killing the Black Body*; Kline, *Building a Better Race*; Briggs, *Reproducing Empire*; Ordover, *American Eugenics*; Carpio, "The Lost Generation"; Stern, *Eugenic Nation*; Lira and Stern, "Mexican Americans and Eugenic Sterilization"; Okrent, *The Guarded Gate*.

29   Segrest, *Administrations of Lunacy*; Burch, *Committed*; Lira, *Laboratory of Deficiency*.

30   Miranda, *Bad Indians*; Hernández, *City of Inmates*.

31   This point was brought to my attention by Joyce Moser (Yurok) in personal communication.

32   Miranda, *Bad Indians*.

33   Takaki, *A Different Mirror*.

34   Hernández, *City of Inmates*.

35   Shah, *Contagious Divides*.

36   Kaniecki et al., "Racialization and Reproduction."

37   Hernández, *City of Inmates*.

38   Hernández, *City of Inmates*.

39   Novak et al., "Disproportionate Sterilization of Latinos under California's Eugenic Sterilization Program, 1920–1945."

40   Chávez-García, *States of Delinquency*; Lira, *Laboratory of Deficiency*.

41   "Report of the State Commission in Lunacy, 1916–18," 37.

42   Hernández, *City of Inmates*.

43   "Report of the California School for Girls, 1916–18"; "Report of the Department of Institutions, 1923–24."

44   "California Department of State Hospitals."

45   Hobson, *Venus in the Dark*.

46   Hobson, *Venus in the Dark*.

47   Harris, "Whiteness as Property."

48   Takaki, *A Different Mirror*.

49   Melamed, *Represent and Destroy*, 11.

50   Fabian, *Time and the Other.*

51   Hall, "The West and the Rest."

52   Somerville, *Queering the Color Line*, 24.

53   "Report of the California School for Girls, 1918–20," 13.

54   Gould, *The Mismeasure of Man.*

55   "Report of the State Commission in Lunacy, 1906–8," 11.

56   Wynter, "Unsettling the Coloniality of Being/Power/Truth/Freedom."

57   This language comes from a question I was asked at the end of a research talk.

58   Various, "Sonoma State Home Case Books."

59   Somerville, "Queer."

60   Chauncey, *Gay New York.*

61   Bookspan, *A Germ of Goodness.*

62   "Report of the California School for Girls, 1914–16," 3.

63   "Report of the State Commission in Lunacy, 1912–14," 17.

64   "Report of the State Board of Charities and Corrections, 1912–14," 19.

65   Various, "Sonoma State Home Case Books."

66   Davis, *Are Prisons Obsolete?*

67   Butler, *Bodies That Matter*, 9.

68   Smith and Stanley, *Captive Genders*; Spade, *Normal Life*; Mogul, Ritchie, and Whitlock, *Queer (in)Justice.*

69   Butler, *Bodies That Matter.*

70   "Report of the Department of Institutions, 1921–22," 37.

71   Various, "Sonoma State Home Case Books."

72   "Report of the California School for Girls, 1916–18," 19.

73   Kunzel, *Fallen Women*, 52.

74   I am baffled by this term. My best guess is that it is a misspelling of *similisexual*, a concept used to describe same-assigned-sex attraction in a 1908 publication written by Edward Irenaeus Prime-Stevenson writing under the pen name Xavier Mayne. Given that the book was published in Naples, Italy, and likely had limited circulation, I am uncertain how the superintendent of a California state school adopted it.

75   Cohen, "Punks, Bulldaggers, and Welfare Queens."

76   The phrase "brutality and immorality" comes from a record in the Sonoma State Home casebook of 1913–20.

77 Gosney and Popenoe, *Sterilization for Human Betterment*; Popenoe and Gosney, *Twenty-Eight Years of Sterilization in California*.

78 Gosney and Popenoe, *Sterilization for Human Betterment*, 57.

79 Gosney and Popenoe, *Sterilization for Human Betterment*, 57.

80 Gosney and Popenoe, *Sterilization for Human Betterment*, 22.

81 Rafter, *Partial Justice*, xi.

82 Rafter, *Partial Justice*, 158.

Chapter 2. The Carcerality of Eugenics

1 "Patton State Hospital Museum," California Department of State Hospitals.

2 "Report of the State Board of Charities and Corrections, 1912–14," 35.

3 "Report of the Department of Institutions, 1921–22," 80.

4 Popenoe, *Applied Eugenics*.

5 Ben-Moshe, "Disabling Incarceration."

6 Davis, *Are Prisons Obsolete?*

7 Yanni, *The Architecture of Madness*.

8 Yanni, *The Architecture of Madness*.

9 "Report of the State Commission in Lunacy, 1910–12," 58.

10 "Sonoma Developmental Center," California Department of Developmental Services.

11 "Report of the California School for Girls, 1914–16."

12 Kelly and Harbison, "Hospital Board Censures Dr. Dolan."

13 Popenoe, *Applied Eugenics*.

14 "Report of the State Board of Charities and Corrections, 1914–16," 32.

15 "Report of the State Board of Charities and Corrections, 1912–14," 101.

16 Black prison abolitionists have deconstructed the notion of an inside and an outside of the prison, given that carceral logics snake into the world more broadly, including into the domestic sphere. One interpretation of the return of the paroled or escaped inmate is the discovery that the outside was no freer than the inside.

17 Fox, *So Far Disordered in Mind*.

18 "Report of the State Commission in Lunacy, 1902–4," 77.

19 "Report of the State Commission in Lunacy, 1902–4," 95–96.

20   Washington, *Medical Apartheid*; Hornblum, *Acres of Skin*.

21   National Commission for the Protection of Human Subjects of Biomedical and Behavioral Research, "The Belmont Report."

22   "Report of the State Commission in Lunacy, 1918–20," 32.

23   Kelly and Harbison, "Hospital Board Censures Dr. Dolan."

24   Kelly and Harbison, "Hospital Board Censures Dr. Dolan."

25   Whitaker, *Mad in America*.

26   "Schulken's Death Was Accidental," *Marin Journal*.

27   "Report of the State Board of Charities and Corrections, 1918–20," 37.

28   Bookspan, *A Germ of Goodness*.

29   "$1 Million for Boiling Prisoner," Prison Legal News.

30   "Report of the State Commission in Lunacy, 1916–18," 77.

31   Kline, *Building a Better Race*.

32   This language is found in the short-lived 1897 insanity law, but it effectively summarizes the legal environment for patients committed after the law was overturned.

33   "Report of the State Commission in Lunacy, 1918–20," 8.

34   "Report of the Department of Institutions, 1921–22," 80.

35   Kline, *Building a Better Race*.

36   "Report of the Department of Institutions, 1921–22," 80.

37   "The California Memorial Project," California Department of State Hospitals.

38   Gilmore, *Golden Gulag*.

39   Kilgore, "COVID-19 Is Turning Prisons into 'Kill-Boxes.'"

40   "Report of the State Commission in Lunacy, 1918–20," 32.

41   Hemarajata, "Revisiting the Great Imitator."

42   "Report of the State Commission in Lunacy, 1918–20," 5.

43   Gilmore, *Golden Gulag*; Kunzel, *Criminal Intimacy*.

44   Tadiar, "Life-Times of Disposability within Global Neoliberalism."

45   "Report of the State Board of Charities and Corrections, 1914–16," 53.

46   James, "George Jackson."

47   "Report of the California School for Girls, 1914–16," 4.

48   Atanasoski, *Humanitarian Violence*.

49   Gilmore, *Golden Gulag.*

50   Aptheker, "The Social Functions of the Prison in the United States," 54.

51   Cacho, *Social Death.*

52   Sears, *Arresting Dress.*

53   Williams, *Marxism and Literature.*

54   Gilmore, *Golden Gulag.*

55   Davis, *Are Prisons Obsolete?*

56   "Report of the State Board of Charities and Corrections, 1914–16," 32.

57   "Report of the State Board of Charities and Corrections, 1918–20," 76.

58   Kunzel, *Fallen Women, Problem Girls.*

59   D'Emilio and Freedman, *Intimate Matters.*

60   Freedman, *Their Sisters' Keepers*; Rafter, *Partial Justice*; Kunzel, *Fallen Women, Problem Girls.*

61   Freedman, *Their Sisters' Keepers,* 45.

62   Rafter, *Partial Justice.*

63   Davis, "Public Imprisonment and Private Violence."

64   Davis, "Public Imprisonment and Private Violence."

65   Haley, *No Mercy Here.*

66   Davis, *Are Prisons Obsolete?*

67   Davis, "Public Imprisonment and Private Violence."

68   Rafter, *Partial Justice.*

Chapter 3. The Political Economy of Carceral Eugenics

1   Smith, *Alice,* 71.

2   Thank you to Viviane Saleh-Hanna for pointing this out to me and inviting me to analyze the racial make-up of the workers at Sonoma State Home.

3   Lira, *Laboratory of Deficiency,* 196.

4   Eisner, *Regulatory Politics in Transition.*

5   Heilbroner and Milberg, *The Making of the Economic Society.*

6   Skowronek, *Building a New American State.*

7   D'Emilio and Freedman, *Intimate Matters.*

8   Glass, *From Mission to Microchip.*

9   Skowronek, *Building a New American State*; Eisner, *Regulatory Politics in Transition*; Skocpol, *Social Policy in the United States*.

10   Leonard, *Illiberal Reformers*.

11   Leonard, *Illiberal Reformers*.

12   Leonard, *Illiberal Reformers*.

13   Kunzel, *Fallen Women, Problem Girls*.

14   Leonard, *Illiberal Reformers*.

15   Gordon, *Pitied but Not Entitled*; Mink, *The Wages of Motherhood*.

16   HoSang, *Racial Propositions*.

17   Leonard, *Illiberal Reformers*.

18   Hong, "Existentially Surplus."

19   Lira, *Laboratory of Deficiency*; Schweik, "Archaeology of the 'Feebleminded.'"

20   Smith, *Alice*.

21   Fitzgerald et al., "The Industrial Farm for Women."

22   Starr, *California*.

23   Norris, *The Octopus*, 50–51.

24   Norris, *The Octopus*, 608.

25   Smith, *Alice*.

26   Kunzel, *Fallen Women, Problem Girls*.

27   Smith, *Alice*, 20.

28   Leonard, *Illiberal Reformers*, x.

29   Leonard, *Illiberal Reformers*, 34.

30   Leonard, *Illiberal Reformers*, 140.

31   Bookspan, *A Germ of Goodness*, 16. Bookspan describes the shoddy establishment of San Quentin, the state's first prison, in the 1850s. Construction and management were originally leased out to a private citizen whose failures to construct or manage a secure building that could house the state's few dozen prisoners led to a protracted struggle during the 1850s. Eventually the state agreed to run its own prison.

32   Smyth, "Psychiatric History and Development in California."

33   Smyth, "Psychiatric History and Development in California," 1225.

34   "Report of the State Commission in Lunacy, 1898-1900," 7.

35   "Report of the State Commission in Lunacy, 1898-1900," 9.

36 "Report of the Department of Institutions, 1923–24," 7.

37 "Report of the State Commission in Lunacy, 1898–1900," 45.

38 "Report of the State Board of Charities and Corrections, 1918–20," 35.

39 Fox, *So Far Disordered in Mind*.

40 "Report of the State Commission in Lunacy, 1900–02."

41 "Report of the State Commission in Lunacy, 1900–02," 29–30.

42 "Report of the State Board of Charities and Corrections, 1916–18," 49.

43 "Report of the Department of Institutions, 1923–24," 5.

44 "Report of the State Commission in Lunacy, 1910–12," 58.

45 "Report of the Department of Institutions, 1923–24," 8.

46 Starr, *California*.

47 "Report of the Department of Institutions, 1923–24," 5.

48 "Report of the State Commission in Lunacy, 1898–1900," 51.

49 "Report of the State Commission in Lunacy, 1898–1900," 51.

50 "Report of the Department of Institutions, 1923–24," 17.

51 "Report of the Department of Institutions, 1923–24," 7.

52 "Report of the State Commission in Lunacy, 1900–02," 29–30.

53 "Report of the State Board of Charities and Corrections, 1916–18," 62.

54 "Report of the California School for Girls, 1916–18," 40.

55 "Report of the State Commission in Lunacy, 1918–20," 5.

56 "Report of the State Board of Charities and Corrections, 1916–18," 67.

57 "Report of the State Commission in Lunacy, 1916–18," 14.

58 "Report of the State Commission in Lunacy, 1916–18," 75.

59 Foucault, *Society Must Be Defended*.

60 In Nicole Hahn Rafter's comprehensive analysis of the women's reformatory movement in the United States, the Industrial Farm for Women in California constitutes just one footnote. The farm is also mentioned briefly in Bookspan's history of California prisons and Cairns's history of the first prison for women in California. Rafter, *Partial Justice*; Bookspan, *A Germ of Goodness*; Cairns, *Hard Time at Tehachapi*.

61 Bookspan, *A Germ of Goodness*.

62 Bookspan, *A Germ of Goodness*.

63 Fitzgerald et al., "The Industrial Farm for Women."

64   "Report of the Department of Institutions, 1921–22," 43.

65   "Journal of the Senate during the Forty-Fourth Session of the Legislature of the State of California," 147.

66   Fitzgerald et al., "The Industrial Farm for Women."

67   Fitzgerald et al., "The Industrial Farm for Women."

68   Fitzgerald et al., "The Industrial Farm for Women."

69   Records of the San Francisco Center of the California Civic League of Women Voters.

70   Fitzgerald et al., "The Industrial Farm for Women."

71   Fitzgerald et al., "The Industrial Farm for Women."

72   Cairns, *Hard Time at Tehachapi*.

73   "Journal of the Senate During the Forty-Fourth Session of the Legislature of the State of California," 251.

74   "Journal of the Senate During the Forty-Fifth Session of the Legislature of the State of California," 867.

75   Robinson, *Black Marxism*.

76   Davis, *Women, Race & Class*; Mies, *Patriarchy and Accumulation on a World Scale*.

77   Hernández, *City of Inmates*.

78   Marx, *Capital*.

79   "Report of the State Board of Charities and Corrections, 1904–6," 129–30.

80   Smith, *Alice*.

81   Smith, *Alice*, 113.

82   Foucault, *The History of Sexuality*, 141.

83   Rafter, *Partial Justice*.

84   "Report of the Department of Institutions, 1929–30," 11.

85   "Report of the Department of Institutions, 1926–28," 53.

86   "Report of the Department of Institutions, 1921–22," 40.

87   "Report of the State Commission in Lunacy, 1918–20," 61.

88   Lira, *Laboratory of Deficiency*.

89   Mies, *Patriarchy and Accumulation on a World Scale*.

90   Lira, *Laboratory of Deficiency*, 107.

91   "Report of the State Commission in Lunacy, 1918–20," 7.

92 Stone, *The Disabled State*; Erevelles, *Disability and Difference in Global Contexts*.

93 Charlton, *Nothing about Us without Us*.

94 "Report of the Department of Institutions, 1921–22," 9.

95 "Report of the Department of Institutions, 1921–22," 38.

96 Russell, *Capitalism & Disability*.

97 "Report of the Department of Institutions, 1923–24."

98 Hong, "Existentially Surplus"; Tadiar, "Life-Times of Disposability within Global Neoliberalism."

99 Hong, "Existentially Surplus," 92.

100 Gilmore, *Golden Gulag*.

101 Russell and Stewart, "Disablement, Prison, and Historical Segregation."

102 Russell, *Capitalism & Disability*.

103 Russell, *Capitalism & Disability*.

104 Gilmore, *Golden Gulag*.

Chapter 4. From Maternalist Care to Anti-eugenics

1 Stuckey, "What Has Become of Jimmy Thornton?"

2 Lira, *Laboratory of Deficiency*.

3 Ben-Moshe, *Decarcerating Disability*.

4 Nielsen, *A Disability History of the United States*.

5 Gilman, *Herland*.

6 Alexander, *Pedagogies of Crossing*.

7 "Report of the State Board of Charities and Corrections, 1916–18," 85.

8 Gilman, *Women and Economics*; Gilman, *The Home, Its Work and Influence*.

9 Lamp, "'It Is for the Mother.'"

10 Gilman, *Herland*.

11 Gilman, *Herland*, 59.

12 Gilman, *Herland*, 71, 77, 82.

13 Gilman, *Herland*, 92.

14 Gilman, *Herland*, 92.

15   "Report of the California School for Girls, 1918–20," 4.

16   Rafter, *Partial Justice*.

17   "Report of the State Board of Charities and Corrections, 1912–14," 31.

18   Sullivan et al., "Grace Maxwell Fernald, 1879–1950."

19   Fernald, "Report of the Psychological Work in the California School for Girls."

20   "Report of the California School for Girls, 1914–16," 57.

21   Gohlke, *Remarkable Women of Stockton*.

22   Gohlke, *Remarkable Women of Stockton*, 63, 62.

23   D'Emilio and Freedman, *Intimate Matters*.

24   "Report of the California School for Girls, 1914–16," 41–42.

25   Smith, *Alice*.

26   "Report of the California School for Girls, 1918–20," 5–8.

27   "Report of the California School for Girls, 1918–20," 5.

28   "Report of the State Commission in Lunacy, 1910–12," 59.

29   "Report of the Department of Institutions, 1923–24," 74.

30   "Report of the State Commission in Lunacy, 1912–14," 68.

31   "Report of the State Commission in Lunacy, 1912–14," 68.

32   "Report of the California School for Girls, 1918–20," 7.

33   "Report of the State Commission in Lunacy, 1912–14," 46.

34   "Report of the Department of Institutions, 1925–26," 61.

35   "Report of the Department of Institutions, 1923–24," 31.

36   "Report of the Department of Institutions, 1926–28," 12.

37   "Report of the Department of Institutions, 1923–24," 31.

38   "Report of the Department of Institutions, 1923–24," 32.

39   "Report of the Board of Prison Directors, 1909–10," 55–56.

40   Foucault, *Discipline and Punish*.

41   "Report of the California School for Girls, 1918–20," 8.

42   "Report of the State Board of Charities and Corrections, 1903–04," 28.

43   Shah, *Stranger Intimacy*; Hartman, *Wayward Lives, Beautiful Experiments*.

44   Hartman, *Scenes of Subjection*.

45   Hartman, *Scenes of Subjection*, 6.

46   Hartman, *Scenes of Subjection*, 5.

47   Spivak, *A Critique of Postcolonial Reason*.

48   Fanon, *The Wretched of the Earth*, 81.

49   Hartman, *Wayward Lives, Beautiful Experiments*.

50   "Report of the State Commission in Lunacy, 1918–20," 8.

51   "Report of the California School for Girls, 1914–16," 41.

52   Mink, *The Wages of Motherhood*; Kandaswamy, *Domestic Contradictions*.

53   Nguyen, *The Gift of Freedom*.

54   Horvat and Štiks, "Welcome to the Desert of Transition!"

55   Leon, *An Image of God*.

56   Schweik, "Eugenic Anti-Eugenics"; Auffrey, "French-Canadian Resistance to and Reformulations of Eugenics in 20th-Century Québec."

57   Hong, "Existentially Surplus."

58   Williams and Shoultz, *We Can Speak for Ourselves*; Dybwad and Bersani, *New Voices*; Johnson and Johnson, *Lost in a Desert World*.

59   Stuckey, ""What Has Become of Jimmy Thornton?"

60   Guha, *Elementary Aspects of Peasant Insurgency in Colonial India*.

61   Blackstone and Gallanis, *Of Private Wrongs*, 89.

62   Kelly and Harbison, "Hospital Board Censures Dr. Dolan."

63   Kelly and Harbison, "Hospital Board Censures Dr. Dolan."

64   "Investigation to Be Made," *Sacramento Union*.

65   "Report of the California School for Girls, 1916–18," 53.

66   Also discussed by Lira, *Laboratory of Deficiency*.

67   "Report of the State Commission in Lunacy, 1910–12," 14.

68   Various, "Sonoma State Home Case Books."

69   "Report of the State Board of Charities and Corrections, 1910–12," 30.

70   Rochlen, "Ventura Revolt Laid to Hearst's Attacks on Institution."

71   Calvanico, "Arson Girls, Match-Strikers, and Firestarters."

72   Various, "Stockton State Hospital Commitment Register."

73   Various, "Ventura School for Girls Inmate History Register."

74   Smyth, "Psychiatric History and Development in California," 1225.

75   Various, "Sonoma State Home Case Books."

76   "Report of the California School for Girls, 1916–18," 6.

77   Simpson, *Mohawk Interruptus*; Benjamin, "Informed Refusal."

78   Muñoz, *Disidentifications*.

79   Whatcott, "Sexuality, Disability, and Madness in California's Eugenics Era."

80   Various, "Sonoma State Home Case Books."

81   Various, "Stockton State Hospital Commitment Registers."

82   Williams, *Marxism and Literature*.

83   Various, "Inmate History Register of Ventura School for Girls."

84   "Report of the State Board of Charities and Corrections, 1914-16," 46.

85   Hernández, *City of Inmates*, 4.

86   Burch, *Committed*.

87   Cacho, *Social Death*, 31.

88   Cacho, *Social Death*, 31–32.

89   Whatcott, "Aiding and Abetting the Unruly Past."

90   Compared to other carceral eugenicists like Miriam Van Waters, there is very little academic writing about Smyth. My source for learning about Smyth's life is Gohlke, *Remarkable Women of Stockton*.

91   Hernández, *City of Inmates*.

92   Muñoz, *Cruising Utopia*.

93   Kafer, *Feminist, Queer, Crip*; Schalk, *Bodyminds Reimagined*.

Chapter 5. Menacing the Present

1   California Senate Resolution 47: Relative to Eugenics.

2   "California Launches Program to Compensate Survivors of State-Sponsored Sterilization," Office of Governor Gavin Newsom.

3   Stern et al., "California's Sterilization Survivors."

4   "30+ Years in a Mental Institution," Disability Rights California.

5   "30+ Years in a Mental Institution," Disability Rights California.

6   Ben-Moshe, *Decarcerating Disability*.

7   Ben-Moshe, *Decarcerating Disability*.

8   "30+ Years in a Mental Institution," Disability Rights California.

9   "Spring 2023 Population Projections," California Department of Corrections and Rehabilitation.

10 Reagan, "A Time for Choosing."

11 Sentencing Project, *The Color of Justice*.

12 Sentencing Project, *Incarcerated Women and Girls*.

13 Kilgore, "Repackaging Mass Incarceration."

14 Ben-Moshe, *Decarcerating Disability*.

15 Braun, *We're Here to Speak for Justice*.

16 Braun, *We're Here to Speak for Justice*.

17 Placzek, "Did the Emptying of Mental Hospitals Contribute to Homelessness?"

18 Braun, *We're Here to Speak for Justice*.

19 "Understanding the Lanterman-Petris-Short (LPS) Act," Disability Rights California.

20 Braun, *We're Here to Speak for Justice*.

21 Bale, "Abuse Findings Continue at Developmental Centers, despite State Scrutiny."

22 Sheridan, "Sonoma Developmental Center Quietly Closes Its Doors."

23 "Sonoma Developmental Center," California Department of Developmental Services.

24 Nishida, *Just Care*.

25 Russell and Stewart, "Disablement, Prison, and Historical Segregation."

26 "State Hospitals," California Department of State Hospitals.

27 "State Hospitals," California Department of State Hospitals.

28 "Understanding the Lanterman-Petris-Short (LPS) Act," Disability Rights California.

29 "State Hospitals," California Department of State Hospitals.

30 "State Hospitals," California Department of State Hospitals.

31 "Koncentration Kamp for Gays," *Gay Flames*; Jackson, "The State and Dr. Frankenstein."

32 "Patient Demographics," California Health and Human Services.

33 "Fairview Developmental Center," California Department of Developmental Services.

34 "Porterville Developmental Center," California Department of Developmental Services.

35 Clare, *Brilliant Imperfection*.

36   Sears, *Arresting Dress*.

37   Focquaert, "Neurobiology and Crime."

38   Ben-Moshe, *Decarcerating Disability*.

39   Bookspan, *A Germ of Goodness*.

40   Gilmore, *Golden Gulag*.

41   Bookspan, *A Germ of Goodness*.

42   Chaddock, "California Medical Facility Was First Prison Hospital."

43   Law, "'Out of Flames and Fear.'"

44   "California Medical Facility," California Department of Corrections and Rehabilitation.

45   Law, "Trans Women Who Report Abuse in Prison Are Targets of Retaliation."

46   Joint Legislative Committee on Prison Construction and Operations, "California's Prisons: California Rehabilitation Center."

47   "California Health Care Facility, Stockton," California Department of Corrections and Rehabilitation.

48   Kilgore, "Repackaging Mass Incarceration."

49   Kilgore, "Repackaging Mass Incarceration."

50   "Compassionate Release in California by the Numbers," Families against Mandatory Minimums.

51   "Letter to the California Governor," UCLA Law Covid Behind Bars Data Project.

52   Baker, "Life without Parole Is America's Hidden Death Penalty."

53   Law, "'Out of Flames and Fear.'"

54   "California Realignment," Stanford Criminal Justice Center.

55   Morris, "The Most Dangerous Place in Alameda County."

56   Villani, "Inmates Oppose Mental Health Settlement for Santa Rita Jail Lawsuit."

57   Ruth Wilson Gilmore, personal communication in graduate seminar, University of California, Santa Cruz, November 9, 2015.

58   Harris, Ben-Moshe, and Moore, "Psychiatric Incarceration Isn't Treatment—It's Violence, Survivors Say."

59   "Governor Newsom Launches New Plan to Help Californians Struggling with Mental Health Challenges, Homelessness," Office of Governor Gavin Newsom.

60   Placzek, "Did the Emptying of Mental Hospitals Contribute to Homelessness?"

61   Kilgore, "Repackaging Mass Incarceration."

62   Howle, *Sterilization of Female Inmates.*

63   Johnson, "Female Inmates Sterilized in California Prisons without Approval."

64   Johnson, "Female Inmates Sterilized in California Prisons without Approval."

65   California Coalition for Women Prisoners, "Charisse Shumate."

66   Eldridge, "Another Hurdle for Former Inmates."

67   Chandler, "Female Offenders, Budget Issues Related to Conditions of Confinement and Illegal Sterilizations."

68   Law, "How Does Incarceration Impact the Spread of HIV?"

69   Californians United for a Responsible Budget, "We Are Not Disposable."

70   Jones, "Cruel and Unusual Punishment."

71   Taylor, "The Emerging Movement for Police and Prison Abolition."

72   Sentencing Project, *Incarcerated Women and Girls.*

73   Sentencing Project, *The Color of Justice.*

74   Gilmore, *Golden Gulag,* 28.

75   Howard et al., *The People's Plan for Prison Closure.*

76   Chávez-García, *States of Delinquency.*

77   Abbott, *I Cried, You Didn't Listen.*

78   Ridolfi, Washburn, and Guzman, *Youth Prosecuted as Adults in California.*

79   "The History of the Division of Juvenile Justice," California Department of Corrections and Rehabilitation.

80   Washburn, "Decades of Abuse at California's DJJ Will End in 2023."

81   Ridolfi, Menart, and Villa, *California Youth Face Heightened Racial and Ethnic Disparities in Division of Juvenile Justice.*

82   Ridolfi, Menart, and Villa, *California Youth Face Heightened Racial and Ethnic Disparities in Division of Juvenile Justice.*

83   Ben-Moshe, *Decarcerating Disability.*

Epilogue

1   Levin, "He Lived in the US for 40 Years."

2 Free Them All San Diego, "About," YouTube, October 29, 2020, https://www.youtube.com/channel/UC-fZrEyVyxlHbdxlgpZmVtg/about.

3 Free Them All San Diego, "Resisting Medical Abuse and Neglect in Detention," YouTube, February 24, 2021, https://www.youtube.com/watch?v=F8yd3DjF2UI.

4 Foucault, *Discipline and Punish*; Davis, *Are Prisons Obsolete?*

BIBLIOGRAPHY

Archives

Sacramento, California

CALIFORNIA STATE ARCHIVES
Appendices to the Journals of the Senate and Assembly of the Legislature of the
State of California
Reports of the Board of Charities and Corrections
Reports of the Board of Prison Directors
Reports of the California School for Girls
Reports of the Commission in Lunacy
Reports of the Department of Institutions
Journal of the Assembly of the Legislature of the State of California
Journal of the Senate of the Legislature of the State of California
Mendocino State Hospital Patient Case Files
Sonoma State Home Case Books, 1900–1920
Stockton State Hospital Commitment Register
Stockton State Hospital Correspondence Files
Stockton State Hospital Records of Operations
Ventura School for Girls Inmate History Register

San Francisco, California

CALIFORNIA HISTORICAL SOCIETY

League of Women Voters of San Francisco, partially processed collection
  Fitzgerald, Mrs. William A., Mrs. Addie Garwood Estes, Miss Marian
    Delaney, Mrs. O. E. Chaney, Curtiss D. Wilbur, William H. Waste,
    E. C. Robinson, et al. "The Industrial Farm for Women." San Fran-
    cisco: League of Women Voters of San Francisco, [1923?].
  Maddox, Edith Walker. "Letter to Members." San Francisco: League of
    Women Voters of San Francisco, 1923.

Government Documents

California Bureau of Juvenile Research

Fernald, Grace M. "Report of the Psychological Work in the California School
  for Girls." *Journal of Delinquency* 1 (1916): 22–32.
Williams, J. Harold, Willis W. Clark, Mildred S. Covert, and Edythe K. Bryant.
  "Whittier Social Case History Manual." Sacramento, CA: California Bureau
  of Juvenile Research, 1921.

California Department of Corrections and Rehabilitation

"California Health Care Facility, Stockton." California Department of Corrections and Rehabilitation. Accessed May 27, 2021. https://www.cdcr.ca.gov
  /facility-locator/chcf/.
"California Medical Facility." California Department of Corrections and Rehabilitation. Accessed May 27, 2021. https://www.cdcr.ca.gov/facility-locator/cmf/.
Chaddock, Don. "California Medical Facility Was First Prison Hospital." Inside CDCR, January 25, 2016. https://www.cdcr.ca.gov/insidecdcr/2016/01/25
  /unlocking-history-california-medical-facility-was-first-prison-hospital/.
"The History of the Division of Juvenile Justice." California Department of Corrections and Rehabilitation. Accessed May 27, 2021. http://www.cdcr.ca.gov
  /Juvenile_Justice/DJJ_History/index.html.
"Spring 2023 Population Projections." California Department of Corrections
  and Rehabilitation, May 2023. https://www.cdcr.ca.gov/research/population
  -reports-2/.

California Department of Developmental Services

"Fairview Developmental Center." California Department of Developmental
  Services. February 7, 2019. https://dds.ca.gov/services/state-facilities/fairview
  -dc/.
"Porterville Developmental Center." California Department of Developmental
  Services. February 7, 2019. https://www.dds.ca.gov/services/state-facilities
  /porterville-dc/.

"Sonoma Developmental Center." California Department of Developmental Services. March 18, 2019. https://www.dds.ca.gov/services/state-facilities /sonoma-dc/.

California Department of State Hospitals

"The California Memorial Project." California Department of State Hospitals. Accessed May 27, 2021. https://dsh.ca.gov/Hospitals/California_Memorial _Project.html.
"Patient & Staff Covid Tracking." California Department of State Hospitals. Accessed August 11, 2023. https://www.dsh.ca.gov/COVID-19/Patient_and_Staff _COVID-19_Tracking.html.
"Patton State Hospital Museum." California Department of State Hospitals. Accessed August 4, 2023. https://www.dsh.ca.gov/Patton/Museum.html.
"State Hospitals." California Department of State Hospitals. Accessed July 30, 2022. https://www.dsh.ca.gov/Hospitals/index.html.

California Health and Human Services

"Patient Demographics." California Health and Human Services. Accessed August 9, 2023. https://data.chhs.ca.gov/dataset/patient-demographics.

California State Auditor

Howle, Elaine. *Sterilization of Female Inmates: Report 2013–120*. State of California, June 2014. https://www.auditor.ca.gov/pdfs/reports/2013–120.pdf.

California State Legislature

"California's Prisons: California Rehabilitation Center." Joint Legislative Committee on Prison Construction and Operations, California Joint Committees. November 29, 1983. http://digitalcommons.law.ggu.edu/caldocs_joint _committees/59.
"Senate Concurrent Resolution No. 47: Relative to Eugenics." California Legislative Information. Accessed October 13, 2023. https://leginfo.legislature.ca .gov/faces/billTextClient.xhtml?bill_id=200320040SCR47.

Office of Governor Gavin Newsom

"California Launches Program to Compensate Survivors of State-Sponsored Sterilization." Office of Governor Gavin Newsom. December 31, 2021. https://www .gov.ca.gov/2021/12/31/california-launches-program-to-compensate-survivors -of-state-sponsored-sterilization/.
"Governor Newsom Launches New Plan to Help Californians Struggling with Mental Health Challenges, Homelessness." Office of Governor Gavin Newsom. March 3, 2022. https://www.gov.ca.gov/2022/03/03/governor-newsom -launches-new-plan-to-help-californians-struggling-with-mental-health -challenges-homelessness/.

National Commission for the Protection of Human Subjects of Biomedical and Behavioral Research

The Belmont Report: Ethical Principles and Guidelines for the Protection of Human Subjects of Research. US Department of Health and Human Services. April 18, 1979. https://www.hhs.gov/ohrp/regulations-and-policy/belmont-report/index.html.

Secondary Sources

Abbott, Dwight E. *I Cried, You Didn't Listen: A Survivor's Exposé of the California Youth Authority*. Los Angeles: Feral House, 1991.

Alexander, M. Jacqui. *Pedagogies of Crossing: Meditations on Feminism, Sexual Politics, Memory, and the Sacred*. Durham, NC: Duke University Press, 2005.

American Friends Service Committee, Detention Resistance, and Pueblo Sin Fronteras. *Compounding Suffering during a Pandemic*. American Friends Service Committee. October 12, 2020. https://www.afsc.org/story/compounding-suffering-during-pandemic.

Aptheker, Bettina. "The Social Functions of the Prison in the United States." In *If They Come in the Morning; Voices of Resistance*, edited by Angela Y. Davis. New York: Third Press, 1971.

Atanasoski, Neda. *Humanitarian Violence: The U.S. Deployment of Diversity*. Minneapolis: University of Minnesota Press, 2013.

Auffrey, Vincent F. "French Canadian Resistance to and Reformulations of Eugenics in 20th-Century Québec, 1912–1945." Paper presented at the American Studies Association Conference, Montreal, Canada, November 2023.

Bailey, Moya, and Izetta Autumn Mobley. "Work in the Intersections: A Black Feminist Disability Framework." *Gender & Society* 33, no. 1 (February 1, 2019): 19–40.

Baker, Brandon J. "Life without Parole Is America's Hidden Death Penalty." Prison Journalism Project, September 21, 2022. http://prisonjournalismproject.org/2022/09/21/life-without-parole-is-americas-hidden-death-penalty/.

Bale, Rachael. "Abuse Findings Continue at Developmental Centers, Despite State Scrutiny." *Reveal*, March 27, 2014. http://revealnews.org/article/abuse-findings-continue-at-developmental-centers-despite-state-scrutiny/.

Baynton, Douglas. "Disability and the Justification of Inequality in American History." In *The New Disability History*, edited by Paul K. Longmore and Lauri Umansky, 33–57. New York: New York University Press, 2001.

Bell, Christopher M. *Blackness and Disability: Critical Examinations and Cultural Interventions*. East Lansing: Michigan State University Press, 2011.

Benjamin, Ruha. "Catching Our Breath: Critical Race STS and the Carceral Imagination." *Engaging Science, Technology, and Society* 2 (July 1, 2016): 145–56.

Benjamin, Ruha. "Informed Refusal: Toward a Justice-Based Bioethics." *Science, Technology & Human Values* 41, no. 6 (November 2016): 967–90.

Benjamin, Walter. "Theses on the Concept of History." In *Illuminations*, edited by Hannah Arendt. New York: Schocken Books, 1968.

Ben-Moshe, Liat. *Decarcerating Disability: Deinstitutionalization and Prison Abolition*. Minneapolis: University of Minnesota Press, 2020.

Ben-Moshe, Liat. "Disabling Incarceration: Connecting Disability to Divergent Confinements in the USA." *Critical Sociology* 39, no. 3 (May 1, 2013): 385–403.

Ben-Moshe, Liat. "Dis-Epistemologies of Abolition." *Critical Criminology* 26, no. 3 (September 1, 2018): 341–55.

Ben-Moshe, Liat, Allison C. Carey, and Chris Chapman, eds. *Disability Incarcerated: Imprisonment and Disability in the United States and Canada*. New York: Palgrave Macmillan, 2014.

Bhatt, Priyanka, Katie Quigley, Azadeh Shahshahani, Gina Starfield, and Ayano Kitano. *Violence and Violation: Medical Abuse of Immigrants at the Irwin County Detention Center*. Atlanta, GA: Project South, 2021. https://projectsouth.org/wp-content/uploads/2021/09/IrwinReport_14SEPT21.pdf.

Bhattcharya, Tithi. "What Is Social Reproduction Theory?" *Socialist Worker* (blog), September 10, 2013. http://socialistworker.org/2013/09/10/what-is-social-reproduction-theory.

Bierria, Alisa, Jakeya Caruthers, and Brooke Lober. *Abolition Feminisms: Organizing, Survival, and Transformative Practice*. Chicago: Haymarket Books, 2022.

Black, Edwin. "Eugenics and the Nazis: The California Connection." *SF Gate*, November 9, 2003. https://www.sfgate.com/opinion/article/Eugenics-and-the-Nazis-the-California-2549771.php.

Blackstone, William, and Thomas P. Gallanis. *Of Private Wrongs*. Book 3 of *The Oxford Edition of Blackstone's: Commentaries on the Laws of England*. Oxford: Oxford University Press, 2016.

Blue, Ethan. *Doing Time in the Depression: Everyday Life in Texas and California Prisons*. New York: New York University Press, 2012.

Bookspan, Shelley. *A Germ of Goodness: The California State Prison System, 1851–1944*. Lincoln: University of Nebraska Press, 1991.

Braun, Theodore. "We're Here to Speak for Justice: Founding California's Regional Centers." Frank D. Lanterman Regional Center, 2007. https://lanterman.org/publications/were_here_to_speak_for_justice_founding_californias_regional_centers.

Briggs, Laura. *Reproducing Empire: Race, Sex, Science, and U.S. Imperialism in Puerto Rico*. Berkeley: University of California Press, 2002.

Brown, Michelle, and Judah Schept. "New Abolition, Criminology and a Critical Carceral Studies." *Punishment & Society* 19, no. 4 (October 1, 2017): 440–62.

Burch, Susan. *Committed: Remembering Native Kinship in and Beyond Institutions*. Chapel Hill: University of North Carolina Press, 2021.

Butler, Judith. *Bodies That Matter: On the Discursive Limits of "Sex."* New York: Routledge, 1993.

Cacho, Lisa Marie. *Social Death: Racialized Rightlessness and the Criminalization of the Unprotected*. New York: New York University Press, 2012.

Cairns, Kathleen A. *Hard Time at Tehachapi: California's First Women's Prison*. Albuquerque: University of New Mexico Press, 2009.

California Coalition for Women Prisoners. "Charisse Shumate: Fighting for Our Lives." Freedom Archives, 2011. https://vimeo.com/19050308.

"California Memorial Project: Remembering Those Who Were Forgotten." Disability Rights California. Accessed August 3, 2023. https://www.disabilityrightsca.org/what-we-do/programs/california-memorial-project-cmp.

"California Realignment." Stanford Criminal Justice Center. Accessed August 1, 2022. https://law.stanford.edu/stanford-criminal-justice-center-scjc/california-realignment/.

Californians United for a Responsible Budget. *We Are Not Disposable: The Toxic Impacts of Prisons and Jails*. Oakland, CA: CURB, 2016. http://curbprisonspending.org/wp-content/uploads/2016/10/CURB-WeAreNotDisposableReport.pdf.

Calvanico, Jessica R. "Arson Girls, Match-Strikers, and Firestarters: A Reflection on Rage, Racialization, and the Carcerality of Girlhood." *Signs: Journal of Women in Culture and Society* 47, no. 2 (January 2022): 399–424.

Carpio, Myla Vicenti. "The Lost Generation: American Indian Women and Sterilization Abuse." *Social Justice* 31, no. 4 (98) (2004): 40–53.

Chandler, Cynthia. "Female Offenders, Budget Issues Related to Conditions of Confinement and Illegal Sterilizations: Testimony Submitted by Justice Now to March 15 Hearing on CDCR." Justice Now, March 13, 2012.

Charlton, James I. *Nothing about Us without Us: Disability Oppression and Empowerment*. Berkeley: University of California Press, 1998.

Chauncey, George. *Gay New York: Gender, Urban Culture, and the Making of the Gay Male World, 1890–1940*. New York: Basic Books, 1995.

Chávez-García, Miroslava. *States of Delinquency: Race and Science in the Making of California's Juvenile Justice System*. Berkeley: University of California Press, 2012.

Clare, Eli. *Brilliant Imperfection: Grappling with Cure*. Durham, NC: Duke University Press, 2017.

Clare, Eli. *Exile and Pride: Disability, Queerness, and Liberation*. Cambridge, MA: South End Press, 1999.

Claremont, Chris. *The Uncanny X-Men #141–42*. New York: Marvel Comics, 1981.

Cohen, Cathy J. "Punks, Bulldaggers, and Welfare Queens: The Radical Potential of Queer Politics?" *GLQ: A Journal of Lesbian and Gay Studies* 3, no. 4 (May 1, 1997): 437–65.

"Compassionate Release in California by the Numbers." Families against Mandatory Minimums, August 1, 2022. https://www.famm.org.

"The COVID Prison Project Tracks Data and Policy across the Country to Monitor COVID-19 in Prisons." COVID Prison Project. Accessed August 11, 2023. https://covidprisonproject.com/.

Davis, Angela Y. *Are Prisons Obsolete?* New York: Seven Stories, 2003.

Davis, Angela Y. "Public Imprisonment and Private Violence: Reflections on the Hidden Punishment of Women." In *Frontline Feminisms: Women, War, and Resistance*, edited by Marguerite R. Waller and Jennifer Rycenga, 3–16. New York: Routledge, 2001.

Davis, Angela Y. *Women, Race & Class*. New York: Vintage Books, 1983.

Davis, Angela Y., Gina Dent, Erica R. Meiners, and Beth E. Richie. *Abolition. Feminism. Now*. Chicago: Haymarket Books, 2021.

D'Emilio, John, and Estelle B. Freedman. *Intimate Matters: A History of Sexuality in America*. 2nd ed. Chicago: University of Chicago Press, 1997.

Dinshaw, Carolyn. *Getting Medieval: Sexualities and Communities, Pre- and Postmodern*. Durham, NC: Duke University Press, 1999.

Dybwad, Gunnar, and Hank A. Bersani, eds. *New Voices: Self-Advocacy by People with Disabilities*. Cambridge, MA: Brookline Books, 1996.

Eisner, Marc Allen. *Regulatory Politics in Transition*. 2nd ed. Baltimore, MD: Johns Hopkins University Press, 2000.

Eldridge, Taylor Elizabeth. "Another Hurdle for Former Inmates: Their Teeth." Marshall Project, June 28, 2018. https://www.themarshallproject.org/2018/06/28/another-hurdle-for-former-inmates-their-teeth.

Erevelles, Nirmala. *Disability and Difference in Global Contexts: Enabling A Transformative Body Politic*. New York: Palgrave Macmillan, 2011.

Fabian, Johannes. *Time and the Other: How Anthropology Makes Its Object*. New York: Columbia University Press, 2014.

Faith, Karlene. *Unruly Women: The Politics of Confinement and Resistance*. Vancouver: Press Gang, 1993.

Fanon, Frantz. *The Wretched of the Earth*. Translated by Richard Philcox. New York: Grove Press, 2004.

Focquaert, Farah. "Neurobiology and Crime: A Neuro-Ethical Perspective." *Journal of Criminal Justice* 65 (2019): 101533. https://doi.org/10.1016/j.jcrimjus.2018.01.001.

Forman, Miloš, dir. *One Flew Over the Cuckoo's Nest*. Berkeley, CA: Fantasy Films, 1975.

Foucault, Michel. *Discipline and Punish: The Birth of the Prison*. New York: Vintage Books, 1977.

Foucault, Michel. *The History of Sexuality*. Vol. 1. New York: Vintage Books, 1990.

Foucault, Michel. "Nietzsche. Genealogy. History." In *Language, Counter-Memory, Practice: Selected Essays and Interviews*. Ithaca, NY: Cornell University Press, 1977.

Foucault, Michel. *Society Must Be Defended: Lectures at the Collège de France, 1975–76*. Edited by Mauro Bertani, Alessandro Fontana, and François Ewald. Translated by David Macey. New York: Picador, 2003.

Fox, Richard W. *So Far Disordered in Mind: Insanity in California 1870–1930*. Berkeley: University of California Press, 1978.

Freedman, Estelle B. *Their Sisters' Keepers: Women's Prison Reform in America, 1830–1930.* Ann Arbor: University of Michigan Press, 1981.

Galton, Francis. *English Men of Science: Their Nature and Nurture.* London: Macmillan, 1874.

Galton, Francis. *Hereditary Genius: An Inquiry into Its Laws and Consequences.* New York: D. Appleton, 1870.

Galton, Francis. *Inquiries into Human Faculty and Its Development.* New York: Macmillan, 1883.

Gilman, Charlotte Perkins. *Herland.* New York: Pantheon Books, 1979.

Gilman, Charlotte Perkins. *The Home, Its Work and Influence.* Walnut Creek, CA: AltaMira Press, 1903.

Gilman, Charlotte Perkins. *Women and Economics: A Study of the Economic Relation between Men and Women as a Factor in Social Evolution.* Berkeley: University of California Press, 1898.

Gilmore, Ruth Wilson. *Golden Gulag: Prisons, Surplus, Crisis, and Opposition in Globalizing California.* Berkeley: University of California Press, 2007.

Glass, Fred B. *From Mission to Microchip: A History of the California Labor Movement.* Berkeley: University of California Press, 2016.

Goeres-Gardner, Diane L. *Inside Oregon State Hospital: A History of Tragedy and Triumph.* Charleston, SC: The History Press, 2013.

Gohlke, Mary Jo. *Remarkable Women of Stockton.* Charleston, SC: The History Press, 2014.

Gordon, Linda. *Pitied but Not Entitled: Single Mothers and the History of Welfare, 1890–1935.* New York: Free Press, 1994.

Gosney, E. S., and Paul Popenoe. *Sterilization for Human Betterment: A Summary of Results of 6,000 Operations in California, 1909–1929.* New York: Macmillan, 1929.

Gould, Stephen Jay. *The Mismeasure of Man.* New York: W. W. Norton, 1981.

Guha, Ranajit. *Elementary Aspects of Peasant Insurgency in Colonial India.* Durham, NC: Duke University Press, 1999.

Haley, Sarah. *No Mercy Here: Gender, Punishment, and the Making of Jim Crow Modernity.* Chapel Hill: University of North Carolina Press, 2016.

Hall, Stuart. "The West and the Rest: Discourse and Power." In *The Formations of Modernity*, edited by Stuart Hall and Bram Gieben, 275–332. Oxford: Polity, 1992.

Harcourt, Bernard E. "From the Asylum to the Prison: Rethinking the Incarceration Revolution." *Texas Law Review* 84, no. 7 (June 2006): 1751–86.

Harris, Cheryl I. "Whiteness as Property." *Harvard Law Review* 106, no. 8 (June 1993): 1707.

Harris, Leah, Liat Ben-Moshe, and Vesper Moore. "Psychiatric Incarceration Isn't Treatment—It's Violence, Survivors Say." Truthout, May 6, 2023. https://truthout.org/articles/psychiatric-incarceration-isnt-treatment-its-violence-survivors-say/.

Hartman, Saidiya V. *Scenes of Subjection: Terror, Slavery, and Self-Making in Nineteenth-Century America.* New York: Oxford University Press, 1997.

Hartman, Saidiya V. "Venus in Two Acts." *Small Axe: A Journal of Criticism* 12, no. 2 (2008): 1–14.

Hartman, Saidiya V. *Wayward Lives, Beautiful Experiments: Intimate Histories of Social Upheaval.* New York: W. W. Norton, 2019.

Heilbroner, Robert L., and William Milberg. *The Making of the Economic Society.* 13th ed. New York: Pearson, 2012.

Hemarajata, Peera. "Revisiting the Great Imitator: The Origin and History of Syphilis." American Society for Microbiology. Accessed March 25, 2023. https://asm.org:443/Articles/2019/June/Revisiting-the-Great-Imitator,-Part -I-The-Origin-a.

Hernández, Kelly Lytle. *City of Inmates: Conquest, Rebellion, and the Rise of Human Caging in Los Angeles, 1771–1965.* Chapel Hill: University of North Carolina Press, 2017.

Hernández, Kelly Lytle. *Migra! A History of the U.S. Border Patrol.* Berkeley: University of California Press, 2010.

Hobson, Janell. *Venus in the Dark: Blackness and Beauty in Popular Culture.* 2nd ed. New York: Routledge, 2018.

Hong, Grace Kyungwon. "Existentially Surplus: Women of Color Feminism and the New Crises of Capitalism." *GLQ: A Journal of Lesbian & Gay Studies* 18, no. 1 (January 2012): 87–106.

Hornblum, Allen M. *Acres of Skin: Human Experiments at Holmesburg Prison.* New York: Taylor and Francis, 2013.

Horvat, Srećko, and Igor Štiks. "Welcome to the Desert of Transition!" *Monthly Review: An Independent Socialist Magazine* 63, no. 10 (March 2012): 38–48.

HoSang, Daniel. *Racial Propositions: Ballot Initiatives and the Making of Postwar California.* Berkeley: University of California Press, 2010.

Howard, Amber-Rose, Brian Kaneda, Felicia Gomez, Liz Blum, Julie Mello, Melissa Rowlett, Fatimeh Khan, Elizabeth Fraser, and Kelan Thomas. *The People's Plan for Prison Closure.* Californians United for a Responsible Budget, April 2021. https://curbprisonspending.org/advocacy/prison-closures/.

Human Rights Program at Justice Now. "Prisons as a Tool of Reproductive Oppression." *Stanford Journal of Civil Rights and Civil Liberties* 5, no. 2 (October 1, 2009): 309–56. https://purl.stanford.edu/hr664xy2767.

"Investigation to Be Made." *Sacramento Union*, September 19, 1907.

Jackson, Don. "The State and Dr. Frankenstein." *San Francisco Good Times*, January 1971.

James, Joy. "George Jackson: Dragon Philosopher and Revolutionary Abolitionist." *Black Perspectives* (blog). African American Intellectual History Society, August 21, 2018. https://www.aaihs.org/george-jackson-dragon-philosopher -and-revolutionary-abolitionist/.

Johnson, Corey G. "Female Inmates Sterilized in California Prisons without Approval." Center for Investigative Reporting, July 7, 2013. https://www.revealnews .org/article/female-inmates-sterilized-in-california-prisons-without-approval/.

Johnson, Merri Lisa, and Robert McRuer. "Cripistemologies: Introduction." *Journal of Literary & Cultural Disability Studies* 8, no. 2 (July 5, 2014): 127–47.

Johnson, Roland, and Karl Johnson. *Lost In a Desert World: The Autobiography of Roland Johnson*. Philadelphia: Speaking for Ourselves, 1999.

Jones, Alexi. "Cruel and Unusual Punishment: When States Don't Provide Air Conditioning in Prison." *Prison Policy Institute* (blog). Accessed March 26, 2023. https://www.prisonpolicy.org/blog/2019/06/18/air-conditioning/.

Kaba, Mariame. *We Do This 'til We Free Us: Abolitionist Organizing and Transforming Justice*. Chicago: Haymarket Books, 2021.

Kafer, Alison. *Feminist, Queer, Crip*. Bloomington: Indiana University Press, 2013.

Kandaswamy, Priya. *Domestic Contradictions: Race and Gendered Citizenship from Reconstruction to Welfare Reform*. Durham, NC: Duke University Press, 2021.

Kaniecki, Marie, Nicole L. Novak, Sarah Gao, Natalie Lira, Toni Ann Treviño, Kate O'Connor, and Alexandra Minna Stern. "Racialization and Reproduction: Asian Immigrants and California's Twentieth-Century Eugenic Sterilization Program." *Social Forces* 102, no. 2 (December 2023): 706–29.

Kelly, Stephen, and R. C. Harbison. "Hospital Board Censures Dr. Dolan, Exonerates Superintendent Campbell." *Los Angeles Herald*, September 10, 1903.

Khanmalek, Tala. "Slavery: The Haunting Legacy of Sterilization Abuse in California State Prisons." *Feminist Wire* (blog), November 14, 2014. http://www.thefeministwire.com/2014/11/slavery-haunting-legacy-sterilization-abuse-california-state-prisons/.

Kilgore, James. "COVID-19 Is Turning Prisons into 'Kill-Boxes.'" Truthout, April 5, 2020. https://truthout.org/articles/covid-19-is-turning-prisons-into-kill-boxes-activists-say/.

Kilgore, James. "Repackaging Mass Incarceration." *Freedom Never Rests* (blog), June 9, 2014. https://www.freedomneverrests.com/2014/06/09/repackaging-mass-incarceration/.

Kim, Eunjung. *Curative Violence: Rehabilitating Disability, Gender and Sexuality in Modern Korea*. Durham, NC: Duke University Press, 2017.

Kim, Jina B. "Toward a Crip-of-Color Critique: Thinking with Minich's 'Enabling Whom?'" *Lateral* 6, no. 1 (Spring 2017). https://doi.org/10.25158/L6.1.14.

Kline, Wendy. *Building a Better Race: Gender, Sexuality, and Eugenics from the Turn of the Century to the Baby Boom*. Berkeley: University of California Press, 2001.

"Koncentration Kamp for Gays." *Gay Flames*, December 1970.

Kunzel, Regina G. *Criminal Intimacy: Prison and the Uneven History of Modern American Sexuality*. Chicago: University of Chicago Press, 2008.

Kunzel, Regina G. *Fallen Women, Problem Girls: Unmarried Mothers and the Professionalization of Benevolence, 1890–1945*. New Haven, CT: Yale University Press, 1993.

Lamp, Sharon. "'It Is for the Mother': Feminists' Rhetorics of Disability during the American Eugenics Period." *Disability Studies Quarterly* 26, no. 4 (2006).

Langarica, Monika Y., Bardis Vakili, and Kimberly Grano. *CoreCivic's Decades of Abuse: Otay Mesa Detention Center*. ACLU Foundation of San Diego and Impe-

rial Counties, April 2021. https://www.aclu-sdic.org/sites/default/files/field
_documents/2021_04_21_final_corecivics_decades_of_abuse_issue_brief.pdf.

Law, Victoria. "How Does Incarceration Impact the Spread of HIV?" The Body: The HIV/AIDS Resource, October 9, 2016. https://www.thebody.com/article/how-does-incarceration-impact-the-spread-of-hiv.

Law, Victoria. "'Out of Flames and Fear': How People with HIV Forced California to Reform HIV Care in Prisons." The Body: The HIV/AIDS Resource, May 23, 2017. https://www.thebody.com/article/out-of-flames-and-fear-how-people-with-hiv-forced-.

Law, Victoria. "Trans Women Who Report Abuse in Prison Are Targets of Retaliation." Truthout, August 23, 2020. https://truthout.org/articles/trans-women-who-report-abuse-in-prison-are-targets-of-retaliation/.

Leon, Sharon M. *An Image of God: The Catholic Struggle with Eugenics*. Chicago: University of Chicago Press, 2013.

Leonard, Thomas C. *Illiberal Reformers: Race, Eugenics, and American Economics in the Progressive Era*. Princeton, NJ: Princeton University Press, 2016.

"Letter to the California Governor: Pass the Compassionate Release Bill to Protect Medically Vulnerable." UCLA Law Covid Behind Bars Data Project, September 16, 2022. https://uclacovidbehindbars.org/letter-to-ca-gov.

Levin, Sam. "He Lived in the US for 40 Years. Then He Became the First to Die from Covid-19 in Immigration Jail." *Guardian*, May 12, 2020. https://www.theguardian.com/us-news/2020/may/12/first-ice-detainee-dies-coronavirus-immigration-carlos-ernesto-escobar-mejia.

Lira, Natalie. *Laboratory of Deficiency: Sterilization and Confinement in California, 1900–1950s*. Berkeley: University of California Press, 2022.

Lira, Natalie, and Alexandra Minna Stern. "Mexican Americans and Eugenic Sterilization." *Aztlan* 39, no. 2 (Fall 2014): 9–34.

Lombardo, Paul A., ed. *A Century of Eugenics in America: From the Indiana Experiment to the Human Genome Era*. Bloomington: Indiana University Press, 2011.

Lombardo, Paul A. *Three Generations, No Imbeciles: Eugenics, the Supreme Court, and Buck v. Bell*. Baltimore, MD: Johns Hopkins University Press, 2008.

Marx, Karl. *Capital*. Vol. 1. Edited by David Fernbach. New York: Penguin Books, 1990.

McRuer, Robert. *Crip Times: Disability, Globalization, and Resistance*. New York: New York University Press, 2018.

Melamed, Jodi. *Represent and Destroy: Rationalizing Violence in the New Racial Capitalism*. Minneapolis: University of Minnesota Press, 2011.

Mies, Maria. *Patriarchy and Accumulation on a World Scale: Women in the International Division of Labour*. London: Zed, 1998.

Minich, Julie Avril. "Enabling Whom? Critical Disability Studies Now." *Lateral* 5, no. 1 (Spring 2016). https://doi.org/10.25158/L5.1.9.

Mink, Gwendolyn. *The Wages of Motherhood: Inequality in the Welfare State, 1917–1942*. Ithaca, NY: Cornell University Press, 1995.

Miranda, Deborah. *Bad Indians: A Tribal Memoir*. Berkeley: Heyday, 2013.

Mogul, Joey L., Andrea J. Ritchie, and Kay Whitlock. *Queer (in)Justice: The Criminalization of LGBT People in the United States*. Boston: Beacon Press, 2011.

Morris, Scott. "The Most Dangerous Place in Alameda County." *East Bay Express*, May 7, 2019. https://eastbayexpress.com/the-most-dangerous-place-in-alameda-county-1/.

Muñoz, José Esteban. *Cruising Utopia: The Then and There of Queer Futurity*. Sexual Cultures. New York: New York University Press, 2009.

Muñoz, José Esteban. *Disidentifications: Queers of Color and the Performance of Politics*. Minneapolis: University of Minnesota Press, 1999.

Nguyen, Mimi Thi. *The Gift of Freedom: War, Debt, and Other Refugee Passages*. Durham, NC: Duke University Press, 2012.

Nielsen, Kim E. *A Disability History of the United States*. Boston: Beacon Press, 2012.

Nishida, Akemi. *Just Care: Messy Entanglements of Disability, Dependency, and Desire*. Philadelphia: Temple University Press, 2022.

Norris, Frank. *The Octopus: A Story of California*. New York: Doubleday, Page, 1901.

Novak, Nicole L., Natalie Lira, Kate E. O'Connor, Siobán D. Harlow, Sharon L. R. Kardia, and Alexandra Minna Stern. "Disproportionate Sterilization of Latinos under California's Eugenic Sterilization Program, 1920–1945." *American Journal of Public Health (1971)* 108, no. 5 (2018): 611–13.

Okrent, Daniel. *The Guarded Gate: Bigotry, Eugenics, and the Law That Kept Two Generations of Jews, Italians, and Other European Immigrants out of America*. New York: Scribner, 2019.

Oliver, Michael. *The Politics of Disablement: A Sociological Approach*. New York: St. Martin's Press, 1990.

"$1 Million for Boiling Prisoner." *Prison Legal News*, October 15, 1994. https://www.prisonlegalnews.org/news/1994/oct/15/1-million-for-boiling-prisoner/.

Ordaz, Jessica. *The Shadow of El Centro: A History of Migrant Incarceration and Solidarity*. Chapel Hill: University of North Carolina Press, 2021.

Ordover, N. *American Eugenics: Race, Queer Anatomy, and the Science of Nationalism*. Minneapolis: University of Minnesota Press, 2003.

Paik, A. Naomi. *Bans, Walls, Raids, Sanctuary: Understanding U.S. Immigration for the Twenty-First Century*. Berkeley: University of California Press, 2020.

Paul, Diane B., John Stenhouse, and Hamish G. Spencer, eds. *Eugenics at the Edges of Empire: New Zealand, Australia, Canada and South Africa*. New York: Springer International, 2018.

Pickens, Therí A. *Black Madness: Mad Blackness*. Durham, NC: Duke University Press, 2019.

Piepzna-Samarasinha, Leah Lakshmi. *Care Work: Dreaming Disability Justice*. Vancouver: Arsenal Pulp Press, 2018.

Placzek, Jessica. "Did the Emptying of Mental Hospitals Contribute to Homelessness?" KQED, December 8, 2016. https://www.kqed.org/news/11209729/did-the-emptying-of-mental-hospitals-contribute-to-homelessness-here.

Popenoe, Paul. *Applied Eugenics*. New York: Macmillan, 1933.

Popenoe, Paul, and E. S. Gosney. *Twenty-Eight Years of Sterilization in California*. Pasadena, CA: Human Betterment Foundation, 1938.

Puar, Jasbir K. *The Right to Maim: Debility, Capacity, Disability*. Durham, NC: Duke University Press, 2017.

Rafter, Nicole Hahn. *Partial Justice: Women, Prison, and Social Control*. 2nd ed. New York: Routledge, 1990.

Reagan, Ronald. "A Time for Choosing." Ronald Reagan Presidential Library and Museum, October 27, 1964. https://www.reaganlibrary.gov/reagans/ronald -reagan/time-choosing-speech-october-27-1964.

Rembis, Michael A. *Defining Deviance: Sex, Science, and Delinquent Girls, 1890–1960*. Urbana: University of Illinois Press, 2011.

Ridolfi, Laura, Renée Menart, and Israel Villa. *California Youth Face Heightened Racial and Ethnic Disparities in Division of Juvenile Justice*. San Francisco: W. Haywood Burns Institute, 2020. https://files.eric.ed.gov/fulltext/ED610669.pdf.

Ridolfi, Laura, Maureen Washburn, and Frankie Guzman. *Youth Prosecuted as Adults in California*. San Francisco: W. Haywood Burns Institute, 2017. https:// www.cjcj.org/media/import/documents/youth_prosecuted_as_adults_in _california.pdf.

Roberts, Dorothy E. *Killing the Black Body: Race, Reproduction, and the Meaning of Liberty*. New York: Pantheon Books, 1997.

Robinson, Cedric J. *Black Marxism: The Making of the Black Radical Tradition*. Chapel Hill: University of North Carolina Press, 2000.

Rochlen, A. M. "Ventura Revolt Laid to Hearst's Attacks on Institution; Mutiny is Quelled, but More Girls Get Away." *Los Angeles Times*, March 2, 1921.

Ross, Loretta, Lynn Roberts, Erika Derkas, Whitney Peoples, and Pamela Bridgewater Toure, eds. *Radical Reproductive Justice*. New York: Feminist Press at the City University of New York, 2017.

Roth, Rachel. "'She Doesn't Deserve to Be Treated like This': Prisons as Sites of Reproductive Injustice." In *Radical Reproductive Justice*, edited by Loretta Ross, Lynn Roberts, Erika Derkas, Whitney Peoples, and Pamela Bridgewater Toure. New York: Feminist Press at the City University of New York, 2017.

Russell, Marta. *Capitalism & Disability*. Edited by Keith Rosenthal. Chicago: Haymarket Books, 2019.

Russell, Marta, and Jean Stewart. "Disablement, Prison, and Historical Segregation." *Monthly Review: An Independent Socialist Magazine* 53, no. 3 (August 7, 2001): 61.

Schalk, Sami. *Bodyminds Reimagined: (Dis)Ability, Race, and Gender in Black Women's Speculative Fiction*. Durham, NC: Duke University Press, 2018.

Schoen, Johanna. *Choice & Coercion: Birth Control, Sterilization, and Abortion in Public Health and Welfare*. Chapel Hill: University of North Carolina Press, 2005.

"Schulken's Death Was Accidental." *Marin Journal*. October 17, 1912.

Schweik, Susan. "Archaeology of the 'Feebleminded': In the Archives with Lee Swearengin." *Osiris* 39, Disability and the History of Science (forthcoming).

Schweik, Susan. "Eugenic Anti-Eugenics." Paper presented at the American Studies Association Conference, Montreal, Canada, November 2023.

Sears, Clare. *Arresting Dress: Cross-Dressing, Law, and Fascination in Nineteenth-Century San Francisco*. Durham, NC: Duke University Press Books, 2014.

Segrest, Mab. *Administrations of Lunacy: Racism and the Haunting of American Psychiatry at the Milledgeville Asylum*. New York: New Press, 2020.

Sentencing Project. *The Color of Justice: Racial and Ethnic Disparity in State Prisons*, 2021. https://www.sentencingproject.org/reports/the-color-of-justice-racial-and-ethnic-disparity-in-state-prisons-the-sentencing-project/.

Sentencing Project. *Incarcerated Women and Girls*, March 2023. https://www.sentencingproject.org/fact-sheet/incarcerated-women-and-girls/.

Shah, Nayan. *Contagious Divides: Epidemics and Race in San Francisco's Chinatown*. Berkeley: University of California Press, 2001.

Shah, Nayan. *Stranger Intimacy: Contesting Race, Sexuality, and the Law in the North American West*. Berkeley: University of California Press, 2011.

Sheridan, Lorna. "Sonoma Developmental Center Quietly Closes Its Doors." *Sonoma Index-Tribune*, December 31, 2018. https://www.sonomanews.com/article/news/sonoma-developmental-center-quietly-closes-its-doors/.

Simpson, Audra. *Mohawk Interruptus: Political Life across the Borders of Settler States*. Durham, NC: Duke University Press, 2014.

Sins Invalid. *Skin, Tooth, and Bone: The Basis of Movement Is Our People: A Disability Justice Primer*. 2nd ed. Berkeley, CA: Self-published, 2019.

Skocpol, Theda. *Social Policy in the United States: Future Possibilities in Historical Perspective*. Princeton, NJ: Princeton University Press, 1995.

Skowronek, Stephen. *Building a New American State: The Expansion of National Administrative Capacities, 1877–1920*. Cambridge: Cambridge University Press, 1982.

Smith, Alice. *Alice: Memoirs of a Barbary Coast Prostitute*. Edited by Ivy Anderson and Devon Angus. Berkeley: Heyday, 2016.

Smith, Nat, and Eric A. Stanley. *Captive Genders: Trans Embodiment and the Prison Industrial Complex*. Oakland, CA: AK Press, 2011.

Smyth, Margaret H. "Psychiatric History and Development in California." *American Journal of Psychiatry*, 94 (1938): 1223–36.

Solomon, Susan Gross, ed. *Doing Medicine Together: Germany and Russia between the Wars*. Toronto: University of Toronto Press, 2006.

Somerville, Siobhan B. "Queer." In *Keywords for American Cultural Studies*, edited by Bruce Burgett and Glenn Hendler, 187–90. New York: New York University Press, 2014.

Somerville, Siobhan B. *Queering the Color Line: Race and the Invention of Homosexuality in American Culture*. Durham, NC: Duke University Press, 2000.

Spade, Dean. *Normal Life: Administrative Violence, Critical Trans Politics, and the Limits of Law*. Boston: South End Press, 2011.

Spillers, Hortense. "Mama's Baby, Papa's Maybe: An American Grammar Book." *Diacritics* 17, no. 2 (1987): 65–81.

Spivak, Gayatri Chakravorty. *A Critique of Postcolonial Reason: Toward a History of the Vanishing Present*. Cambridge, MA: Harvard University Press, 1999.

Starr, Kevin. *California: A History*. New York: Modern Library, 2005.

Stepan, Nancy Leys. *The Hour of Eugenics: Race, Gender, and Nation in Latin America*. Ithaca, NY: Cornell University Press, 1996.

Stern, Alexandra Minna. *Eugenic Nation: Faults and Frontiers of Better Breeding in Modern America*. Berkeley: University of California Press, 2005.

Stern, Alexandra Minna. "From Legislation to Lived Experience: Eugenic Sterilization in California and Indiana, 1907–1979." In *A Century of Eugenics in America: From the Indiana Experiment to the Human Genome Era*, edited by Paul A. Lombardo, 95–116. Bloomington: Indiana University Press, 2011.

Stern, Alexandra Minna, Nicole L. Novak, Natalie Lira, Kate O'Connor, Siobán Harlow, and Sharon Kardia. "California's Sterilization Survivors: An Estimate and Call for Redress." *American Journal of Public Health* 107, no. 1 (January 2017): 50–54.

Stone, Deborah A. *The Disabled State*. Philadelphia: Temple University Press, 1984.

Stuckey, Zosha. "'What Has Become of Jimmy Thornton?': The Rhetoric(s) of Letter-Writing at the New York State Asylum for Idiots, 1855–1866." *Disability Studies Quarterly* 31, no. 3 (August 8, 2011). https://doi.org/10.18061/dsq.v31i3.1669.

Sullivan, Ellen B., Roy M. Dorcus, Bennet M. Allen, and Louis K. Koontz. "Grace Maxwell Fernald, 1879–1950." *Psychological Review* 57, no. 6 (November 1950): 319–21.

Tadiar, Neferti X. M. "Life-Times of Disposability within Global Neoliberalism." *Social Text* 31, no. 2 (Summer 2013): 19–48.

Tajima-Peña, Renee, dir. *No Más Bebés*. Los Angeles: Virginia Espino and Moon Canyon Films, 2015.

Takaki, Ronald. *A Different Mirror: A History of Multicultural America*. New York: Back Bay Books, 2008.

Taylor, Keeanga-Yamahtta. "The Emerging Movement for Police and Prison Abolition." *New Yorker*, May 7, 2021. https://www.newyorker.com/news/our-columnists/the-emerging-movement-for-police-and-prison-abolition.

Theobald, Brianna. *Reproduction on the Reservation: Pregnancy, Childbirth, and Colonialism in the Long Twentieth Century*. Chapel Hill: University of North Carolina Press, 2019.

"30+ Years in a Mental Institution." Disability Rights California, May 13, 2021. https://www.disabilityrightsca.org/latest-news/30-years-in-a-mental-institution.

"Understanding the Lanterman-Petris-Short (LPS) Act." Disability Rights California, 2018. https://www.disabilityrightsca.org/publications/understanding-the-lanterman-petris-short-lps-act.

Villani, David. "Inmates Oppose Mental Health Settlement for Santa Rita Jail Lawsuit." *Daily Californian*, February 1, 2022. https://www.dailycal.org/2022/02/01/inmates-oppose-mental-health-settlement-for-santa-rita-jail-lawsuit/.

Villarosa, Linda. *Under the Skin: The Hidden Toll of Racism on American Lives and on the Health of Our Nation*. New York: Doubleday, 2022.

Washburn, Maureen. "Decades of Abuse at California's DJJ Will End in 2023." Center on Juvenile and Criminal Justice, February 16, 2021. http://www.cjcj .org/news/13081.

Washington, Harriet A. *Medical Apartheid: The Dark History of Medical Experimentation on Black Americans from Colonial Times to the Present*. New York: Doubleday, 2006.

Whatcott, Jess. "Aiding and Abetting the Unruly Past: Queer and Critical Disability Approaches to American Political Development." *Politics, Groups & Identities* 11, no. 1 (2023): 37–54.

Whatcott, Jess. "No Selves to Consent: Women's Prisons, Sterilization, and the Biopolitics of Informed Consent." *Signs: Journal of Women in Culture and Society* 44, no. 1 (2018): 131–53.

Whatcott, Jess. "Sexuality, Disability, and Madness in California's Eugenics Era." In *The Routledge Handbook of Disability and Sexuality*, edited by Russell Shuttleworth and Linda Mona, 121–31. London: Routledge, 2021.

Whitaker, Robert. *Mad in America: Bad Science, Bad Medicine, and the Enduring Mistreatment of the Mentally Ill*. Cambridge, MA: Perseus, 2002.

Williams, Paul, and Bonnie Shoultz. *We Can Speak for Ourselves: Self-Advocacy by Mentally Handicapped People*. Bloomington: Indiana University Press, 1984.

Williams, Raymond. *Marxism and Literature*. Oxford: Oxford University Press, 1977.

Wynter, Sylvia. "Unsettling the Coloniality of Being/Power/Truth/Freedom: Towards the Human, After Man, Its Overrepresentation—An Argument." *CR: The New Centennial Review* 3, no. 3 (2003): 257–337.

Yanni, Carla. *The Architecture of Madness: Insane Asylums in the United States*. Minneapolis: University of Minnesota Press, 2007.

INDEX

carceral eugenics, definition, 3

carceral humanism, 151, 161, 163, 165, 169, 176

carceral-industrial complex, 3, 11–15, 24, 62, 82, 84, 117. *See also* prison-industrial complex

carceral logics, 78–80, 163, 176, 188n16; and care, 165; in institutions, 3–4, 21, 76

carceral state, 3, 67, 118, 132, 176; gendered, 52, 82, 84; and pathologization/criminalization nexus, 11, 25; resistance to, 19, 27, 139; studies of, 14, 51

care: by the state, 25, 122, 124, 132; crip care work, 10

Carey, Allison, 11

Chapman, Chris, 11

Charlton, James I., 114

Chávez-García, Miroslava, 11, 170

chosen family, 9–10, 17, 21–22, 144. *See also* kinship

chronic illness, xvi, 16, 31, 159, 165; people with, 10, 18, 22

civil commitment, 12, 32–33, 68, 156

Civil War (US), 64, 87, 116

Clare, Eli, 158

Clark, Asa, 98, 102

clubwomen. *See* women's club movement

Coalinga State Hospital, 155–56

Cohen, Cathy, 22, 54

Community Assistance, Recovery, and Empowerment (CARE) Act (2022, CA), 164

compassionate release, 162

consensual eugenics, 25, 123–24

conservatorship, 156, 164

CoreCivic, xiv–xv, xvii, 175. *See also* Otay Mesa Detention Center (OMDC)

COVID-19 pandemic, xvi, 70, 149, 162, 167, 173–75

criminalization, 3, 67, 70, 150, 158–59, 163–66, 169; of HIV-positive people, 162; of mental illness, 156, 160, 172; of migrants, xiii, xv; and pathologization, 5, 11, 25, 62, 79, 156, 162; and racialization, 13–14, 79–80, 156–57; of sex work, 110–11; of vagrancy, 109

criminal legal system, xv, 3, 8, 12–13, 45, 150, 156–58. *See also* prison-industrial complex

crip futurity, 19–21, 23, 122, 146, 159

cripistemologies (Johnson and McRuer), 17–18, 135–37, 143

critical disability studies, 23, 39, 90, 120–21, 164; as methodology 15–19

custodial care, 73; cost of, 101; and deinstitutionalization, 152, 159; and racism, 13–14; and rehabilitation, 114–15, 130; and reproductive control, 3, 61, 66; of women, 37, 78, 81

Davis, Angela Y., 11, 14, 25, 63, 80, 83–84

deafness, 14, 39

debilitation, 75, 88, 165, 168, 183n77; Jasbir Puar's theorization of, 19. *See also* disablement

decarceration, 163, 172

"defective class," 60, 73, 99, 100, 112, 168; and anti-eugenics, 142–45; creation of, 24, 28–57; criminalization of, 150, 156–58, 163, 166; dysgenic people, 22–23, 25, 121, 134; and eugenics, 5, 10, 12, 20–21, 61, 66, 73–81, 102–4, 107–8, 121, 134–39, 169; feminized, 127, 131–33; and surplus value, 25, 90, 96, 114–18; "unfit" discourse, 2, 13, 59, 123

deinstitutionalization, 4, 116, 155–57, 164

delinquency. *See* juvenile delinquency

dementia, 14, 38, 75, 161

deportation, xiii–xvi, 7, 43–46, 79, 99–101, 174–75

Deukmejian, George, 160

DeWitt State Hospital, 153

diagnosis: for commitment, 32, 38; and family history, 36; of immorality, 17, 51–53, 55; resistance to, 138, 141; and sexuality, 47; of trauma, 133

Dinshaw, Carolyn, 22–23

disability confinement, xviii, 3–4, 22, 25, 43, 84, 86, 120, 128, 158–59; and abuse, 26; and civil commitment, 12; and deinstitutionalization, 155–56; and eugenics, 34, 60, 176; and pathologization, 14; and psychopathology, 68, 160; and race, 45, 49, 80, 157; and segregation, 11, 149, 150–51; and surplus value, 90

disability justice, 4, 18–19, 41, 176–77

Disability Rights California: Peer Self-Advocacy Program (PSAP), 148–49

disability rights movement, 121, 135, 143

disability studies. *See* critical disability studies

disability terminology, 183n77

disablement, 14, 20, 24, 26, 56, 117, 169; and "defective class," 31, 39–42; institutionalization as, 15, 18; prisons causing, 151, 159, 165; by slavery, 39–40

discipline (Foucauldian), 10, 109, 125, 127–29, 132–34
Dortch, Vaughn, 72
Down syndrome (Trisomy 21), 39, 183n77
Dybwad, Gunnar, 135

electroshock therapy, 59
elimination, logic of (Kelly Lytle Hernández), 11, 16, 20, 46, 102
Elise (Sonoma State Home inmate), 141–42, 145
enclosure, 3, 10, 20–21, 131
epilepsy, 14, 30, 36, 39, 70; colonies for people with, 3, 10, 17, 79
Erevelles, Nirmala, 39–41
escape, 19, 66, 121, 135–36, 138–39, 188n16
Escobar Mejia, Carlos Ernesto, xvi–xvii, 173
eugenics family history, 22, 24, 34–36, 49, 141
Eugenics Record Office, 35; and Cold Spring Harbor laboratory, 6
existentially surplus (Grace Hong), 40, 116

Fabian, Johannes, 47
Fairview State Hospital, 152, 156–57
"fallen woman" discourse, 50, 81–84, 89, 95, 108, 113
Federal Bureau of Prisons, xvi
feeblemindedness, 30, 103–6, 112, 152; and anti-eugenics, 121, 136, 141; and "defective class," 30, 36–37, 39, 133, 158; and eugenics, 2–3, 12, 59–63, 66, 73–74, 77, 133; and maternalism, 125, 128; and methodology of book, 17; racially gendered, 13, 37, 48, 50, 53–54, 56, 84, 98–99; and segregation, 3, 50
feminism, 7, 56, 133; abolitionist, 14–15, 19; Black, 14, 22, 50, 63; intersectional, 32; Marxist, 9, 109; second-wave, 82; white, 122–23; women of color, 18
Fernald, Grace Maxwell, 37, 126–27
Folsom State Prison, 62–63, 82, 160
Forced or Involuntary Sterilization Compensation Program (2022, CA), 148
Foucault, Michel, 11, 104, 131; on biopolitics, 15, 103, 106, 111; on discipline, 10, 109; on genealogy 22–23
Fox, Richard, 12

Galton, Francis, 2, 4–5
gender, 5, 68, 88, 145, 161–62, 174; and ableism, 56; and capitalism, 10, 81, 111; and the carceral state, 11, 52, 80, 82, 84; and "defective class," 31, 35, 81, 127, 131–33; and delinquency, 53, 78, 103–5, 125; in detention centers, xv; and disability, 14, 17–19, 21, 41, 54–55; and feeblemindedness, 13, 37, 48, 50, 53–54, 56, 84, 98–99; and insanity, 11–12; and institutionalization, 51, 56, 59–67, 80–84, 102–4, 108, 125–26, 131; and labor, 89–91, 109–18, 155; policing of, 9; and queerness, 22; and race, 13–14, 31, 56–57, 83–84; and rehabilitation, 56, 83, 103, 105, 108, 124, 131; and sex segregation, 50–52, 180n1; and sexuality, 50–57, 141. See also heteropatriarchy; womanhood
gender nonconformity, 18, 21, 26–27, 31, 84. See also trans and transgender people
genealogy (Foucauldian), 22–23
genocide, 42–43, 102, 109, 123, 132, 158; and Holocaust, 6
Gilman, Charlotte Perkins: Herland, 24–25, 122–27
Gilmore, Ruth Wilson, 75, 80, 116, 163, 169
Gold Rush, 42–43
Gosney, Ezra, 55; Sterilization for Human Betterment, 6
group homes, 4, 117, 155

habeas corpus, 136
Haley, Sarah, 22, 83
handicapitalism, 117
Harcourt, Bernard, 12
Hartman, Saidiya, 22, 132, 184n89
Hatch, F. W., 74
heredity, 39, 48, 124, 169; and "defective class," 30, 74; dysgenic, 22–23, 25, 121, 133–34; and eugenics, 2, 4, 10, 13, 20, 35–36, 169. See also inheritance, biological
Hernández, Kelly Lytle, 11, 45, 109, 144
heteropatriarchy, 10, 13–14, 31, 41, 56, 88, 95
HIV/AIDS, 160–62, 165, 168
homes for the feebleminded. See Pacific Colony; Sonoma State Home
homosexuality, 6, 47, 156, 160; and homophobia, 163
Hong, Grace, 40, 116
Hottentot Venus. See Baartman, Sarah ("Hottentot Venus")
Human Betterment Foundation, 6, 8. See also Gosney, Ezra; Popenoe, Paul
humanitarianism, 11, 48, 61, 66, 80, 102, 162; and reformism, 9, 14; as violence, 78

Spillers, Hortense, 39–40
Stanford-Binet intelligence test. *See* IQ tests
Stanford University, 6, 37, 126
state homes. *See* Pacific Colony; Sonoma
    State Home
state hospitals. *See individual state hospitals*
State Normal School, California, 126
state prisons. *See individual state prisons*
Stephens, William, 105, 107
sterilization, 41, 59, 126, 145, 154, 165, 169,
    176; apology for, 147–48; as disable-
    ment, 55; economics of, 102; and eugen-
    ics, 2, 6–10, 13, 39, 60; forced, xiii–xiv,
    1–2, 7, 9, 148; and hysterectomies, 1, 9,
    72; and making good, 127; of migrants,
    xiii–xiv, 6; and oophorectomies, 9, 167;
    racialized, 13, 43, 114; as release condi-
    tion, 72–74; resistance to, 134, 142, 144;
    and salpingectomies, 6; and tubal liga-
    tions, 14, 166. *See also* Asexualization
    Act (1909, CA)
Sterilization and Social Justice Lab, 44,
    182n57
Stocking, Leonard, 64–65, 99
Stockton State Hospital, 6, 31, 62, 75, 102,
    126, 140, 145; closure of, 154; construct-
    ing defectiveness, 38; correspondence
    from, 120–21, 135; deaths at, 75, *149*; and
    disability confinement, 12; resistance
    at, 142
Stuckey, Zosha, 120
substance users: confinement of, 26, 105,
    107, 139, 157, 159, 161, 163–64, 169
surplus populations, 90–91, 101, 109,
    116
syphilis, 36, 52, 54–55, 73; Salvarsan treat-
    ment of, 75; Wassermann test for, 35

Tadiar, Neferti, 76, 116
Terman, Lewis, 6, 37
trans and transgender people, 9, 52, 159;
    and incarceration 162–63. *See also* gen-
    der nonconformity

Trisomy 21 (Down syndrome), 39, 183n77
Tuitel, Johnnie, 117

The Uncanny X-Men, 184n99
undocumented people, xiii–xv, 114
University of California, Los Angeles, 126
"unruliness," 19, 25, 30, 71, 84, 121, 125, 137, 145
US Border Patrol, xv, 7
US Constitution, 33, 136, 167; Eighth
    Amendment, 166; Thirteenth Amend-
    ment, 79. *See also* habeas corpus
US Marshals Service, xiv–xv
US-Mexico border, xiv–xv, 44, 174. *See also*
    California cities and regions

vagrancy, 68, 89, 105, 109–10, 143
Van Waters, Miriam, 197n90
venereal disease. *See* sexually transmitted
    infections (STIs); syphilis
"vice industries," 30, 89, 91–96, 105–6, 110–
    11, 123, 127, 140

Wagner, W. D., 99–101
Warren, Earl, 126, 160
white supremacy. *See* racism
Whittier State School, 35–36, 44, 52, 62, 139,
    141, 170–71
Williams, Paul, 135
Williams, Raymond, 80, 142
womanhood, 47, 82–83, 124; and whiteness,
    13, 46
women's club movement: California
    Federation of Women's Clubs, 106;
    and reformatory movement, 83, 149;
    Women's Legislative Council of
    California, 104–5; Women's Political
    League of California, 104. *See also*
    League of Women Voters of San
    Francisco
World War I, 44, 63, 103, 105, 112
World War II, 45, 46, 62, 134, 153

Yanni, Carla, 64